Celebrate the Wheel of Life

Just as the seasons change with the cycle of life and death, so it is with our own lives. Each new stage, from birth to adolescence, coupling to midlife, elderhood to the final passage, carries with it the turbulence of transition. It is during these transitions that we experience our own cycle of life and death; death of ideas, of desires, of ways worn thin. And it is here we experience rebirth . . . through new ideas, new desires, and new ways of living.

All of life's transitions can now be personally marked through the time-honored rituals in *Rites of Passage*. This groundbreaking book provides supportive structure when life presents chaos, and it offers channels for the myriad emotions born of change. *Rites of Passage* illuminates the uniting cycles of life and death—in nature as well as in our own lives.

Learn about the Gift of Beauty. Recognize a Coming of Age Rite. Recount the legend of your own life. Understand the meaning of Handfasting. Prepare for Elderhood's inward turn of energies. Initiate a healing memorial rite when it is needed, and much more. Written for those new to the Pagan path, as well as for seasoned practitioners, Rites of Passage is a guide for anyone who desires to celebrate the Wheel of Life.

The Circle at Brescia
1285 Western Road
London, Ontario, Canada
N6G 1H2

About the Author

Pauline and Dan Campanelli are the author and illustrator of *Wheel of the Year*, *Ancient Ways*, and *Circles, Groves & Sanctuaries*, and have contributed to *Llewellyn's 1991 Magickal Almanac*. Pauline has also written for *Witchcraft Today: The Modern Craft Movement*, and *The Witches Almanac 1991*.

The Campanellis have been practicing Wiccans since 1968. Because of their deep religious beliefs they have evolved a lifestyle based on Natural Magick. In their 18th century home in western New Jersey, Magick is a part of their everyday life.

Pauline and Dan have written and illustrated articles on Witchcraft, as well as their personal experiences with the Spirit World for *Circle Network News* and Fate magazine. Other paranormal experiences shared by Pauline and Dan have been included in *Haunted Houses: U.S.A.*, and *More Haunted Houses*, and in Alan Vaughan's *Incredible Coincidence*.

Both Dan and Pauline are professional artists. Dan works in watercolor, Pauline in oils. They are each listed in 13 reference books, including *Who's Who in American Art* and *The International Dictionary of Biographies*. Their home and artwork were featured in *Colonial Homes*, March/April 1981 and *Country Living Magazine*, April 1985 and October 1992. New Jersey Network produced a program on their artwork and lifestyle for PBS in 1985. Their paintings have been published as fine art prints and are available throughout the United States and Europe.

To Write to the Author and Artist

If you wish to contact the author and artist, or would like more information about this book, please write to them in care of Llewellyn Worldwide and we will forward your request. We appreciate hearing from you and learning of your enjoyment of this book and how it has helped you. Llewellyn Worldwide cannot guarantee that every letter written to the author can be answered, but all will be forwarded. Please write to:

Dan and Pauline Campanelli
c/o Llewellyn Worldwide
P.O. Box 64383-119, St. Paul, MN 55164–0383, U.S.A.
Please enclose a self-addressed, stamped envelope for reply, or $1.00 to cover costs.
If outside the U.S.A., enclose international postal reply coupon.

Free Catalog From Llewellyn Worldwide

For more than 90 years Llewellyn has brought its readers knowledge in the fields of metaphysics and human potential. Learn about the newest books in spiritual guidance, natural healing, astrology, occult philosophy, and more. Enjoy book reviews, new age articles, a calendar of events, plus current advertised products and services. To get your free copy of the *Llewellyn's New Worlds of Mind and Spirit*, send your name and address to:

Llewellyn's New Worlds of Mind and Spirit
P.O. Box 64383-119, St. Paul, MN 55164-0383, U.S.A.

Llewellyn's Practical Magick Series

Rites of Passage

The Pagan Wheel of Life

Written by Pauline Campanelli

Illustrated by Dan Campanelli

1994
Llewellyn Publications
St. Paul, Minnesota, U.S.A., 64383-0383

First Edition
Second Printing, 1995

Cover Painting by Dan Campanelli
Interior design and editing by Connie Hill

Library of Congress Cataloging-in-Publication Data
Campanelli, Pauline, 1943 –
    Rites of passage: the Pagan wheel of life. / written by Pauline Campanelli : illustrated by Dan Campanelli.
        p.   cm. —(Llewellyn's practical magick series)
    ISBN 0-87542-119-9
        1. Witchcraft. 2. Paganism—Rituals. 3. Rites and ceremonies.
4. Religious calendars—Paganism.   5. Life cycle. Human—Religious aspects—Paganism.   I. Title. II. Series.
    BF1566.C267   1994

                                                  94-30677

    291.3'8—dc20

CIP

Llewellyn Publications
A Division of Llewellyn Worldwide, Ltd.
P.O. Box 64383, St. Paul, MN 55164-0383

About Llewellyn's Practical Magick Series

To some people, the idea that Magick is practical comes as a surprise. It shouldn't. The entire basis for Magick is to exercise influence over one's environment. While Magick is also, and properly so, concerned with spiritual growth and psychological transformation, even spiritual life must rest firmly on material foundations.

Magick can, and should, be used in one's daily life for better living! Each of us has been given Mind and Body, and surely we are under spiritual obligation to make full use of these wonderful gifts. Mind and Body work together, and Magick is simply the extension of this interaction into dimensions beyond the limits normally conceived. That's why we commonly talk of the "super-normal" in connection with the domain of Magick.

The Body is alive, and all Life is an expression of the Divine. There is god-power in the Body and in the Earth, just as there is in Mind and Spirit. With Love and Will, we use Mind to link these aspects of Divinity together to bring about change.

With Magick we increase the flow of Divinity in our lives and in the world around us. We add to the beauty of it all—for to work Magick we must work in harmony with the Laws of Nature and of the Psyche. Magick is the flowering of the Human Potential.

Practical Magick is concerned with the Craft of living well and in harmony with nature, and with the Magick of the Earth, in the things of the Earth, in the seasons and cycles, and in the things we make with hand and Mind.

OTHER BOOKS BY THE AUTHOR

Wheel of the Year

Ancient Ways

Circles, Groves & Sanctuaries

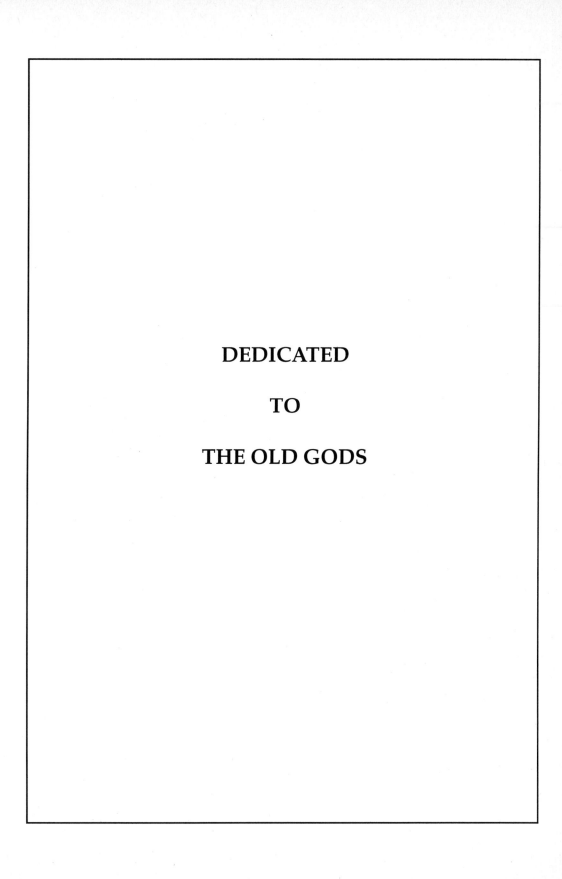

DEDICATED

TO

THE OLD GODS

Table of Contents

Illustrations

Photos

Tables and Diagrams

Introduction

Among the cards and letters that come to Flying Witch Farm every year, there are always a number that ask us how to conduct various Rites of Passage. Those most often asked about are the Wiccaning or Paganing of a new born child, Coming of Age, Self-Dedication or Initiation, Handfasting, and Burial Rites for both Pagans and non-Pagans.

Meanwhile, as the seasons change and the years roll by, Dan and I have experienced several transitions in our own lives, some of which were ritually celebrated, and some of which should have been. It became apparent that, for all of us on the Pagan path, there is a need for a complete system of rites to celebrate the inevitable changes in our lives, both physical and spiritual.

Just as the wheel of the year marks the cycles of Birth, Death, and Rebirth as celebrated at the solar sabbats, so does it mark the transitions of our lives. Just as we dance the magick circle, from East to South, West to North, so do we dance the dance of life.

We are born in the North as the Divine Child of the Great Goddess is born at Yule. We come of age in the Northeast with the stirrings of adulthood at Imbolc. We are reborn spiritually in the East at Initiation and are married in the Southeast like the Lord and Lady at Beltane. Like the Sun at Midsummer, we reach our Middle years in the South, and consecrate the harvest of our lives at Lammas in the Southwest. In the West our bodies begin to wither as we sip the wine of spirit in Autumn, and join the ancestors in Caer Arianrod in the Northwest at Samhaintide, but the wheel turns only Sunwise and never stops. The dance of life continues and we are born anew, like the Winter sun at Yule.

If you, like many Pagans, have ever held your own infant in your arms and wanted to rejoice with the immortal Gods over the birth, or witnessed a wedding and cringed at the shallowness of the words, "till death do you part," knowing that the two about to be joined have been soul mates for several lifetimes, and will be for many more to come, or sat among mourners at the funeral of a loved one, receiving no comfort from the words of the minister who never knew the person in life, then you have known the need for such a book as this. It will give you a framework to ritually mark the momentous transitions of life, in terms that are in keeping with your Pagan beliefs both intellectually and spiritually, and enable you to channel these powerful emotions into pure magick.

Here is a complete system of the Pagan Rites of Passage which are based on the ancient traditions of our Pagan ancestors. Written for the Wiccan or Pagan, solitary or coven practitioner, beginner or advanced, the series of rituals given here are general enough to be adapted into any tradition.

Flying Witch Farm
Yuletide 1993

Chapter One
Birth/Paganing

Birth/Paganing

As the setting sun ends the shortest day, so begins the longest night of the year. Snow settles in hollows and covers a sleeping Earth, and tiny lights begin to flicker. All through the darkness candles are lit, and rainbow lights flicker on fragrant evergreens adorned with silvered pine cones, gilded walnuts, blown glass fruits and birds with spun-glass tails. Then, at midnight's darkest hour, the Yule Log is kindled and the darkness brings forth the light, the Divine Child of Promise, the newborn Sun of the solar year. And, as the sun comes up early on Yule morning, it brings the promise of life renewed.

In a softly illuminated chamber, figures of goddesses move gently across a wall. White candles flicker before a figure of an ancient fertility goddess in a tiny shrine, and glossy cowrie shells reflect the candlelight. Charms and amulets hang from the pine headboard of a bed generations old and a quilt pieced and stitched with designs of protection lays across it. All of the preparations have been made, some months in advance, for the magickal event that soon will take place here, the magick of birth.

As Pagans, we believe that everything in Nature is a manifestation of the Gods and that everything has a spirit which is a spark of the divine, and so the moment of birth, when the new spirit emerges from darkness into the mundane world, is a reenactment of the birth of the Divine Child, the moment of birth involves two entities, the mother and the child, and, like Yule, the moment of birth is a reenactment of the myth of the Great Goddess, who in the beginning was the darkness, and who brought forth from herself the Light. At the moment of birth each mother is the Great Goddess, each child the Divine Child.

While the act of giving birth is in itself a Rite of Passage for both mother and child, it is not a convenient time to celebrate for either party, and so the actual Rite of Passage is usually put off to a day in the near future. Although birth is a mainly physical event, there is much that can be done to

Planting the Birth Tree.

mark it as a spiritual and magickal event for the mother, and this can be especially important for a woman if it is her first child.

In ancient Egypt when a woman was about to give birth, the public room of the house, what we today would call the living room, where guests would be entertained, was entirely redecorated for the occasion. The walls were repainted with white wash and then adorned with figures of Gods and Goddesses who presided over childbirth: Taueret, Bes, and Isis. On the platform that served as the family altar, the figures of the Gods were removed, and two columns of bricks were constructed, upon which the woman gave birth in a squatting position similar to that being used again today in some cases. It was here, in the most important room of the house, upon the family altar, that the mother brought forth her child.

In certain forms of early American architecture, there was a room built especially for childbirth, called the "borning room." It was built against the central chimney of the house and had no windows or outside doors. The only source of heat for this room was the bricks of the chimney, the fireplace openings being elsewhere in the house. Historians tell us that the purpose for this was to protect the newborn from drafts, but it is just as likely that this archaic bit of architecture was devised to prevent the spirit of the infant, just now bound to a physical body, from escaping, especially up the chimney, a traditional exit for spirits.

While modern homes do not usually have "borning rooms," and only the most fanatic of Pagan women would repaint their living rooms just for the occasion, many contemporary Pagan woman elect to have natural childbirth and many of those choose to do so at home. For those who choose to give birth in a hospital, many hospitals are now providing a more cozy, home-like room for childbirth. Whether home birth or hospital room is chosen, there are still many things that can be done to help the mother-to-be focus on the magickal and spiritual side of the process whenever possible.

There are many charms and spells that have been made or performed through the ages in order to insure a smooth delivery. On islands in the South Pacific where colorful and beautiful sea shells are abundant, shells of the genus Cypraea, commonly known as cowrie shells, famous for their smooth, glossy exteriors, were used by island women for this purpose. Pregnant women would rub their abdomens with the glossy surface of the shells to transfer the magickal quality to themselves. Necklaces of these shells possess the same magick. On the other side of the world, in the ancient countries of the Mediterranean, shells of the same genus were sacred to the fertility Goddess Aphrodite, because of both their incredible beauty and the resemblance of the shell's aperture to a woman's vagina. The Latin name for the genus comes from the island of Cyprus where they were left as offerings at the temple of Aphrodite. Charms and necklaces of cowrie shells can be worn or carried throughout the pregnancy for their magickal property of smoothness, and kept in the birthing room when the time comes.

Another object from the sea that was used to ease childbirth is the large brown seed, smooth and shiny, called the sea heart (*Entada gigas*). In Norway women in labor would drink a potion served in a cup made of the outer shell of the sea heart. It is possible that the potion contained rue, which stimulates the action of the smooth, involuntary muscles, including the uterus, but whatever the ingredients, the smoothness of the seed and its association with the sea gave its own special magick to the brew.

So closely associated with the sea is childbirth, especially in coastal villages such as in Brittany and Wales, that it was believed that children were born during an incoming tide, and death occurred as the tide was going out.

The ancient Egyptians made numerous charms and amulets that invoked the protection of the divinities that preside over childbirth. Paramount among these is Isis, she who was called the Divine Mother. It was Isis who, after the resurrection of her consort Osiris, Lord of the Underworld, gave birth to Horus, the Sun God.

She has been portrayed suckling the infant Horus, who usually appears to be more of a miniature pharaoh than an infant; as a vulture-winged Goddess with her protective wings outspread; and simply as her sacred animal, the vulture.

Cowrie shells, sacred to Aphrodite, insure an easy delivery.

Three other Egyptian deities who presided over childbirth were Bes, Taueret, and Bast. Bes, the fat jolly dwarf who is friend to all women, was believed to have originated in the Sudan. With feathered headdress and pointed ears, his image was carved on the headboard of the marriage bed to insure his blessings for wedded bliss and his presence was welcomed in the birthing chamber where he protected both mother and child by driving away evil spirits. Tiny amulets of faience that were clutched or worn thousands of years ago by birthing mothers are fairly numerous and can still be found at galleries that deal in antiquities, and excellent reproductions are being made today.

Taueret is the Hippopotamus Goddess who presided over child-birth and who protected the expectant mother beforehand. She is sometimes portrayed as a hippopotamus standing upright on her hind legs and wearing a ceremonial wig. Her full, round shape in this pose is one that almost any woman in the final weeks of pregnancy can identify with, but it is the gorgeous blue faience hippopotamus walking on four feet and decorated with deeper blue lotuses is the image of this Goddess with which most people are familiar. This popular museum reproduction powerfully conveys the feeling of cool water, soothing, supporting, and freely flowing.

Of all of the Egyptian deities, one of the most beloved, now as then, is Bast. Depicted either as a cat, sometimes adorned with jewels, or as a cat-headed woman, Bast is one of the most powerful of all Egyptian deities. A sister to Sekhmet, the Lion Goddess who is associated with the sun, Bast is naturally associated with the moon, and for this reason the Greeks identified her with Artemis, the Moon Goddess who presided over childbirth. To the Romans She was Diana, the Moon Goddess, who also took the form of a cat to seduce her brother Lucifer, and give birth to Aradia. Often portrayed with a litter of kittens, Bast embodies the feminine principles of fertility and motherhood.

It was these three divinities, Bes, Taueret, and Bast, whose images were painted on the walls of the birthing rooms of ancient Egypt, and their images still possess the powers of protection for women who are about to give birth, especially those who have leanings toward Egyptian magick. It is still possible today to find authentic ancient Egyptian amulets for a surprisingly affordable price, and those of Bes and Bast are fairly common. There are also wonderful museum reproductions of larger altar pieces being produced as well, and it seems that one of the industries of modern Egypt is to reproduce Egyptian charms and amulets that look 3,000 years old. The only real difference between the authentic ancient ones and the new ones, aside from the prices, is that the new ones have not been enchanted by priests. There were two kinds of Egyptian amulets, those that were inscribed with magickal words of power and those that were not. Those amulets not inscribed depend on the image or the material they are made of for their power.

Once the amulet of the proper image has been found, it might already be inscribed with hieroglyphics. If not, it might be inscribed later with hieroglyphic runes, astrological signs, or any other magickal alphabet that expresses the purpose of the charm. Then in a simple ritual, within a Circle, the amulet can be enchanted with words like:

> *Taueret, Goddess of the Nile*
> *protect this mother and this child.*

or

> *Lady of Life, Bast divine*
> *Help me bring forth this child of mine.*

Authentic ancient amulets do not need to be cleansed, inscribed, or enchanted. They have a magickal power all their own.

There is an amulet made today of stone, lapis, obsidian, or malachite, in the image of a bear. This amulet is especially appropriate to wear during pregnancy because the bear, one of the most powerful of animals, is sacred to the Mother Goddess. The bear gives birth during hibernation, while she is deep in sleep. She usually bears a pair of cubs, suggesting the divine twins, and she usually does so in a cave, associating her with the Earth Mother. She births her cubs and suckles them about the time of Yule, the birth of the Divine Child. Contemporary bear amulets, or fetishes, are made of a variety of stones, each with their own power to add to the charm, but I have recent-

The hippo is sacred to the Goddess Taueret, the divine midwife,
and protector of pregnant women.

ly seen an original Plains Indian version of this amulet. It is carved of wood a bit larger than the modern stone ones, and the wood was dyed a pinkish red. Around the bear's middle are several strands of twine made of dark animal hair, each ending with a bit of polished stone or shell and in at least one case a shell of the genus Olividae which had to be traded all the way from Florida and which is known for its naturally glossy exterior. This is a very powerful amulet with many associations with the Great Goddess and with a smooth and easy delivery that would have a place in any birthing room, especially if, for one reason or another, a woman chooses to give birth in a hospital, under anaesthetic.

Another traditional amulet to be worn during pregnancy is a key. This might be an antique key to an ancient door long fallen from its hinges, or a tiny gold key to a diary or jewel box. The magick of the amulet, of course, is in its ability to open that which has been locked tight. The key, like the other amulets described here, can be worn throughout pregnancy, and then hung up in the birthing room when the time comes.

To choose a key to a door, lock, or jewel box, you must also have the lock. Skate or clock keys will not do, as their purpose is to tighten, not to unlock.

As early in the pregnancy as possible, on the third night before the Full Moon, place the key in a bowl of lightly salted water and leave it in moonlight overnight. Then, on the night of the Full Moon remove the key from the water and pour the water on the ground. Then insert the key in its lock and gently turn it, saying words like:

> Key with the Power to unlock
> I shall call upon you soon
> Not to open this lock
> But to unlock my womb.

Repeat this charm each Full Moon and wear or carry the key at all times. Then, when the time has come, mentally call upon the power of the key.

Opening and unlocking as a magickal charm to facilitate childbirth has been practiced in a great variety of ways in just about every culture. In many European villages, when a woman was about to give birth, all of the doors and windows in the house, if not the town, were opened wide and every lock unlocked. In other cultures lids were removed from pots and pans, and chests and boxes were opened. Pliny tells us that it was considered unfortunate for anyone to sit with their hands clasped or their legs crossed when a woman was giving birth.

Probably the most important magickal act performed when a woman was about to give birth was the untying of all knots. Ropes, belts, curtain ties, every knot in the house and preferably the village was untied. The birthing room is definitely no place for Celtic knot designs.

So important was the untying of knots at the time of childbirth, that at the rites of Juno Lucina, the Roman Goddess who presided over childbirth, participants had to untie any knots in their garments.

In some cultures all sharp or pointed tools and weapons were removed from the house in which a woman was about to give birth, in order not to harm the delicate new spirit of the infant. In other cultures it was forbidden to work with sharp tools at that time for the same reason.

In some ancient cultures it is believed that to make any preparations for the child, such as buying baby furniture or clothing before the child is born, is to invite the Evil Eye and will surely bring bad luck. This belief is especially prevalent in countries around the Mediterranean, and so in many of these countries there are to be found charms for protection against the Evil Eye.

In Italy there is the Sprig of Rue Charm. This might be an actual sprig of the herb *Ruta gravelonensis*, or a bronze, silver, or gold replica of the plant, as shown in *Ancient Ways* (page 83). In Greece and the Greek Islands small stones or pebbles, or glass beads are painted with a simple drawing of an eye, neither right nor left (suggesting it is the third or center eye), and used as a protection against the Evil Eye.

One of the most popular of all Egyptian amulets is the Eye of Horus, or Udjat. It has been made of almost as many kinds of materials as could be found in the ancient world, but the original and most correct material was lapis lazuli, or *mak stone*, and this was sometimes inlaid with gold. These amulets were buried with the dead, in order to give back life and vitality to the deceased, and they were worn by the living for acquiring or preserving health, strength, vigor, and in general protection from just about anything. Unlike the Greek eye amulets, Udjats were made in two varieties, a left and a right usually associated with the Sun and the Moon. Left eye Udjats, those associated with the Moon, are rare, the great majority being the right eye associated with the Sun and especially the Sun at Midsummer, when Udjat ceremonies involving twelve altars were held.

The Udjat is, of course, sacred to Horus, the Divine Child of the Egyptian pantheon, being the son of Isis and Osiris after Osiris was resurrected from the dead to become the Lord of the Underworld. Udjats made of the ancient lapis or the later faience are the protective blue color of heaven, and are powerful charms for protection against the Evil Eye, but these amulets of the Divine Child are especially appropriate for children.

Another popular charm for protection against the Evil Eye, from the ancient lands of Phrygia (Turkey) and Sumer (Arabian States), is the "Hand of Fatima." Fatima is the Arabic name for Ishtar or Inanna. Pronounced *Fa-ti-ma* in Arabic, it is pronounced *Fat-i-ma* in Italian, which makes one wonder just who the Lady was that appeared to three children in Portugal, and whose message was to be revealed in 1961.

Be that as it may, the "Hand of Fatima" is an amulet in the shape of a hand, with an eye of some sort in the palm. The eye may be engraved or made of stone or glass. In the latter cases it is usually blue in color, blue being, in Islamic countries, the color of heaven and therefore protective. The hand may be anatomically correct or so abstract as to seem not to be a hand at all, but the knowledgeable observer will recognize the five digits, no matter how unhand-like and decorative the amulet is.

By the late fifteenth and sixteenth centuries, when Europeans began to explore the Pacific Ocean, a new charm was added to the arsenal of weapons against the Evil Eye. The genus of seashells known as *Turbos* possess a small trap door called an operculum. In life they are attached to the flesh of the animal but can be found on beaches among the empty shells. Each species of Turbo produces its own uniquely ornamented operculum, but that of Turbo petholatus, or tapestry turban, is a deep, rich vitreous green. Popularly called "cats eyes," these objects, one inch in diameter, were set in rings of gold or silver and worn as protection against the Evil Eye. These cats eyes have additional magickal power because on their reverse side there is inscribed by nature the most perfect spiral.

Before leaving the subject of "eyes," a Native American belief is that if the wing feather of a blue jay is found, (it must not be one taken from a bird) it should be left to stand in a vessel of water. The water then may be sprinkled on the eyes of a baby, insuring that the child will in the future awaken early with the jay and not grow up to be lazy.

A traditional charm for an infant in Mediterranean countries, to insure protection and good fortune, is three tiny objects knotted onto a length of red thread or cord long enough to be a bracelet. The first of the three objects is a bit of precious red coral, the second is a tiny image of a cat or a cat's head, usually black, and the third is a tiny pair of scissors that actually work. At first glance the symbolism of these three objects seems a bit confused, but a second look can clarify the picture.

The number three of the objects suggests that this charm invites the protection of the Triple Goddess and therefore it is likely that each of the objects represents one of Her aspects. The red coral might, because of its color, seem to represent the Mother aspect of the Goddess, but since coral comes from the sea, it is most likely to represent the Maiden aspect who was called Aphrodite, "foam born," or "born of the sea" by the Greeks, and Venus by the Romans and Italians. The cat, especially if it is black, is usually associated with the Crone aspect of the Goddess, but it was Diana who took the form of the cat in order to seduce her brother Lucifer and give birth to Aradia. To the Greeks, Diana was Artemis who presided over childbirth and who was identified with the black cat goddess of Egypt, Bast, who presided over fertility and maternity. This leaves the scissors to represent the Crone aspect of The Goddess.

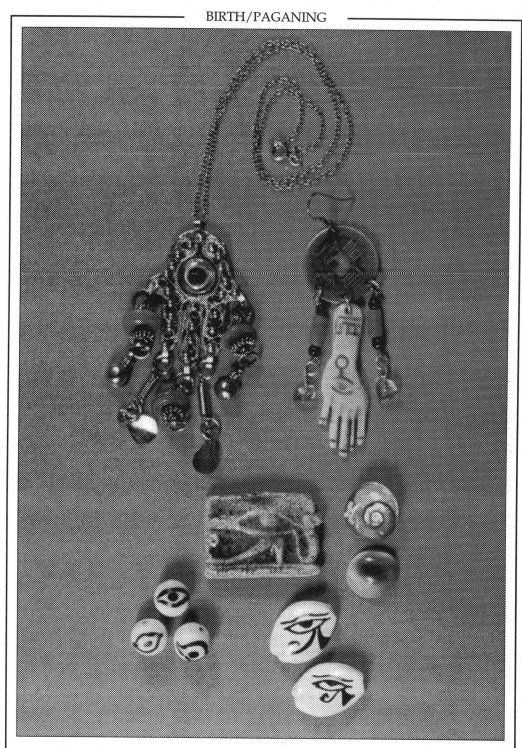

An assortment of charms for protection against the Evil Eye.

But there is another element to this charm and that is the cord itself. Traditionally the cord is red, the color of life, and so this ancient and deceptively simple charm consisting of a bit of red coral, the figure of a cat, and a tiny scissors knotted together on a red thread or cord representing life itself, not only invites the protection of the Triple Goddess but the blessings of the Goddess in her aspect as the Three Fates. In Greek they are called the Moirae; Lachesis who spins the thread of Life, Clothe who weaves the patterns of it, and Atropos who cuts the thread of Life at death. To the Romans they were known as the Parcae; Nona, the spinner, Decima, the measurer (who is identified with the Moon Goddess who measures time with her phases), and Morte, death. To the Norse they are the Norns; Urdr, Skuld, and Verdandi, and to the Anglo-Saxons the Wyrd whose individual names have been lost.

And so this simple little charm of a piece of red coral, a cat figure, and a tiny pair of scissors calls upon the protection of the Triple Goddess and the blessings of the Three Fates as well, and may be the original charm bracelet.

This charm is traditionally made by the child's mother or grandmother. To make such a charm it is necessary first to find the objects. The red coral might be found in a gem and mineral shop, pre-drilled for stringing, or as a piece of antique jewelry.

A single antique coral earring yielded enough red coral for me to have a lifetime supply. The cat figure might be found as an antique charm or as a new one, and the tiny scissors are also popular charms in sterling silver or could also be found in a shop selling dollhouse miniatures.

(Scissors play an important part in other Italian charms for protection against jealousy or the Evil Eye. One simple charm is to place an open pair of scissors somewhere in the home where they will not be seen. Be sure they are facing the door or entrance to the home. The function seems to be that the scissors, symbols of Morte, or the Crone, cut or "kill" the spell of the Evil Eye. I have been told, by a close family member, that she has seen the scissor closed after a certain person has left her house.)

Since this charm invokes the blessings of the Three Fates who are portrayed as spinners in almost every culture, it would be most appropriate to hand spin the length of yarn if that is at all possible, and dye it red with madder root, which is native to many Mediterranean countries. (Cochineal is the native red dye of the Americas.) As the yarn is being spun it can be enchanted with words like the following:

> *Fleece and flax spin around*
> *As you do the magicks bound*

Whether this charm is seen as invoking the protection of the Triple Goddess or the blessings of the Three Fates, it is calling upon the magick of the Goddess of the Moon. Therefore, as the Moon is waxing, seek the tiny charms

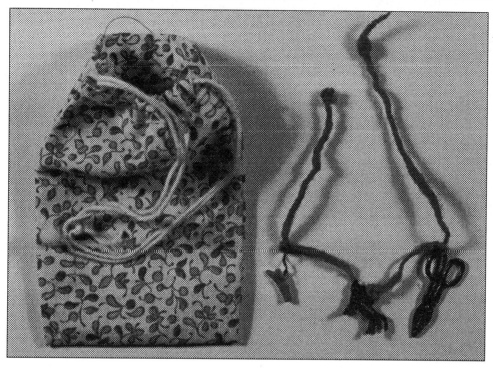

An ancient Italian Charm of Protection for an infant.

and spin the yarn, and on the night that the Moon is full, gather together all of the things you will need. Light a white candle, cast a simple Circle, and in the light of the Moon begin knotting the charms one at a time, contemplating their meaning and speaking your wishes aloud with words like;

> *Aphrodite, born of the sea, protect this child*
> *And grant her (or him) your gifts of Love and Beauty*
> *Diana, mother of Aradia protect this child*
> *And grant her your gifts of Wisdom, Power, and Prosperity*

and finally,

> *Morte, Goddess of Death, protect this child*
> *And grant her your gift of a long, healthy life.*

Needless to say, any of these charms for the protection of the child should be hung well out of the reach of the most active child.

As the time of birth approaches, and all the charms and amulets have been made for the protection of both the mother and the newborn child, one final preparation might be made, a small shrine or altar to the Mother Goddess, in the room where the birth is to occur. This need not be elaborate, just a figure or representation of the Goddess in her Mother aspect, a pair of white candles, a red candle to be lit later on, and perhaps flowers. (In a hospital candles are not permitted because of the presence of oxygen.)

Some appropriate representations of the Goddess are the Venus of Willendorf or the Venus of Laussel, Demeter with her torch and golden sheaves of wheat, Artemis with her pine cone-tipped wand, or Isis, the Divine Mother, with her protective feathered arms outspread, to name only a few. The figure ideally can be placed where it can be a focal point from the birthing bed and illuminated by the two white candles. The candles might be anointed with Altar Oil (olive oil in which frankincense and myrrh have been dissolved) and inscribed with magickal signs such as the Rune ᛒ.

One of the fundamental beliefs of most Pagans and Wiccans is reincarnation, and it is hoped that we will be reborn within our own clan or tribe or village, to be reunited with those we love and who have loved us. If this is a part of your belief system, it might be appropriate to place upon the altar a family album containing photos of your ancestors, as a sign that the ancestral spirits are welcome to at least witness the rebirth, if not to be reborn.

Finally, the unlit red candle, anointed with oil and inscribed with symbols of life such as the Rune ᛋ, might be placed before the image of the Goddess. This candle does not represent the element of Fire, but the Divine spark of the life of the newborn child. It may be placed in a glass or silver bowl of sea water containing a few cowrie shells, or in a cauldron, and be lit when the child is born. Allow the candle to burn down completely, signifying a life lived to the fullest, and to give strength and energy to the child, much like the Yule log gives strength to the newborn Sun at Yule.

In ages past, when all babies were born at home with the aid of a midwife, many of these women were as skilled at reading signs and omens as they were at delivering babies. Any strange occurrences that coincide with the time of a birth should be noted and may possibly be an omen that predicts something about the future of the child. A friend of ours relates that on the night she was born, the hospital called her father to announce the blessed event, and at that moment a bat flew in his window!

The Pagan interpretation of this would be something like: a bat is a creature of the night and therefore associated with the Spirit World, and so this bat would be either a message from the Spirit World or a sign that the newborn child is the spirit of a deceased ancestor reborn. Her father had a different interpretation!

A dog howling is a sign that Hecate, Queen of the Witches, is nearby. A dog howling as a child is born would be a sign that the child will have extraordinary powers of magick. The appearance of an unusual animal at the

A Birthing Shrine with a figure of Gaia.

moment of birth may be a sign that the child will be endowed with the powers of that animal, or that this is the child's totem animal or spirit guide. (For more information on signs and omens and the symbolic meaning of various animals, see *Ancient Ways*.)

One of the most prevalent beliefs is that if a child is born with a caul he will have "second sight," clairvoyance or the gift of prophecy, or the ability to see ghosts.

There are a number of rites that, in ages past, were almost universally performed in the days following the birth of a child, and many of these involved the navel cord. In some cultures, the navel cord, when it finally fell off, was dried and carried as an amulet by one of the parents. In others, it was tied into a necklace, to be worn by the infant for protection. In still other cultures the navel cord was carefully hidden away to protect the child for its entire life, and it was believed that harmful magick could be worked against the child by anyone who gained possession of the cord. This is, of course, true of any body parts, the afterbirth, hair, or nail clippings of any individual, at any age.

One of the most universal rites, then, to be performed for the protection of the child by protecting the navel cord, was, and still is, to bury it under a tree which was also planted for the protection of the child. If for any reason the navel cord is not available, a knotted red cord might be substituted for it.

Tree planting is one of the most important of all of the rituals performed after a child's birth, and was practiced from the North of Europe to the South Pacific. In Switzerland, it was traditional to plant an apple tree for each son born, and a pear tree for each daughter. In every culture that ritually planted trees for the protection of a newborn child, it was believed that the well-being of the tree and of the child were one, and as the tree flourished and grew, so did the child. If the tree was blighted or struck by lightning, so would the child be diseased or struck down.

In today's transient world, it is unfortunate that such beliefs that unite us with the Earth and all life upon it must be abandoned. But perhaps this is not true. Such ideas need not be abandoned, but only altered slightly to fit circumstances. For every tree planted in a suburban backyard, only to be cut down in later years by the newest resident of the tract house, two more trees must be planted to insure the well-being of the child, because today, more than ever, our children's lives depend on the planting of trees.

For anyone who has both the place and the desire to plant a tree for the protection of their child, there are many things to be considered. Since the well-being of the tree will be in some way connected with the life and well-being of the child, a tree of long life would be a logical choice. Bristle cone pine and sequoia aside, oak trees live for many years and of course have associations with magick. Oak is usually associated with the God, or Male Principle, and so would be a bit more appropriate for a boy. Pine and fir, including the above mentioned sequoia and bristle cone pine are associated with the Goddess, especially in her aspect as Goddess of Childbirth, and so all pines and firs are appropriate for children, especially girls. Maple trees are long-lived hardwoods and bring with them the magick of all the beauties of life.

The apple tree is associated with love and beauty and with healing. It is the tree of Avalon, and there is a New England legend of an apple tree called *Seek-no-Further* that was planted in the 1700s, and is still producing fruit. Each time the old tree died, its trunk toppled over and a few of the uppermost branches, still living, took root and grew into a new tree, each resurrection growing several feet from the last. The apple is a perfect tree for a girl.

Two other trees that would be especially good birth trees are the rowan and the hawthorn. Both trees are known for their magickal properties, and both are favored by Faeries.

There are two trees that in European traditions are considered the "Tree of Life," the ash and the yew. Both trees are thought of as connecting the mundane world of the living with the underworld of the spirits of the dead, and the spiritual planes of the high Gods. While the ash is the "Tree of Life," the yew is also a tree of death, more often planted in graveyards than as birth trees in cottage gardens. It is this quality of the ash as a tree of life, connecting the world of the living with the realms of the spirits, that makes it the chosen wood for many a shaman's staff, the Stang of several British traditions of the Craft, the traditional shaft of the Witches' besom or broom, and the simplest version of all of these, the most ancient of magickal tools, the magick wand. Trees are of such vital importance today that if you live in an apartment and do not know of anyone who would allow you to plant a Birth Tree on their property, you might consider contributing something to an organization such as "Global Releaf" in the child's name.

As Pagans, we know that it would be immoral to deprive our children of their right of religious expression. Still, it is hoped that they will choose the Pagan Path when they come of age, and if that should turn out to be the case, the birth tree would provide the wood for at least one of their basic tools of the Craft later in life.

There are a few trees to be avoided in choosing a birth tree. As already mentioned, yew is associated with death and graveyards, and therefore not a good choice. All members of the willow family are sacred to Hecate, but weeping willow is also associated with death and mourning, so it too would not be the best choice. Birch is sacred to the Goddess and is a symbol of rebirth, but white birch has a tendency to break in ice storms, so in a climate where this is likely to happen it is not a good choice either.

Still, there are many wonderful trees to choose for a birth tree, and the planting of it might be the central point of the Rite of Passage, along with the ritual burial of the navel string. In the years to come, other body parts such as baby teeth might be ritually buried here. In other times a child's first teeth were buried under the hearth, or near a mouse or rat hole. The ritual burial was accompanied by a chant requesting that the mouse take the tooth and give in exchange the hardness and strength of its own teeth to the child. Today, for better or for worse, most of these pests have been exterminated, but a similar ritual can be accomplished. After the "Tooth Faerie" has purchased the tooth for a reasonable sum, the parent might then bury the tooth under the birth tree, intoning words like:

> *Earth I give you bone,*
> *Give* (child's name) *stone,*
> *So mote it be.*

Considering that the dental profession is still pretty much back in the Burning Times, this is a spell that should be worked at every opportunity.

A child's first haircut might also have its final resting place under the birth tree.

It has been traditional, for longer than anyone can remember, to give gifts to the newborn. While such gifts as savings bonds and certificates of deposit are useful, valuable, and will certainly be appreciated, they are outside the scope of a book about magick. Recall the story of Sleeping Beauty and the 12 Witches who were invited to her "christening." Each Witch gave the princess a magickal gift, the gift of Love, the gift of Wisdom, the gift of Happiness, and so on (see *Ancient Ways* for more on the story), and this is a magickal tradition that can and really should be continued, whether you are a Pagan parent or a Pagan friend of the family.

The gift of Wisdom, for instance, could be symbolized by a book. What more perfect gift for a child than a book of Faerie Tales or mythology, that will be enjoyed for years to come and treasured for a lifetime afterward, to be handed down to the next generation. To make the gift a more valuable one on several levels, it might be an antique book containing stories and secrets no longer in print; but a book, no matter how rare and full of Wisdom it might be, is only a gift on the mundane level, unless it is an enchanted book.

To enchant the book, perform a simple ritual. Cast a Circle according to your tradition and light candles of blue and indigo. Burn sweet incense and invite the Goddess, in her aspect as Athena, Goddess of Wisdom (for example). Ask her to grant your desire to bestow upon the child, with this book the gift of Wisdom. Direct the magick of your spell into the book with your wand, and then, holding the book close to your lips, intone words like:

Faerie Book
Be thou enchanted
The gift of Wisdom
Will be granted
So mote it be:

Then inscribe the book to the child, letting the inscription express the wish.

The gift of Beauty can be a questionable one. Some feel that there is too much emphasis placed on physical beauty, and that, even in the old Faerie Tales, a beautiful maiden could win the treasure and the handsome prince by virtue of her good looks alone. Let us hope that the Beauty referred to in these ancient tales is simply the outward manifestation of true inner beauty, and a pleasing countenance is simply the physical expression of a good person. "Pretty is as pretty does," the old nursery rhyme tells us, and there is a certain magickal truth to this. If we believe that we are beautiful, and act accordingly, with grace and confidence, others will believe it too and see us as beautiful, regardless of our physical features.

One way to practice this is mirror gazing, and so the gift of Beauty can be given symbolically as a mirror. The comb and mirror as symbols of the

Old Faerie Tale books impart the gift of Wisdom.

Goddess of Beauty and fertility, Aphrodite, or Venus, are lovely symbolic gifts of Beauty for a girl-child. For a boy, perhaps the rearview mirror of a '57 Chevy, or just a handsome wall mirror that would be a valuable piece of furniture. In mythology, Perseus was given, by Zeus, a shield of bronze which he later used as a mirror when slaying the Medusa, thereby saving his life. In most Pagan traditions, however, it is the mother who traditionally arms her son, so the gift of a magickal shield would be an inappropriate gift from a Pagan friend. But, like the book that represents the gift of Wisdom, an 18th century wall mirror or a rearview mirror from a 1949 Mercury is just a mirror unless enchanted.

To magickally transform a mundane mirror to one that will bestow the gift of Beauty, first cleanse it with an infusion of a purifying herb such as vervain. Then, on a night when the Moon is Full, cast a Circle according to your ways, and within its boundaries catch the moon's reflection in the mirror's depths, and, gazing at it, chant words like these:

> *Mirror of the midnight sky*
> *Cause the glass to show the eye*
> (Child's name) *beauty deep and hidden*
> *Mirror do as you are bidden.*

Then wash the glass once more, this time with dew, and wrap it in silk or linen until the time for it to be presented.

To paraphrase Benjamin Franklin, "Wine is proof that the Gods love us and want us to be happy." He was right! Furthermore, Dionysus, or his Roman counterpart, Baccus, was the God of Wine and of Joy (as well as resurrection), showing the ancient and mythical connection between wine and joy. This makes wine a perfect symbolic gift of Joy, and one that might be appreciated for years to come. A case of wine vinted in the year of the child's birth will mellow and age in the bottle, over the years becoming a valuable collectors' item, providing that the wine chosen is one that keeps well. Generally speaking, red wines keep for many years, while white wines do not. Among the imported wines, Bordeaux (including the Medocs etc.) will keep and improve for many many years, while the Burgundies (Beaujolais, etc.) are best enjoyed at three to ten years of age. A case of fine wine, given to the Pagan parents of a child, can be stored and a bottle opened and ritually used at each of life's passages, with a few bottles left over for personal celebrations. The bottles will have to be properly stored, at cellar temperature (about 50°–55°), and slanted so that the cork is kept wet with the wine while any sediment falls to the bottom of the bottle (i.e., lay the bottles down, don't stand them on their heads).

There is just one problem with the gift of wine vinted in the year of the child's birth, and that is that it will have to be given at a later date because any good wine vinted in that year may not be bottled for one to three more years. On the plus side however, there is so much magick involved in the growing, harvesting, pressing, and fermenting of wine that very little ritual is required, just the verbal expression of your wish that this wine be the gift of Joy in the name of the Gods. Also, many small local wineries will make up special custom labels.

One of the most charming of handmade gifts is a quilt for a child. It need not be a huge quilt to fit an old fashioned double bed, but a traditional 36" by 36" crib quilt, which could double as a receiving blanket.

A quilt is the symbol of warmth, comfort, and security. For the infant and child, the sleeping and the sick, it is the magician's cloak of protection. Pulled up over the head it provides us with protection from cold drafts that chill our ears and noses, keeping us awake at night, as well as from the unseen terrors of the darkness that lurk in the corners of childhood bedrooms.

A quilt is made of three parts, the top, or quilt cover, the filling or batting, and the backing. All three layers are stitched together with a simple running stitch which is the quilting, and which may form a design of its own. The cover may be patchwork, that is, made up of pieces of materials of contrasting colors that have been stitched together to form a design; applique, in which pieces of material cut into shapes have been stitched onto the quilt cover to form a design; or it may be plain, adorned only with the quilting stitches.

Large or small, a handmade crib quilt (whether handmade or "store bought," or even made by an entire coven) can become the "security blanket" of early childhood, a playroom wall decoration, and if it should survive, aged beyond its years by the rigors of childhood, it might become a family heirloom.

There are an infinite number of patterns from which to choose in both patchwork and applique, any of which might have special meaning for the Pagan. (For more on this, see *Wheel of the Year*.) There are also endless color combinations. Traditionally, pink is for girls, blue is for boys. It is interesting to note that some years ago, in an experiment, it was learned that if the walls of a prison cell were painted pink, the prisoner within behaved less aggressively. Perhaps the traditional roles of separationism are inflicted upon us as early as pink and blue nurseries, so let's forget those traditional colors. Yellow is the color of cheerfulness and intellect, green is the color of nature and of growth, and violet is the color of spirituality. People seem to prefer pastel colors for infants' rooms, while infants themselves seem to prefer bright colors, which also make more stunning quilts. Whatever colors and patterns are chosen, the pattern of the quilting stitches will be superimposed over this to form another design and this, too, can be a magickal design. The Rune ᛉ

meaning growth and fertility can be the basis of the quilting pattern and impart its magickal power. It also incorporates the Rune X or gift.

Whatever patterns, colors, and designs are chosen, a quilt is still just a quilt, unless it is a magickal quilt. See ritual given in *Wheel of the Year*, pages 26–28.

In parts of Old Europe a traditional gift is, of course, a Pysanky, or Ukrainian Easter Egg. Those made especially for a newborn are predominantly white or light in color, and of simple design. A perfect motif for such an egg is the Tree of Life, usually a stylized evergreen with a variety of birds in the branches, and a pair of deer at its base. This design bears an incredible resemblance to the Norse myth of the pair of harts that nibble away at the roots and branches of Yggdrasil, the Nordic Tree of Life. Both symbols have the same meaning as Aping, an infinitely varied design that is awarded as a tattoo among the as-yet unChristianized natives of Sumatra at initiations or other rites of passage.

There is one gift, of course, that only the Gods can give, and that is the gift of Immortality. When the Goddess, in her aspect as Demeter, roamed the Earth in search of her daughter Persephone, who had been abducted by the Lord of the Underworld, she stopped to weep at the well of Eleusis. Still today deep scars can be seen on the well where, for thousands of years, ropes have cut deeply into its walls as buckets of water have been drawn up. So bitterly did Demeter weep, that three sisters who came to draw water from the well took pity on her and took her to their home. Here, at the home of the King of Eleusis, she was shown much kindness. One night she decided to repay the kindness. As she held the king's infant in her arms and thought of her own child, now lost, she decided to give him the gift of immortality. This she would accomplish by holding the child in the purifying flames of the hearth fire, flames which burn away that which is mortal and mundane leaving only the immortal. But she was interrupted in her purpose by the child's mother who was terrified by the sight, and the spell was not completed.

Years later, after she had been reunited with her beloved daughter, Persephone, the Great Goddess, as Demeter, still remembered the kindness she had been shown at Eleusis. She returned to the city and there established her temple, where she taught her mysteries of immortality to all who would come to learn them. A similar tale is told of Isis. The secrets of the Mysteries of Eleusis have never been revealed by its initiates, but through the magick of the God and Goddess, through their descents into the Underworld, we are all given the gift of Immortality in the eternal cycle of Birth, Death, and Rebirth.

Sometime after the child's birth, preparations for the Rite of Paganing begin to be made. It is important at this time to be fully aware of what this

22

Pysanky with the Tree of Life design are appropriate gifts for the newborn.

rite means, and what it means is entirely different from what the new religion's rite of Christening or Baptism means. In fact, the purpose of Baptism and Christening is two-fold, the Baptism being a ritual of purification to cleanse the child of "original sin" (the hereditary curse due to Adam and Eve having disobeyed God's condition that they not eat from a certain tree), and Christening being the dedication of the child's spirit (or soul) to Jesus Christ.

On the contrary, the Rite of Paganing is not a purification ritual. What could be more pure than this newborn entity that has just come to us from the Spirit realms? Nor does the Rite of Paganing in any way dedicate the spirit of the child to our Pagan Gods. That is a decision that the child can only make for himself after he has come of age, and no one else has that right. The Rite of Paganing is simply the ritual naming of the child, a spiritual bonding of the child to its self, and the introduction of the child, by the name by which it will be known, to the Gods and Guardians, spirits, friends, and family members. For these reasons it is obvious that the selection of a name is of great importance. This is not a secret or Craft name but the legal name by which all the world will identify the child for the rest of his or her life, and by which the child will identify her- or himself. There are many things that might be considered.

In the main line religions it is expected that a child will be named after a recently deceased ancestor or a character in the Bible. To a Pagan, naming a child after a recently deceased ancestor has far deeper implications than it does for other religions, and should be carefully considered. Names chosen from mythology can be as inconspicuous as names from the Bible, and can invite the protection of a particular deity without binding the child spiritually. Two of the most popular names for children today, Samantha and Daniel, certainly have Pagan and Wiccan connections. The fact that Samantha was the name of the lovable Witch on "Bewitched," a popular television program of the early 1960s, is no coincidence. Samantha is a traditional Witch name and probably comes from the Celtic name for Halloween, which is still spelled Samhain, no matter how it is pronounced. Daniel, one of the two most popular Irish names for boys, of course is in honor of the Celtic Mother Goddess, Danu, for whom Denmark and the Danube River are also named. Names like Diane, Diana, and Selena honor the Moon Goddess. Arthur is a traditional boy's name that honors one of our mythology's greatest heroes, who is also a representative of the Sun God. There are many other names with Pagan associations that would not embarrass a second grader in the public school system.

Here are a few other ideas for girls: Morgan, Fay (for Fee or Faerie), Sheila (na-gig), Bridgett or Brita (Bride), Elva, Mae (May), Cybele, Bel, etc. For boys the choices are far fewer. There are, as mentioned, Daniel and Arthur. Jason is a popular name, after a Greek hero. Dion might be for Dionysus, or in the Celtic tradition Durwood, for Duir (oak) and Wyd (to see or to know), is related to the word Druid.

There might be other elements, too, to be considered when choosing a name—numerology, for example. Simple numerology is based on the idea that each letter of the alphabet has a numerical value from one to nine (see chart) and that the numerical value of a name, when the values of all the letters have been added together and reduced to a single digit, will set up a certain "vibration" that will continue to affect the owner of the name for life.

The name Diane, for example is traditionally spelled D-I-A-N-E, numerologically 4+9+1+5+5, which equals the number six. (In the system of addition that I use, based on an old magickal system, I automatically drop out any 9s, because they cancel themselves out anyway, for example 9+5= 14=5.) Six is a number of love, beauty, and harmony. It is sacred to the Goddess Venus (Aphrodite). This is a very nice number for any girl. A variation of the spelling of this name is D-IA-N, with a numerical value of one. One is a number sacred to the Sun and having attributes like grand, outgoing, magnanimous, and leadership abilities. While these are usually considered "Masculine" traits, a woman can do well with them in today's world. The only

1	2	3	4	5	6	7	8	9
A	B	C	D	E	F	G	H	I
J	K	L	M	N	O	P	Q	R
S	T	U	V	W	X	Y	Z	

Letters of the alphabet and their numerical equivalents.

problem might be that Dian is still a variation of the name of the Moon Goddess, and having a Sun number with it might cause either conflict or balance. Another variation, in fact the original, is Diana, with a numerical value of 2, which brings with it the qualities of passive receptivity and psychic intuition, qualities altogether in keeping with the name of the Moon Goddess, but before being reduced to 2, the numbers of the name D-I-A-N-A, 4+9+1+5+1, add up to eleven, and in most systems of numerology, eleven is considered a "master number." It gives the qualities of mysticism and spirituality, as well as spiritual leadership.

Once the name has been chosen, a date for the Wiccaning can be set. This too might be carefully considered. The date may be selected according to the phases of the Moon; either the Full Moon for the completion of a project or the New Moon for new beginnings. Astrology might also be considered. If you or someone you know is versed in astrology, then an auspicious date might be selected on that basis.

In Bali, the date for naming a child is placed on the 105th day of the child's life. In this land of spiritually aware people, infants are considered to come directly from heaven, and are treated with the same reverence as a god. They are thought of as still belonging more to heaven than to earth until this time, and for this reason are not permitted to touch the earth prior to their naming day. On the day that the child is named he is given magick symbols inscribed on flower petals, and gifts that symbolize wealth.

Among the Maori, a child is not named until its navel string drops off. This then is buried under the tree planted to protect the child's life.

In the Catholic and other Christian traditions, when a child is being Christened, a man and a woman are appointed to be the "godparents" of that child. The sole purpose of these godparents is to see to it that if anything should happen to the child's natural parents, the child would be brought up in the same belief system as the parents.

As Pagans, we believe it is wrong to force our own beliefs on others, even our own children. However, most Pagan parents do instruct their children in the basic beliefs and joys of the Pagan faith, if only to dispel the intentional lies about Paganism and Witchcraft that they might be taught in school.

If you are Pagan or Wiccan parents of children, you might consider asking a trusted Pagan friend to act as Faerie Godmother to your children, instructing them in Pagan ways, in the event that you are unable to. This might also be included in a will. Again, this is not to say that a Faerie Godmother would raise the child as a Pagan, only offer cultural and spiritual instruction, perhaps on a seasonal basis, as an alternative religion that the child might choose when he or she comes of age.

As the date for the Wiccaning approaches, preparations for the rite begin to be completed. Friends, family, and coven members prepare to present their gifts, and the ritual area is adorned with seasonal decorations suitable to the occasion. Regardless of the time of year, pine or fir branches are always appropriate for a Wiccaning, and are always available. Sprays of baby's breath make a beautiful and delicate contrast for both the altar and the Circle itself. If this is a first child, then just within the Circle there might be a red cape to be ritually presented to the new mother, and next to it the Birth Tree. The following rite is written for a solitary couple, but can be altered to suit a solitary practitioner or a group.

The priest/husband/father, casts the Circle by himself and stands within it while the priestess/mother/wife awaits outside the Circle at the Southern Quarter, and the child in a basinette is just outside the East Quarter.

When the Circle is cast the priest invites the priestess into the Circle with words like:

> Lady ____ enter now this Circle,
> But not as before through the Eastern Gate.
> As that is the direction of Birth.
> For now you yourself have given birth.
> And now, to mark your passage from Maiden
> To Motherhood, enter this Circle through
> The Southern Gate, the Gate of Life.
> And the Element of the Fire of Life.

The priestess/mother enters the Circle and takes her place at the altar holding high her athame, saying words like:

> By the magick of the Mother Goddess (name, in your tradition),
> And that of the Father God (name),

Through my priest and consort (name) *here,*
Has the magick of new life flowed through me,
And to our newborn child.

By the power of the Lord and Lady (names),
Do I leave behind the flower of my Maidenhood,
For I have born the fruit of Motherhood.

The priestess then lights the red taper on the altar from the white one, and extinguishes the white one, replacing it with the red one. The priest takes up the red cape and holding it across both his arms, he says words like:

Here do I hold the symbol of the Great Mother
Red like the fire of Life
As I place it on the shoulders of my priestess (name)
Divine Mother of all Life, grant her your gifts
Of Wisdom and Love,
For she has entered your sacred realm.

The priestess accepts the red mantle and both priest and priestess meditate for a moment on the spiritual implications of the life changes that have taken place. The priest then goes to the altar and, raising both arms, intones words like:

Lord and Lady, Father and Mother, God and Goddess
We have cast this Circle on this night
To celebrate a new life
Which through your magick has come to us.

The priestess goes to the East Quarter and carries the infant into the Circle. The child is placed before the altar in the center of the Circle with the priest and priestess standing on either side. Both parents meditate for a long moment on the spiritual presence of the child. Then the priestess intones words like:

Divine child, conceived in love
Through the Magick of the Gods, I name you _____.

Then the priest carries the infant to the East Quarter and holds it high while the priestess, with arms raised, intones words like:

Spirits of the East, know this child whose name is (name)
Bless him with the Breath of Life
And give him strength of mind.

The priest then holds the incense up before the child and gently blows some of the smoke in the child's direction, saying words like:

(Child's name) *be clear of mind and strong of purpose,*
That you may know and fulfill your destiny.

The priest and priestess then carry the child to the Southern Quarter, and the priestess intones words like:

Spirits of the South
Know this child whose name is _____
Bless him with the Fire of Life
And give him a passion for life.

The priest then holds up the Fire candle, moving it so that the child's eyes follow it.

(Child's name) *let the passions of life burn fiercely in you,*
That you may know and fulfill your destiny.

At the Western Quarter the priestess might intone words like:

Spirits of the West
Know this child whose name is _____
Bless him with the Magick of Life
And give him the gift of Hidden Knowledge.

The priest then dips his finger in the cup of water and anoints the infant's forehead saying words like:

(Child's name) *listen to the inner voice*
And follow your intuition
That you may know and fulfill your destiny.

And finally at the North Quarter the priestess speaks words like these:

Spirits of the North
Know this child who's name is _____
Bless him with the Strength of Life
And give him the gift of Physical Well-being.

At the North Quarter the priest takes a few grains of salt on his finger and puts it on the child's tongue.

(Child's name) *taste the joys of life*
And honor your physical being
That you-may know and fulfill your destiny.

Now the priest and priestess carry the baby back to the altar, and together they intone words like:

Lord and Lady (names)
Father and Mother of all
Behold this child whom we call (name)
Conceived in love
And by your divine law.
We ask that you protect
This new and fragile life
And infold him in your love.

Priest and priestess take up the green and red altar candles, and, holding their flames together, light the short red candle on the altar, saying:

By your power
Lord and Lady
We light the purifying flame
May its transforming magick
Grant the gift of immortality to (child's name).

Then the child is carried around the Circle and if other Pagan friends, family members, or coven members are present, the child is introduced to each one and each presents his or her magickal gifts. If others are not present but gifts have been sent, this is the time for them to be presented by the parents.

Finally it is time for the ritual planting of the Birth Tree. Ideally the Circle has been cast in a place outdoors where the tree can be planted at its very center, This is announced by the priest with words like:

Now is the time to plant the Birth Tree!

If others are present they may form a circle around a hole which has previously been dug, and the soil prepared. Then the priest, holding high the tree, speaks words like:

Lord and Lady
Spirits of the East, South, West, and North,
From this time on, this child (name),
And this tree are Magickally bound.
As one flourishes, so does the other.
May the Elements of Earth, Air, Fire and Water
nurture this tree.
As I will So Mote it be.

Now the priestess places the navel string or a substitute in the prepared soil, and gently places the tree in with it. If necessary, the priest shovels the soil back around the tree roots. Then priest and priestess dance around the child and the tree. Around and around, everyone joining in and dancing around the tree. If the tree is big enough, charms of protection and symbols of good fortune might be hung from its branches. When everyone has finished dancing, it is time to sit and feast around the tree end celebrate the new arrival.

From now until the Coming of Age are the golden carefree days of childhood. For the next few years, the child will seem to be suspended somewhere between the gentle world of Faerie folk from which he or she has just been so abruptly ejected, and the material world of physical reality. These are days of openness and exploration, of imagination and learning, of adventure and experiences. These too, are the days of Faeries and princesses, knights and dragons, scarecrows and playmates unseen. Many of us on the Wiccan or Pagan Path realize what we had almost forgotten ourselves, these days, and now must work to recapture them in our rituals and in our Magick.

It is the spiritual realities of these magickal days that others, on other more mundane paths, try to deprive us of and to replace with their own incomplete but ever so tangible realities, but it is the memories of these golden days of childhood that keep alive the Divine Child of the Great Goddess in all of us.

Chapter Two
Coming of Age

Coming of Age

The waxing Sun of winter has not yet risen in a cold, gray morning sky. Across the road a neighbor's horse stands, like a painting on a cave wall, in a field of white. With her back to the wind, thick winter coat and long chin whiskers, she stands dark and still in the swirling snowflakes. Down the valley, hearth fires are rekindled and the smoke drifts and mingles with the scent of freshly brewed coffee. The world awakens to another winter day. And beneath the blanket of snow, still silent and unseen, new life begins to stir.

And so it is with children. Like the maiden Goddess at Imbolc, beneath the innocence and laughter and carefree play, at some point something else begins to stir.

Like constellations in the midnight sky, bison and caribou migrate across the ceiling of a cave and vanish into darkness as a torch light is withdrawn. Here, among bats and scorpions, in the absolute blackness of a tomb-like cave, lurk terrors unknown. How long will it be, for the boy about to become a man, until the light of day again is seen?

Elsewhere in time and space, a girlchild who has recognized the first sign of puberty is confined to a specially built hut where she will eat and drink from special utensils for an entire moon. When her confinement has ended, the hut and its contents, her clothing, and eating vessels will be burned and she will be welcomed as a woman of her tribe, able to perform the rites and traditional dances of her people, as well as bear children.

In cultures that are today called "primitive" by those who have lost touch with that other side of reality, when a boy or a girl comes of age physically, they are also, and often at the same time, initiated into the religio-magickal traditions of their people. In our society today this is impossible, and in many cases that is just as well. In so-called primitive cultures where shamanistic forms of spirituality are practiced, religions are not differentiated, but in our culture today there is a distinct difference between a Catholic and a Bap-

Coming of Age.

tist, a Jew and a Lutheran, even though they may all live in the same village, along with a few Buddhists, and even a Pagan or two. Within these various traditions it seems to be assumed that young people will simply grow up in the same faith as their parents, as if a belief system was a matter of genetics.

Pagan parents, however, do not take this for granted. When the child of Pagan parents comes of age, the physical aspects of coming of age are celebrated, and this is done completely separately from any spiritual initiation.

But when does a child "come of age"? For a girl, the exact moment is quite obvious. It is when she first begins to menstruate. For a boy, the transition from boyhood to manhood is slower, more subtle, and so the date is usually fixed at the time when he has completed 12 solar cycles, 12 being a solar number and therefore, one associated with the God and male aspects of divinity. And so, a boy is generally thought of as coming of age on his 13th birthday. This is the case with the Jewish tradition of the Bar Mitzvah, in which a boy on his 13th birthday, becomes a man.

Among some Native American people, a boy came of age before he went into his first battle, and among other people who live in hunter/gatherer societies, a boy has to come of age before participating in his first hunt of an especially dangerous animal. It is interesting to note that both of these activities, hunting and doing battle, involve drawing blood, one's own possibly, as well as another's, while the purpose of the activity is to take the life of another. Even within the extremely conservative and ultra-civilized traditions of the British upper classes, it is customary to be "blooded," that is, anointed with animal blood, when one first participates in a successful hunt, usually the atrocious so-called sport of the fox hunt.

So coming of age, for both girls and boys, involved, since ages past, the shedding of blood. For a girl it was the shedding of her own blood, a sign that she now possessed the magickal power to bring forth life, while for a boy it was the risk of shedding his own blood, while performing the magickal act of taking a life.

In the pages of the *Golden Bough*, it is stated that among so-called primitive peoples, sacred priest/kings, murderers, mourners, pregnant women, girls at puberty, and menstruating woman, all had to obey similar laws of ceremonial purity. What is it that these people all have in common? They all stand at a portal, a place between the worlds of the living and of the spirits; pubescent girls and pregnant or menstruating women, at the portal of birth; mourners, homicides, and hunters, at the portal of death.

As the hunter/gatherer way of life gave way to the agrarian way of life, as hunting was no longer a necessity, and treaties replaced battles, blood letting became a symbolic act, an ordeal of pain rather than the taking of a life. These rites might have consisted of such painful ordeals as beatings, mutilations, starvation, or circumcision.

Even today there are ordeals of pain that are associated with coming of age. One of these is ear piercing. In my grandmother's day, girls had their ears pierced when they reached a certain age, but my mother's generation seems to have considered ear piercing "barbaric." One aunt of mine compared it to "wearing a bone through your nose." I well recall my own piercing, which I desperately wanted done years before it had come back into fashion, so there were no professional jewelers to do it, and doctors refused on the grounds of "barbarism." Finally, a neighbor volunteered. The ordeal took place in the warm, yellow light of my mother's kitchen, the ritual tools a threaded needle, a cork, an ice cube and some rubbing alcohol. Mother handed me libations of dark rum, and by the time my ordeal was over, the tingling in my ears was nothing compared to the throbbing in my head.

Ear piercing eventually became popular again, and in the 1980s multiple piercing was in vogue. This multiple piercing, resulting in a neat row of tiny holes in the earlobe, reflects almost exactly images of the Goddess from two ancient cultures a world apart, one the Eastern European Karanova cul-

Ancient examples of ear piercing from the Karanova culture of Bulgaria, ca. 5000 B.C.E., the Valdavian culture of ancient Peru, and the Syrio-Hittite, ca. 2200 B.C.E.

ture of Bulgaria 5000 B.C.E., and the other the Valdavian culture of ancient Peru. In both of these cultures, the Goddess figures are portrayed as having about five holes in each very predominant ear, and in one figure from Kara- nova there are still rings in some of the holes.

While the act of piercing is symbolic and very appropriate for a girl who has just come of age, happily, boys are having their ears pierced too, and why not? The pharaohs of Egypt had their ears pierced, as did men of the Romany Gypsies.

Another ordeal of pain, one that was traditionally a sign of manhood, is tattooing. Tattooing seems to have originated in the South Pacific, where it was done as a part of a coming of age/initiation ordeal. In Samoa, where the old ways were allowed to linger a bit longer by missionaries of the new faith, the traditional tattooing designs are still being employed. Symbolic designs about the thighs and navel represent the completion of the birth process, and the rite ends with the breaking of an egg over the initiate's head.

In Sumatra and Borneo, men are tattooed by the elder women of their tribes, to commemorate all of the passages and initiations of life. All of these tattoos, while infinite in variety of design, have but a single theme, the supreme god, Aping, the Tree of Life. With a highly stylized human face at its center, surrounded by spiraling tendrils of roots and branches, symmetrical- ly arranged, the tattoo of Aping, Supreme God, is undeniably the foliate mask of the Lord of the Greenwood. The sacred art of tattooing is not con- fined to the South Pacific, however. The priestesses of the Celtic Druids wore tattoos as well as stained their bodies blue. In fact, the word "picture" comes from the name Pict.

Tattoos may be worn as signs of rank, or symbolic ones can act as a link with certain spirits or aspects of divinity. Today, young woman are getting themselves tattooed, and young men are having their ears pierced, while only a generation or two ago both ear piercing and tattooing were considered signs of the "lower classes" or the "criminal element." This probably is all due to a reference in the Bible forbidding "making any cuts on the flesh or tattooing, because of the dead." While Pagans certainly do not feel bound to obey any laws put forth in the Bible, it is wise to be aware that many do still hold these preconceived ideas, and such body markings can be held against you, affecting your social standing or even your job, later in life. So if you, or your children choose to be pierced or tattooed as a sign of coming of age, as an ordeal of pain, or simply as a way of adorning the Pagan temple of flesh, keep this in mind.

Aside from the ordeal of pain, another tradition associated with the rites of coming of age is a period of isolation. This period may range in length from a month (moon) to a fortnight (two weeks or half a moon) to a few days or just a 24-hour period. While women today might object to the idea of

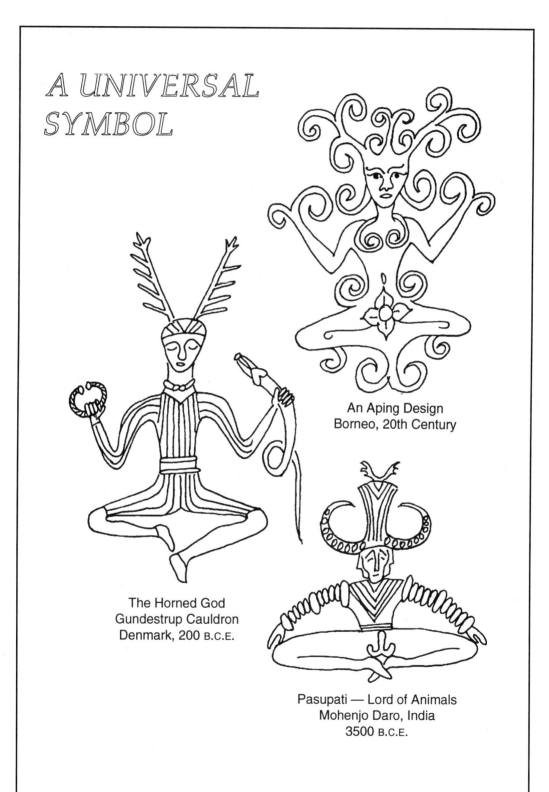

A UNIVERSAL SYMBOL

An Aping Design
Borneo, 20th Century

The Horned God
Gundestrup Cauldron
Denmark, 200 B.C.E.

Pasupati — Lord of Animals
Mohenjo Daro, India
3500 B.C.E.

being isolated because one is menstruating, and rightly so, this period of isolation from friends and family, both for boys and for girls, has the benefit of separating the time of life that has ended from the time of life that is about to begin. In many of the so-called primitive cultures, this period of isolation also took place in darkness. One reason for this in the case of girls was that it was thought a girl might be impregnated by the Sun.

In any case, whether there will be an "ordeal of pain" or not is entirely up to the individuals involved. However, a period of isolation prior to the rites of Coming of Age can only enhance the magick of the rite.

When a boy becomes a man, or a girl becomes a woman, it is an appropriate time for fertility charms, since Coming of Age is the celebration of sexual maturity. While most Pagans today are environmentalists, and are fully aware that the last thing this planet needs is more people on it, it is still everyone's right to have children if they choose to. Fertility charms are not just for the purpose of promoting reproduction, they are also to enhance sexuality, whether it is manhood or womanhood. Many of the traditional fertility charms are amulets of protection as well.

Among Italian people there are two very popular charms. One is a tiny replica of a human hand in a fist, with the index and little fingers extended, making the sign of the horns. This amulet, known as the *manu in cornu,* or the hand in horns, is a popular protection against the Evil Eye, but it is also a sign of the Horned God and a charm of masculinity. The manu in cornu charm is sometimes carved of red coral, mentioned in the previous chapter as being protective of children. Such a charm would be ideal for presentation at a boy's coming of age rite, as it invokes the powers of manhood and the protection of the child at the same time.

For a girl's Coming of Age, there is a similar charm or amulet called *manu in fica* or the hand in the fig. This charm is a human hand in a fist with the tip of the thumb protruding from between the index and middle fingers. It symbolizes the Goddess and female sexuality. Carved of red coral, the charm is also one of protection for a child. Another traditional Mediterranean charm for male sexuality is a red coral horn.

Among Anglo-Saxon and Celtic people, the same principles of male and female sexuality can be expressed with an acorn or a pine cone. The acorn, symbolizing the Oak God and the masculine attributes of strength and power, might be an actual acorn or one of iron or gold. It has the added fertility symbolism summed up in the phrase, "An entire forest is contained in a single acorn."

The pine cone is symbolic of the Mother Goddess and childbirth. Like the acorn, the pine cone contains within itself an entire forest, but its scales (or petals) are arranged in spirals, identifying it with the Goddess and female sexuality.

In Eastern Europe, there are eggs with specific designs for enhancing masculine or feminine sexuality and fertility. For men the rooster or the oak tree might be inscribed upon a raw egg, itself a symbol of fertility. For a woman a bird or a number of other animals would be appropriate, but there is also an ancient symbol called "the princess," which seems to be the symbol of the Goddess in her "maiden" aspect.

Other ancient fertility charms were of mandrake or mandragora roots. The roots of the plant were once said to let out such a blood-chilling scream when being pulled from the earth that it could cause a person to die of fright. Old grimoires recommended tying a dog to the crown of the plant and leaving a plate of food just out of its reach. Apparently, either dogs were not affected by the screams of the mandrake, or dogs were considered expendable. In any case, mandrake is grown commercially now for occult use, and I doubt that the roots are harvested by hounds! While any mandrake root has some magickal power, it is the roots that are shaped like a man or a woman (with a bit of imagination) which are to be used as male or female fertility charms. When these were not available in ancient times, an ordinary man-

Mandrake Roots

drake root was simply carved into the likeness of a man or a woman. Considering the effort, the focus, and the intent required to do this, these man-made amulets probably possessed as much, if not more, power than those formed by Nature.

If you decide to make such a charm to give to someone who has come of age, or to increase your own sexuality, here is a charm that can enhance its magick.

Find a mandrake root thick enough to carve. Take it and a small carving tool suitable for the job to a place where you can work at midnight. Light a red candle, and as you work chant words like:

> *Mandrake root, stem and flower*
> *A charm I make at Witching hour*
> *Born of Earth*
> *Given Birth*
> *Give to* (whoever the charm is intended for)
> *Your Magick power.*

Be sure to carve the root to be very obviously male or female. It will also add to the power of the charm if you are slightly sexually aroused as you carve.

When the carving is complete (it need not be realistic), breathe life into it by blowing on it three times, then slip it into a small pouch, red for a female charm, green for a male one.

There are gifts suitable for a child about to come of age that are symbolic rather than magickal. For boys, a watch has been traditional. With today's digital watches, the symbolism is no longer apparent, but a watch face that has 12 hourly divisions of the solar year, rather than the 13 divisions of the Lunar year, makes it a truly masculine symbol.

For girls, a birthstone ring or pendant might be given. In the myth of Ishtar's descent into the underworld, one of the last of her jewels to be removed as she moved through the gates was her "girdle of birthstones." These probably were 13 in number, relating to Ishtar's association with the moon and fertility.

In one tradition of the Craft with which I have been acquainted, female initiates wear "Witches' jewels" of 13 symbolic stones as a necklace, probably for this same reason. The myth of Ishtar is probably the earliest recorded reference to birthstones, a tradition that has continued, in various forms, for at least 4,500 years.

A cameo is another suitable gift, as most depict a lovely young lady. I was given a pair of cameo earrings for my newly pierced ears. Each of the earrings had a woman's face; the pair seemed to be mother and daughter. Today I think of them as Demeter and Persephone. True cameos are carved of

A pair of cameo earrings from Naples, representing mother
and daughter, Demeter and Persephone.

shell, but only of one particular species of shell, *Cassis rufa*, which has natural layers of red and white. Red and white are the colors of the Maiden and the Mother—mother and daughter.

While it is understood that a Coming of Age rite celebrates and acknowledges the transition from boyhood to manhood, or from girlhood to womanhood for the one about to make that passage, what is not so apparent, and in fact often forgotten, is that the family, tribe, or community is also about to change in its relationship with the subject of the rite. This is especially true for the parent/child relationship, which is about to end. This transition is symbolized in some so-called "primitive" cultures when a boy is ritually kidnapped, often right from his mother's arms.

From this rite of passage onward, the father/son relationship is transformed to one of man to man, and the mother/daughter relationship becomes one of woman to woman. From this rite onward, the girl who has become a woman and the boy who has become a man have earned the right to be treated with a certain degree of respect and equality, by parents and elders of the family, tribe, or community. The individual who has undergone a Coming of Age rite deserves to be treated as an adult, a young adult, to be sure, but still an adult, by members of the group.

One way to impress this upon the adult members of the group or family is to ritually grant the one who has just come of age the right to address all members of the group by their first names as part of the ceremony.

When the certain night arrives, when the charms have been made, when the ordeal has been completed, and a period of isolation has ended, it is time to celebrate the Coming of Age of the young man or woman. The following rite is based on some ancient customs, as well as on traditional Wicca.

This rite should be performed as soon as possible after a girl's first menses, and, if possible, on the night of the New Moon. It is a rite for women only and would best be performed with four or five women, one of whom is the mother of the girl. If, however, mother and daughter are solitaries, the rite can be performed just as easily by the two.

A Circle is cast according to the mother's ways and adorned with ears of corn, corn dollies, birch branches, colored eggs, or other symbols of female fertility. A simple altar arranged at the center of the Circle contains a three-armed candelabra (if possible) with a white taper in the center socket, a red one in the left socket, and a black one in the right socket. If a candelabra symbolizing the three who are one is not available, then the three colored candles can be placed in separate holders on a round plate or on a triangle of parchment.

Other items necessary for the rite are: a bit of red body paint, a vial of food coloring, red lipstick or washable magick marker, a silver crescent charm or pendant, about two yards of black cloth, and symbolic gifts at each of the four quarters. These gifts could be a feather or small bottle of perfume for Air, a heart locket or fire opal for Fire, a seashell or shell cameo for Water, and a stone or rock crystal for Earth, as examples. There should also be a mirror which will be kept covered or hidden on the North side of the Altar.

When the Circle has been cast and consecrated, the mother stands between the North and East points of the Circle, facing outward, and summons her daughter with words like:

> Woman-child, you are about to enter
> The Circle of Women.
> Kneel and receive your mark.

The mother then marks her daughter's forehead with red pigment in the shape of a triangle, saying:

> Bear the mark of womanhood proudly,
> But first kneel and contemplate
> The transformation that is taking place.

The mother then places the black fabric over her daughter, covering her completely as if with a shroud, and she and the women in the Circle drum or chant Goddess (of fertility) names for a length of time, until the mother feels the time is right, or a sign is given.

When the time has come, the women of the Circle line up with their legs spread to form a traditional birth tunnel through which the girl must pass, chanting or drumming as they move into position. Then the music should end abruptly and at the same instant the veil be removed from the girl by her mother, who is the woman closest to her, and who then pushes her firmly through the tunnel of women's legs. The mother then leaves the line of women and walks to the altar where her daughter will confront her as she emerges from the tunnel. (If the rite is a solitary one, the mother simply walks around the girl to face her at the altar. If it is a group rite, the other women take up their positions at the four quarters.

The mother, confronting her daughter at the altar, now solemnly intones words such as:

Now you kneel in the Circle of Women
Do you know what this means?
(The answer should be "not yet")
Stand now and walk the Circle with me
And you will learn.

The mother puts her arm around her daughter and gently guides her to the Eastern quarter where either the mother or one of the women of the Circle, representing the East and the element of Air, will intone words such as:

(Girl's name), *know that as a woman*
Once in the month when your blood flows
Or the Moon is full, your mind will be
Open and receptive to things unseen.
Learn to see with the mind's eye,
And listen to the wind
Heed your inner voice,
To be a woman is to gain Wisdom.
Take this gift (symbolic of Air and Wisdom)
So that you will always
Remember this.

The mother then leads her daughter to the South quarter, where words such as these will be intoned:

(Girl's name), *know that to be a woman*
Is to know the joy of passions flame
Learn to open your arms and heart to love
And to return it freely.
Be guided always by your mind's vision
And your heart's desire.
To be a woman is to know Love
Take this gift (symbolic of Fire and Love)
So that you will always remember this.

Mother and daughter then proceed to the West quarter, where such words as these might be spoken:

> (Girl's name), *know that to be a woman*
> *Is to feel the ebb and flow of the tides of life*
> *Learn to move to the gentle rhythms of your own body*
> *And to flow with the current of your life*
> *To be a woman is to feel the flow of life.*
> *Take this gift* (symbolic of Water and Intuition)
> *So that you will always remember this.*

And finally, mother and daughter proceed to the North quarter, where words such as these might be spoken:

> (Girl's name), *know that to be a woman*
> *Is to possess the magick of making.*
> *Learn to bring forth and to nurture*
> *That which the mind can envision,*
> *The heart love and the spirit sense.*
> *To be a woman is to possess the power to create.*
> *Take this gift* (symbolic of Earth and creativity)
> *So that you always remember this.*

Mother and daughter now walk to the East quarter again and then, the Circle having been completed, they return to the Altar. Now the mother instructs her daughter in the following ceremony.

> *From this night onward shall your life*
> *And the cycles of the moon*
> *Be Entwined.*
> *Light now the candles of the Triple Goddess*
> *The Three who are one.*
>
> *White as snow or the flowers of May,*
> *Is the color of the waxing Moon.*
> *Light the White candle for the Maiden.*
>
> *Red as the flowing blood of Life*
> *Is the color of the Moon at Full.*
> *Light the Red Candle for the Mother.*
>
> *Black as the darkest winters night*
> *Is the color of the waning Moon.*
> *Light the Black candle for the Crone.*
>
> *Now the Three who are One are within you,*
> *And you are in them.*

Then taking up a mirror which has been hidden from sight, the mother holds it so that her daughter can gaze at her own reflection in the candle light, saying words like:

Behold the girl who has become a woman.

After she has gazed at her reflection for a time, her mother will replace the mirror and take up the silver crescent charm:

We stand now, woman to woman,
At the center of the Circle
Where all things meet their opposites.
Take this charm of the silver crescent
As a reminder of this:
That as the Horned Moon represents
The Goddess, giver of Life,
So does it symbolize the horns of the Lord of death.
She who has the power to create life
Also has the power to take it.
The magickal power of Womanhood
Is to accept responsibility.

Mother places the charm of the silver crescent about her daughter's neck and kisses her as the other woman of the Circle gather about to kiss her, congratulate her, and present her with gifts.

This rite might be followed by a small feast, usually a "pot-luck" dinner these days, during which conversation will probably turn to tales of young womanhood, woman's strengths, and heroines.

In the years that follow this magickal night there will be many transformations of body, mind, and spirit. Not the least of these will be a transformation of the very special relationship between mother and daughter, wherein the mother will eventually have to acknowledge her daughter as a woman, mature and equal.

The following is a similar rite that might be used for a young man's Coming of Age. This rite should be performed as close to the boy's 13th birthday as possible. It is a rite for men only, and, like the rite for girls, it is best performed with four or five men, one of whom is the boy's father or spiritual guardian. However, if the parent or guardian is a solitary, the rite can be performed by the two alone. Each of the men might be masked.

The boy should have spent the previous time period alone, in a tent in the forest, in the desert, on a cot in a cellar, or at least alone in his room. The Circle is cast, preferably in a darkened room, and delineated with branches of oak and/or ash. A simple altar arranged in the center of the Circle has upon it two lighted altar candles, a cup of wine, and a knife such as a hunting knife or a pen knife. This knife should have been purchased by the boy's mother, and it is important to note too that this is a knife made to cut with, it is not an athame. Each man will hold a small container of body paint of a different color. As before, a mirror is hidden behind the altar. There will also be appropriate symbolic gifts at each of the four quarters.

Once all is prepared, one of the men, and it should be the one least known to the boy, shall go for him wearing a mask, and blindfold the boy. Then the man will carefully lead him to the Circle, causing him to stop at the Eastern gate. Here he will be confronted by his father or guardian with words like:

> Boy, you are about to enter
> The Circle of men.
> Stand tall and bear the mark.

The father marks the boy's forehead with the paint, making a solar cross, upward-pointing triangle, vertical bars, lightning streak, or other masculine symbol. Still blindfolded, the boy is then led to the center of the Circle where his shirt is removed and his upper torso is painted by the other men of the Circle with masculine signs and symbols. (If for any reason body paint is objectionable, the ash of burnt corn cobs is a traditional material for this purpose, and there are several native herbs that yield natural dyes for body staining such as bloodroot, pokeberries, and celendine.) When this is finished (it should only take a minute or two), the containers of paint should be hidden away and traces of paint wiped from everyone's fingers. Then each man, is stationed at one of the four quarters, and the father removes the boy's blindfold, saying words like the following:

> You now stand in the Circle of Men
> Do you know what this means?

The boy should answer;

> Not yet.

And the father replies with words like:

> Then come and walk the Circle with me
> And you will learn.

Father then gently leads his son to the Eastern quarter, where either he, if this is a solitary ritual, or one of the men of the Circle will represent the element of Air, speaking words such as:

(Boy's name), *know that to be a man*
Is to have courage and never fear.
But know too, that knowledge overcomes fear.
Learn to confront that which causes fear
And in so doing, gain wisdom.
To be a man is to learn courage.
Take this gift (an owl's feather perhaps wound with
beads is perfect)
So that you will always remember this.

The father then leads his son to the South quarter, where words such as these might be intoned:

(Boy's name), *know that to be a man*
Is to know the fire of passion.
But know too that the element of fire
Is the element that transforms.
See to it always
That the flames of your passion
Forge the forms that you desire.
Learn to harness the power of the flame
To forge your own destiny.

When a boy comes of age.

Take this gift (of something forged of iron, an antique key
or tiny labyrs is perfect)
So that you will always remember this.

Father and son then walk to the Western quarter, where a man representing the element of water may speak words like:

(Boy's name), *know that to be a man*
Is to be called upon to make decisions.
But always remember too that deep within yourself
Lies the intuition that will enable you
To decide wisely and well.
Follow your deepest instincts
And you will always choose well.
Take this gift (of something masculine yet symbolic of
water, such as a shark's tooth)
So that you will always remember this.

And finally, the father guides his son to the north quarter, where a masked man representing the element of Earth speaks words such as:

(Boy's name), *know that to be a man*
Is to be strong in body and mind.
But remember, too, that you also possess
The power to plant the seed of Life.
Use your strength always
With courage, wisdom and intuition,
To live the life that you desire
Free of regrets and filled with rewards.
Take this gift (an acorn is perfect)
That you will always remember this.

Now the father leads his son back to the altar, where the other men gather close around. The father speaks:

Every ending is a new beginning,
And so, on this night of transition,
As this boy becomes a man
His childhood has ended.
As a sign of this does he leave behind a token.

The boy places the token of his childhood in a cauldron to burn, or in a fireplace or firepit (if it is not something that will cause vast amounts of air pollution to burn), or simply places it in a wastebasket. Remember that this is not a sacrifice. The boy is not being asked to give up a childhood treasure, just to discard a token of his childhood. It might even be something he detested.

When the token has been burned, or otherwise disposed of, the father then takes up the knife:

> *Down through the ages*
> *It has always been so,*
> *That as women are the bearers of life,*
> *Men are the hunters and the warriors.*
> *Accept this token, then*
> *Of your manhood* (handing his son the knife)
> *Carry it always with you,*
> *And with it a single thought*
> *That the hand that has*
> *The power to take life*
> *Also has the power to preserve it.*

After a moment of silence, the father holds up the mirror and commands:

> *Now behold the boy*
> *Who has become a man!*

After the boy has gazed at his own reflection by firelight, body painted and knife in hand, it is time for all of the men to sit in the Circle, sharing food and drink, stories of heroes, and their own experiences.

In the years that follow a person's Coming of Age, there are many changes, both physical and spiritual. Childhood's playthings will be replaced by computers, cars, and clothes. For the moment, fantasies of knights and maidens, warriors and princesses, will recede to the mind's darkest corners and dustiest attics, to be replaced by those of music, rock stars, and sex. New self-images emerge as old ones are banished, but when the transitions are all complete and the mature butterfly emerges from the cocoon of childhood, one day there is another stirring, a fleeting recollection of another time and place, a tiny spark of light shining in a darkened corner where it was left since the close of childhood. This will not happen for everyone, only for the fortunate few.

Chapter Three
Initiation

Initiation

The eastern sky is flushed with pink, and rosy rays of light pierce clouds of lavender-gray. As the sun comes up over the horizon, changing from pink to gold, illuminating and warming, robins forage in the greening grass, daffodils thrust themselves upward through the frosty earth, soft gray pussy willows burst from dark-brown buds and newborn lambs browse for tender shoots. Everywhere life is reborn, in response to the light of the waxing sun as it climbs higher in the springtime sky.

As we stand on the threshold of the Vernal Equinox, balanced between darkness and light, we recognize both sides of life, both the warm, sunny days of physical life and the dark, mysterious nights of spiritual life, and we realize that we dwell in both worlds, as each of us is a vortex where the two worlds meet and join as one.

For many, this simply means the idea of some sort of life after death and the acceptance of the religious doctrines they were taught as children. But, for the few of us who have heard the ancient call, who know the truth of the old tales and legends, who have laughed with the Faeries in the forest, or have recalled the long forgotten dream, the process is a much deeper one.

"American by birth, Rebel by choice," so quips a Harley Davidson tee shirt, but this slogan could easily be paraphrased to describe the majority of Pagans, "Christian by birth, Pagan by choice." These words express a fundamental difference between Pagans and the followers of most other faiths. That is, that Pagans, even those who call themselves hereditary, have chosen this particular path of spirituality, rather than having just been brought up in it, and this act of free will is usually the result of serious intellectual investigation. Once the choice has been made, the next of life's passages is Initiation. Like Nature herself at the Vernal Equinox, to be initiated is to be reborn.

It is traditional to allow a waiting period of "a year and a day," to elapse from the time a person decides to become a Pagan or a Wiccan and the time that person actually is initiated into a coven, tradition, or "inner circle." "A

Taking the Measure

year and a day" is actually a lunar year of 13 months of 28 days and several hours each. This waiting period is a time of learning and study, a time for challenging your decision, to be sure you have made the right choice, and it is a time of preparation for a life-altering event. The traditional waiting period of a year and a day, is recommended for the solitary practitioner as well as one about to join a coven, and for one who plans to perform a self-initiation, as well as one who will eventually be initiated by a recognized priest or priestess.

Before even beginning the year and a day period, it is wise to do some honest self-questioning about *why* you are considering the Pagan path as your spiritual expression. Are you rebelling against Christian parents or trying to please Pagan ones? (We are never too old to rebel against, or seek the approval of our parents.) Do you think being a "Witch" is an interesting persona that will help you get dates? Are you a feminist interested in "Goddess worship" because you dislike the male-dominated mainstream religions? (While a pantheistic religion like Paganism certainly allows for the worship of a single aspect of divinity, many of us on the Pagan path deeply resent those who use our religion for their political purpose). If any of these or similar questions strike a chord, you probably will change your mind before a year and a day have passed, and even a solitary Witch has to sleep with herself.

But if none of these questions make you in the least uncomfortable, then you, like the majority of us, have probably always followed the ways of Nature, honored the Old Ones, celebrated the seasons, and believed in Faerie tales.

You have already taken the first step on the hidden path, so mark the date on the calendar, and mark it well! To ritualize this commitment, after marking the date on the calendar, pour a small amount of water in a bowl and add a pinch of salt to it. Using your finger pointing toward the ground, draw an imaginary Circle about yourself and visualize it glowing a silvery blue Faerie fire.

Then, holding the bowl of salted water, intone words like these:

> *With this potion I dedicate myself*
> *To the Ways of the Ancient Gods.*
> *When a year and a day has passed*
> *I shall be fit to celebrate at their altars.*

Then using your fingertip, anoint your forehead, making the sign of the Sun wheel, the Crescent Moon or the Pentagram. When a year and a day have come to pass you will become one of the initiated.

There is much to be learned in the days ahead and one of the best ways to learn is under the instruction of a competent teacher. Of course, if you come from a Pagan background, or have already read many books on the subject, you probably are way ahead, but it is always best to begin at the beginning, just in case there is something that you have missed somewhere along the way, some little piece of the puzzle. If you really are quite knowledgable, a good instructor will recognize this and speed you along. A good instructor also will not be an "authority figure." She will simply be someone who has already been through a training program and knows what basics are necessary and in what order. Above all, a good instructor is one of the greatest shortcuts. She can hand you a list of recommended reading that could save you years of "hit and miss" research and a fortune in books that did not live up to their titles. Finally, a good instructor is one who will simply help you put the pieces you probably already possess together in the proper order, and fill in the spaces if any of the pieces happen to be missing. As one of my most influential instructors once told me, "It is not how much you know, it is how well you know the basics." This is true of many things.

Now then, how does one go about finding a good teacher, especially if you do not know any Wiccans or Pagans personally? One of the easiest ways is to ask at a local "Occult" or "Esoteric" book store. If there are none conveniently located, the next-best place to look is in the personal ads in the back of a Pagan journal, or place an ad in one yourself.

Once contact has been made, the first step is usually a phone conversation. This enables the instructor to get a sense of the sincerity and level of knowledge of the student, while the student can learn if the teacher is working with the tradition the student is interested in, and if she or he is truly more knowledgable than the student. Furthermore, both parties can learn what they have in common. While a degree of mutual respect is essential, both will gain in wisdom if there is a genuine fondness for one another. If the phone call is successful, usually a meeting in a public place is scheduled. Often, a priestess or instructor with a well-developed psychic sense will skip this step, but there are a lot of "weirdos" out there who still equate Witchcraft with satanism, and Paganism with human sacrifice, so caution is always advisable.

One old tradition that should be followed, if at all possible, is that the student and the instructor be of opposite sexes. This is because, when magickal information is being given under the proper circumstances, between individuals of opposite sexes, there is also a transmission of magickal power.

One of the proper conditions is that student and instructor sit facing one another within a consecrated Circle whenever magickal information is being given. This, of course, is not necessary when discussing, for example, the mechanical "how-to's" of engraving the handle of an athame, but it can be tremendously enhancing when a magickal charm or formula is being given. For this same reason, it is suggested in some traditions that no one teach the secrets of their magick verbally to more than three students in a lifetime, or they may give away too much of their power. Of course, no real "secrets of the Craft" will be given at this time, they will be given at Initiation, and afterward, but there will be an exchange of energy. Likewise, it is an old belief among Witches that a Witch cannot die until she has passed on her knowledge or power to someone else.

There is one pitfall to be avoided. It is inherent in human nature to take the first thing we learn about a subject, or the teaching of our first instructor, as (you should pardon the expression) "gospel." No one is all-knowing or without fault, so no matter how dearly you loved your instructor, keep an open mind.

It is said by many on the yogic path that, "when the student is ready the teacher will appear." This does not, of course mean that the day you decide to study Pagan ways a certified teacher will walk into your life. What it does mean is once you have a clear understanding of what the questions are, the answers are more easily found. The "teacher" then need not be a person at all, but a book, a friend, a television program, a dream, or an oak tree. It is as if, when the student is ready, a veil is lifted and some things can be seen for what they really are, not just what they were thought to be.

For those on the solitary path, books might substitute for an instructor. While it is still true that an instructor can save the student a lot of time that might otherwise be wasted, an instructor will usually recommend books. There will not only be a list of recommended reading, but a student is also encouraged to seek new books on his own. For the student working with an instructor, this can help to develop intuition, even psychometry, but for the student on the solitary path, without guidance, this quest can be a part of the Initiation process itself.

A friend recently commented that, "there are a lot of books out there (on Paganism); every one has something to say." This seems to be a natural by-product of Paganism. So many have found the love, the joy, the beauty, and the truth—everything one looks for in a religion—in the Pagan ways, that there is this natural outpouring and desire to share. However, the plethora of books now available does not make it easier for the student on a quest.

Here is a charm to help in the quest for books, or knowledge in general. It was given in our book, *Ancient Ways,* but is necessary to repeat here. Place one drop of magnet oil (olive oil in which a magnet or lodestone has been placed for a length of time) on the point between the eyebrows, usually referred to as the "third eye," saying:

> *That I may recognize* (place a drop on your purse or wallet),
> *That I may afford* (place a drop between your palms),
> *That I may possess*
> *O gracious Goddess*
> *That which I seek.*

Aid me in my quest as I go forth
That ere I return I find
That which I desire.

But there is much more to be done than just reading and studying. Aside from the basic knowledge of the fundamental beliefs of the Old Religion, every student is encouraged to learn at least one magickal skill, and there are many to choose from. The following is a partial list:

Divination by means of:

Tarot Cards	Numerology
Runes	I Ching
Astrology	Scrying
(or other methods)	

Spirit Communication by means of:

Ouija board or Wine Glass	Mediumship
Automatic Writing	Shamanism
(or other means)	

Herbcraft or Wortcunning for:

Health and Healing	Magickal Charms

Developing other psychic skills such as:

Psychometry	Psychokinesis
Clairvoyance	Astral projection
Telepathy	Dream Magick

Developing such creative talents as:

Drawing or painting traditional designs	Singing or composing new or old magickal tunes
Poetry	Traditional Folk Dancing
Learning and telling folk tales and legends	Traditional needlework Learning an ancient language

Even if you only master one of these skills, you should also have some knowledge of most of them.

While learning the basics of the Craft and developing one or more magickal skills, this is also the time to be filling the pages of what is usually called the "Book of Shadows." This book is usually divided into two parts; the first part being the Sabbat Rites and the second part being charms and spells, etc. (This may also be done with two separate books.) This is probably not the last time you will be writing this book as you walk the hidden path of the Pagan life, but one has to begin somewhere.

The first factor that has to be considered is what the book will look like, physically. There are several options today that can make a very attractive book fairly easy to produce. One is a simple looseleaf binder that can be covered with anything from needlepoint or flamestitch, to hand-tooled leather, as very early Bibles, diaries, and probably Books of Shadows were. A looseleaf has the obvious feature of making the pages easy to rearrange. Another option is the blank hard-cover books available in artist's supply stores, and a third option is the sometimes beautifully bound blank books filled with faintly lined paper that are available in some bookstores.

Once the book style has been selected, it is necessary to decide how the pages will look. I suppose something like the "Book of Kells" is really the goal of most Pagans. However, the Book of Kells is difficult to read in daylight, let alone candlelight, so if you plan to write your rituals in calligraphy, be sure that the letters will be large enough and simple enough to be readable in the subdued light of the sacred Circle. If you are not a skilled calligrapher, neat printing can be quite attractive.

Once the style of the book has been decided upon, the pen must also be selected. The earliest writing implements, of course, were reeds and quills. In *Wheel of the Year* I gave simple instructions for making a magickal quill pen. These are fine for writing brief charms on bits of parchment or drawing magick signs or symbols, but they will make writing a Book of Shadows unnecessarily difficult.

Instead, there are so many simpler tools to choose from. There are calligraphy pens and fountain pens, ballpoint pens and felt tip markers. If you do choose a felt tip marker, a calligraphy, or fountain pen, do be sure that the ink is waterproof, as the book is very likely to be sprinkled when the Circle is being consecrated, and it will probably receive its share of libations as well.

It is advisable to have a planned layout for the Book of Shadows, one that will be convenient in the years to come. The following is the way our Book is arranged, and it has proven to be quite convenient: the first page is left blank, or simply adorned with a Pentagram. The second page is a title page containing the title of the book, the day it was begun, and your Craft name, but this page will be discussed in detail shortly. The following pages will contain the rituals themselves.

Our own Book of Shadows begins with the opening rituals, or the Casting of the Circle, the Calling of the Spirits of the Four Directions, the Invitation to the Lord and Lady, all of the rites that are always performed prior to the sabbat or esbat rites. The opening rituals are followed by the Charge, a traditional Wiccan prayer recited at most rituals. Then the actual rites of each of the Solar Sabbats, beginning with whichever sabbat your tradition considers the beginning of the magickal year, in order: Samhain, Yule, Imbolc, Spring Equinox, Beltane, Midsummer, Lammas, and Autumn Equinox. A

The Book of Shadows, and a book of charms and spells.

paragraph or so at the beginning of each sabbat should describe the preparations for that sabbat. For example: "Yule—A log adorned with sacred greens is on the hearth, and candles on the altar are unlit since Samhain." It is a huge inconvenience to realize in the middle of the Lammas Sabbat that you forgot the Lammas loaf!

The Sabbat Rites are followed by the Blessing of the Cakes and Wine, and that is followed by the banishing of the Circle. Following this are the Lunar Rites: the Full Moon Esbat, the New Moon Esbat, Drawing Down the Moon, and then special rites for each of the 13 moons, beginning with the first full moon of the year, the Wolf Moon, Storm Moon, Chaste Moon, Seed Moon, Hare Moon, Dyad Moon, Mead Moon, Wort Moon, Barley Moon, Wine Moon, Blood Moon, Snow Moon, Oak Moon. These might be followed by a rite for banishing the Esbat Circle.

Following the cycles of the Solar Sabbats and Lunar Esbats there are charms and spells, herb lore and moon lore, and magick of all sorts.

This arrangement of text and several well-placed bookmarks is really quite convenient. The Opening Rites are the first pages of text in the book. A bookmark at the sabbat being celebrated is left at the end of that sabbat rite and is therefore at the place of the next sabbat when the time comes. A second bookmark is kept at the Blessing of the Cakes and Wine, so when the rite is ended it is easy to flip the pages to the next part of the ritual, and finally, just turn the page to banish the Circle. A third bookmark might be kept at the beginning of the Lunar Cycle, and another be moved from one moon to the next.

All of the actual rites, of course, might be copied from an instructor's Book of Shadows, from a book that gives a complete cycle of rites, or the rites may be newly created, based on ancient tradition and personal desire.

Finally, it is advisable to write the rituals and charms, rites, and incantations first in pencil, inking them in only after they have been proofread several times and all the "kinks" have been eliminated.

In the early days of the Witchcraft revival (the 1960s) it was often advised that the Book of Shadows be written in one of the magickal alphabets such as the Runes, Ogham, or Theban. This was next to impossible to read, however, and is no longer necessary, but it did help to create that "other world" atmosphere within the circle.

Once the book and the writing implement have been selected, they might both be consecrated with a simple ritual. On the night of the New Moon, by candlelight, gather together the book, the pen and the ink, if any, and draw a bowl of water, to which add a pinch of salt. Cast a Circle as done previously and place in the center of it the writing equipment. Then, holding hands out and palms downward, incant words like these:

> *Book of Shadows, leaves of white*
> *Pen of art with point so fine*
> *Soon be filled with Sabbat rite,*
> *Magick charm and chanted spell.*
> *Day by day and night by night,*
> *White pages pen of art will fill.*

Then anoint each, the book (provided it will not be harmed by the water), the pen, and the bottle of ink with a finger dipped in the salted water, making the sign of the Crescent Moon, the Sun wheel, or the Pentagram, and speaking words like:

> *From this night of the moon,*
> *I dedicate this book and this pen, (etc.)*
> *To the Mysteries of the Ancient Ways.*
> *As I will, so mote it be!*

Now inscribe the first page of the book with its title; Book of Shadows "Book of Rites," "The Tree of Many Leaves," or whatever you choose to call it, using the pen and ink. (This may have already been carefully laid out in pencil.) Below the title write the date in Pagan terms, such as "The first night of the Barley Moon, 1993," and whatever other information you feel is perti-

Quills, a quill pen, and a pen knife.

nent. Do not, however, write your own name here just yet. This will be reserved for the night of your initiation, and then it will be your Craft name that will be inscribed.

Along with a Book of Shadows, and possibly a separate book of Charms, Spells, and Magick, many Witches, as well as practitioners of other magickal traditions, also keep a Magickal Journal. This is often divided into the phases of the Moon or astrological Sun signs, rather than just the days of the year. In this book are written meaningful dreams and synchronistic experiences, omens and portents, their interpretation and fulfillment, experiences with the spirit world, magick charms that were performed along with their results, success or failure, rune or Tarot readings and their fulfillment, premonitions and all of those strange and wonderful things that help us to know that we are on the right path. Pressed between the pages of this magickal journal might be photos and news clippings, herbs and flowers, any of the artifacts that might pertain to the experiences recorded upon the pages themselves.

The purpose of this journal is a subtle but important one, associated with the purpose of this particular spiritual path itself. That is that the practitioner learns to travel between the worlds of the spirit and that of mundane reality. While in an altered state, lit by flickering candles, scented by incense, stirred by the chanting of sacred names and ancient dances, it is easy enough to accept that the spark of white light that appeared in the dark corner of the room, or the three herons that flew overhead looking just like a symbol on an ancient seal were manifestations of the spirit world. But, when the candles have been extinguished, the robes replaced by street clothes and the chanted prayers drowned out by traffic sounds, it is all too easy to dismiss these spiritual experiences with mundane explanations, and in doing so, forget them altogether. The purpose of the Pagan spiritual path is to keep open that doorway between the two worlds, and by carefully recording all experiences of the "other world" in this journal it will become an aid to that purpose, and help to reaffirm those experiences and the other side of reality, whenever mundane reality would deny spiritual reality and lock the door between the worlds forever. In the mundane world apparently devoid of magick, it is easy to forget, but, by opening the pages of your magickal journal, devoid of mundane reality, it becomes easier to remember.

As the night of Initiation draws closer and the pages of the Book of Shadows are being filled with the sabbat rites of the wheel of the year, and charms and spells for every purpose you might have, there are other things that might become the subject of a quest. One of these is the above mentioned "Craft Name."

The taking of a new name at Initiation symbolizes the rebirth of the individual being initiated. Among the aborigines of Southeast Australia, when a child is about to be initiated he is given a new secret name, which is not to be revealed to strangers, nor even mentioned by friends or family without cause.

The sanctity and magickal power of a name is so great that, in the Hebrew tradition, whenever the "unspeakable name of god" appears in a text, the name Adoni (meaning Lord) is spoken instead. In the Roman Catholic tradition, whenever the name Jesus is spoken aloud, heads are reverently bowed. In both of these traditions, it is forbidden to take the name of god in vain.

So great is the link between the individual's name and one's true self, among those who follow ancient traditions, that when a friend visited Papua, New Guinea, not too long ago, she was warned before leaving the ship, not to give her name to any native who might ask, lest she wind up in a cannibal's cauldron.

In the Roman Catholic religion, when a child is born she or he is given a name at baptism and the soul is cleansed of "original sin." The child is Christened, or made Christian, but when the child has "come of age," he or she is confirmed, that is, has agreed to be a Catholic by their own free will. A part of this ritual is the taking of a new name, a "Confirmation name," which becomes the person's middle or third name. This name is carefully chosen by the individual from a lengthy list of saints' names prior to the Confirmation ritual, and the child is then confirmed by that name.

In the Pagan Celtic tradition a boy was given his name by his mother when he came of age (and a girl most likely by her father). In the myth of Llew Llaw Gyffs, the boy was denied by his mother, the Goddess Arrianrhod, and she had to be tricked into giving him his name.

There are many methods for choosing a Craft name, the simplest of which is to take the name of your favorite character or deity from Pagan myths or legends, or the name of the animal totem, gem, or mineral that you seem to identify with.

A second method is to open to the index of a book on the mythology of your chosen tradition, Celtic, Norse, Mediterranean, or worldwide if you are eclectic, and then, using a pendulum, dowse the list of names of the mythological figures. Note which names caused the pendulum to respond, usually by changing the direction of its swing, and choose your favorite from among these names.

An improvement on this method is to write the names selected by the pendulum on a piece of paper, fold it, and sleep with it under your pillow. When you awaken in the morning you will *know* your name to be.

Another method of choosing a Craft name is to cast the runes or draw a number of cards from a Tarot deck. The number of cards or Runes is determined by drawing one card or rune first and using its numerical equivalent as the number of letters to be selected. Then draw that number of cards or runes and lay them out in a row, from left to right. Each card has a number from Ace (one) to ten, Page, Knight, Queen and King are 11, 12, 13, and 14, respectively, and the Major Arcana cards are also numbered.

The number on each card tells which letter of the alphabet it represents; Ace = A, two = B, XXI = u, etc. Each rune has a phonetic value, so it is fairly easy to just read the name.

Any of these methods will be enhanced if they are performed within a magick Circle. This would best be done during the Full or waxing Moon when magickal powers are strongest. When the Circle has been cast you might state your purpose with words like:

> *Lord and Lady, guardian spirits of the Four directions,*
> *I have cast this Circle on this night*
> *That I might be given a name,*
> *A name by which I will be known*
> *To the Gods, and those within the Sacred Circle.*

If you have chosen a name by using the Tarot or the runes, also make note of the prophetic meanings of the runes or cards that were selected. This will give some insight into the nature of the work you will be called upon to do when you have been initiated into the service of the Gods.

If you chose a name by the dowsing method, or simply chose a name, you may use the numerology chart in the previous chapter to gain some knowledge of the magick of that name. (A more in-depth explanation of the Pagan meanings of the numbers is given in *Ancient Ways.*)

From the time you have chosen your Craft name until the night of your Initiation when you are given the name in the sight of the Gods, you will learn to identify with it as the name of your other self in the spirit world. For this reason this is a secret Craft name, traditionally to be known only by coven members, and used only within the magick Circle. While most Pagans and Wiccans have a secret Craft name, many also have a public one which they use when interacting with other Pagans in a public context, such as a Pagan gathering. This name serves a dual purpose. It simultaneously tells something of the individual's tradition and magickal interests, while it also protects the privacy of the individual by not revealing his secret Craft name or his legal name by which he might be harassed by those not friendly to our Pagan ways.

As the year and a day progresses, as the pages of the book are gradually filled and a Craft name has made itself known, there are other items to be sought. For those about to join a coven, in some traditions these tools are given at Initiation, but for most, and especially for the solitary practitioner, they all might be the objects of quests.

The two most important personal tools of the Craft are the Cup and the knife, or athame. The cup, a simple vessel, symbolizes the Goddess. It is the Holy Grail of Arthurian legend, the Cauldron of Cerridwen. It represents the eternal cycle of birth, death, and rebirth. The sacred knife is the symbol of the God. Usually called the athame, this sacred symbol of spirit is never used to cut anything but air. As the cup is the Grail of Arthur, so the athame is Excalibur. The cup and the athame together are used to perform the most sacred symbolic act, which is the very core of most Wiccan sabbat rites.

While some traditions use a sword as well as a knife or athame, this is really rather redundant, except in the case of a sword owned collectively by a coven, while each member owns their own personal knife.

It is also true that some traditions require that figures or images representing the Lord and Lady be present on the altar, while other traditions hold that the Lord and Lady cannot be portrayed, but only represented symbolically, as with candles. This is a matter of personal taste, something that each person, group, or coven must decide for themselves, but whenever the sanctified cup and knife are on the altar, the Lord and Lady are well-represented.

What could be a more suitable object for a quest than the perfect ritual cup and knife—at antique shops or yard sales, second-hand stores, or grandmother's attic, and when all else fails, the old reliable religious article shop or occult suppliers catalog. Cups may be made of various materials, but silver or a silver-colored metal is traditional. Those sold in religious article stores are usually intended to be the chalices of Catholic priests, and are often very expensive, since they are traditionally made, in part, of pure gold.

The finest athames are usually to be found in antique stores, and are often one-of-a-kind. The traditional athame has a double-edged blade and a black handle, and may be as simple or as ornate as personal taste dictates.

When the cup and the athame both have been found or obtained, the ritual that follows might be performed.

On the night of the New Moon, cast a Circle with your finger. Have within it a bowl of water with some sea salt and a bowl containing an infusion of wormwood, a clean towel, and some white linen, as well as the cup and the athame, and an extra vessel that the liquids can be poured into afterward. Light a candle and focus your energies, then take up the cup (which has previously been washed with soap and water). Hold the cup in both hands saying words like:

> *Silver Cup, symbol of my Lady*
> *Be thou now cleansed!*

Pour a little of the salted water into the cup and swirl it around. Visualize the cup glowing with white light, then pour the water into the empty vessel and pour some of the wormwood infusion into the cup saying words like:

Silver cup, sacred vessel
Be thou free of the negativity
Of the mundane world.

Pour the herbal infusion into the vessel, then take up the athame.

Shining bladed Athame
Symbol of my Lord
Be thou now cleansed.

Plunge the blade into the salted water and stir it around three times, withdraw the blade from the salted water, and put it into the wormwood infusion, saying something like:

Weapon of power I cleanse thee
Of the negativity of the mundane world.

Stir the herbal liquid and visualize a phosphorescent glow, as the negativity that once clung to the blade now reacts with the wormwood.

When this is done, dry both the cup and the athame with the towel, and then wrap them in the white linen and put them in some quiet place, until the night when the Moon is Full. Pour the salted water and the herbal bath into the third vessel from which the combined liquids can eventually be poured out onto the earth.

On the night when the Moon is full, remove the cup and the knife from their hiding place and cast a Circle with your finger, this time having within the Circle a fresh bowl of salted water, a candle, and an herbal brew of mugwort. Remove the tools from their linen wrappings and pour the salted water into the cup until it is half full, saying words such as:

Earth Mother, Queen of the Sea
I dedicate this Cup to Thee.
Ancient Goddess of the Moon
As I will so mote it be.

Then taking up the athame, pass its blade through the candle flame and hold it high above, saying words like:

Sky Father, Lord of Light
In your name, and on this night,
I dedicate this blade to Thee.
As I will so mote it be!

Now place the blade in the cup, intoning words such as;

Ancient Goddess, Lord of Light,
Your two symbols I unite.

In your union all things grow
From your union life does flow.

If the athame will stay with its blade in the cup, leave it that way, but if not, place its blade across the bowl of the cup and slowly pour the mugwort infusion over the blade until the cup is full. When this is done, enchant them with such words as:

Magick Mugwort, moonlight bright
By your power on this night,
Work your magick to empower
These tools before the morning hour.
So mote it be!

Leave the cup and the athame thus united in the moonlight, and before sunrise the following morning wrap them again in the linen cloth, or place them where they will be kept between the sabbat rites and ritual uses.

Some traditions require that the handle of the athame be inscribed with certain signs or symbols, while in earlier times, during the persecution, such signs and symbols would certainly have condemned the owner of this knife to death. One way to safely inscribe the handle then, was to inscribe the signs

The Cup and the Athame.

on a piece of paper, burn the paper, and rub the ashes on the handle of the athame.

There is also a white-handled knife, which, in contrast to the athame, must be very sharp, because it is only used for harvesting herbs, carving Runes, cutting cords, or any kind of magickal work that requires a sharp blade.

Other objects which might be the subject of a quest are those which represent the four Elements, Earth, Air, Fire, and Water. For the Pagan about to join a coven, while it is true that the coven already probably owns its own symbols of the four elements, usually those of the priest and priestess, it will still be necessary to have your own for private devotions, rituals, and rites. For the solitary, of course, it is fairly essential.

These four symbolic objects are traditionally placed either on the altar, or at the corresponding quarters of the Circle, depending on the tradition.

The Element of Air, which corresponds to the direction of East, is traditionally symbolized by either incense or feathers, often a finely made medicine fan. A Japanese silk or paper fan might be just as appropriate, or perhaps more so, considering Japan lies in the East, about as far East as you can get. The Element of Air is associated with mental qualities, clearness of thought, and inspiration. East is the direction of Birth.

The Element of Fire is associated with the direction of South. It is usually represented simply by a candle, often red or orange in color. The Element of Fire is associated with the passionate emotions such as love and anger. South is the direction of life and fertility.

The Element of Water is associated with the direction of the West. It is usually represented by a cup or a bowl of water. It is associated with the deep emotions of sympathy, love, and intuition. West is the direction associated with death.

The element of Earth is associated with the direction of North. It is often represented by a bowl or a dish of salt or soil. It should be mentioned here that salt is a soil pollutant and should be used sparingly. My preference for the symbol of Earth is an earthenware dish lightly sprinkled with salt. The Element of Earth is associated with the physical body, with strength and solidity. The direction of North is considered the dwelling place of the Spirits.

In many Pagan and Wiccan traditions the fifth element, Spirit, is represented by the pentacle, usually a disc of silver or copper, engraved with a pentagram. This might also be of stained glass, in symbolic colors. The pentacle is placed at the center of the Circle or altar. (In our own tradition, Dan and I use the more ancient symbol of the Sun wheel rather than the pentagram, which probably was incorporated into Wicca, along with much Near Eastern magick, during the Middle Ages.)

Aside from the cup and the athame, and the symbols of the four elements and the Book of Shadows, there are other tools and equipment that may or may not be desired. There are altar cloths which may be purchased simply as lengths of cloths, or magnificently embellished with embroidery in intricate Celtic knot designs or pentagrams in gold and silver threads. There are also ritual robes which may be made or purchased by those who choose not to worship skyclad. There will be candles to anoint with oils for various purposes and incenses appropriate for the changing seasons, and there are a few other basic tools that some consider necessary.

One of these is the Wand. The wand is a simple length of wood. That is all, but it has a long and subtle history and a deep association with Witchcraft, from the Faerie Godmother who can grant a wish with her star-tipped stick to the royal monarch, latest in an unbroken chain of priest/kings, whose symbol of power is the jewel-tipped scepter. from the wizard's twisted staff to the broomstick of the Halloween Witch, the wand, this simple length of wood, is a personal tool of power.

Its origins are in the ancient shamanic beginnings of Paganism, when a shaman would use a length of wood, whether it was made into his walking

Objects representing the four elements.

stick, bent into the rim of his drum, or thrust up through the smoke hole of his tent as a ladder to the spirit world. This length of wood was considered an offshoot of the World Tree, the trunk of which connects the world of the living with the spirit worlds above, and the realm of the ancestors below. In some Anglo-Saxon covens, a length of ash, forked or horned at the top, is used in ritual. This Stang, as it is called, represents the male principle. Great care is taken in finding or selecting this length of wood. The traditional Maypole, a fir tree stripped of all but its uppermost branches, is again the symbol of the male principle, the venerated phallus. Such trees have been discovered by archaeologists in sacred wells in Europe, placed there as ladders to and from the underworld, or as a symbolic union of the Sky Father with the Earth Mother—or both. Likewise the traditional ashen handle of the Witches Besom, upon which the Crone rides at Samhaintide, from the Earth plane across the Moon to the world of spirits, is the same world tree, and it appears again at Yuletide as the fragrant fir tree adorned with ornaments, symbolizing the return of life; of birds and flowers, and of fruit in the coming year.

The wand is an offshoot of the world tree. What type of tree the world tree is depends upon your tradition. To the Norse or Anglo-Saxons, it is ash or yew. To the Celts—oak or holly, to others it is a fir, and so on. Another traditional wood for the wand is hazel. The length of the wand varies. It may simply be the length of a given piece of wood, whatever that might happen to be, or it may be personalized by making it as long as the distance from your elbow to the tip of your little finger. (This is approximately the length of that ancient measurement, the cubit.)

The wand might be inscribed with runes or other magickal alphabets along its length, elaborately carved or inlaid with a spiral of copper or silver wire. (Flat wire for this kind of inlaying is available from gunsmith suppliers.) The wand might have copper wire, magickal herbs, or crystals inserted in its length, and finally, it might be tipped with a quartz or other type of crystal. This idea of the crystal-terminated wand is not the innovation of the "New Age" movement or the power crystals of Edgar Cayce's Atlantis. The rare jewels mounted on the head of Europe's royal scepters are really just crystals, rare and precious though they may be, and the scepter is the wand of the priest/king.

The particular combination of quartz crystals and copper wire is an interesting one. If a quartz crystal is wound with copper wire it becomes an electromagnet, and electromagnetism seems to be a vehicle for psychic ability.

In many ways, the wand and the athame are interchangeable. Both, for example, are associated with the God, or male principle, and both may be used to cast the Circle, but they also have their differences. The wand is associated with the element of Air, while the athame is associated with the trans-

TRADITIONAL CORRESPONDENCES

Direction	North	East	South	West
Element	Earth	Air	Fire	Water
Season	Winter	Spring	Summer	Autumn
Symbolic Object	Salt Stone Earth	Incense Feather Fan	Candle Lamp Fire	Cup Bowl of Water Shell
Part of Self	Physical	Mental	Emotional	Spiritual
Stage of Life	Death	Birth	Midlife	Old Age
Time of Day	Midnight	Dawn	Midday	Sunset
Color	Green	Yellow	Red	Blue

forming element of Fire in which it was forged. The wand is a gentle, passive tool, used to draw energy to itself and its user, rather like an antenna, and it is traditionally used to invoke or invite the Lord and Lady, while the athame is a tool of power used to direct energy and to charge objects.

The wand is one of the few tools that can easily be made. When it is completed it can be consecrated in the same way as the athame.

Two other tools that are coming to be more widely used are the cauldron, and the broom or besom. The cauldron has been used recently as an object in which to burn incense, simmer fragrant herbs, burn inscribed symbols, and probably for many other things as well; but like the cup, the cauldron is a symbol of the Goddess and is associated with the elements of water and earth. The cauldron is, again, the holy Grail, from the Latin *gradalis*, meaning an all-providing dish or cauldron, a horn of plenty. Such cauldrons are a common element in early Celtic literature. One of the 13 magickal treasures of Britain was the Cauldron of Dyrnwch, and one of the four magickal treasures of ancient Ireland was the Cauldron of Plenty. At least two of the tales in the Mabinogion, a collection of Welsh tales which were recorded in the eleventh century, but which come from a much earlier oral tradition, refer to such magickal cauldrons. These tales are "Branwen, daughter of Llyr," and "Culhwch and Olwen." The Grail is also the Cauldron of the Goddess Cerridwen, from which one drop of potion caused Taliesin to become a wizard. However, this concept is not confined to the Celtic traditions alone. In the earliest Roman mythologies the Earth Mother Ops, from whose name we have derived the word "opulent," and whose Greek counterpart is Gaea, is symbolized by the cornucopia or horn of plenty. This object, representing an inexhaustible supply of the fruits of the harvest, bears a stunning resemblance to the horn-shaped drinking vessel held by the French Venus of Laussel, in an ancient stone carving which dates to paleolithic times. The Grail is a major element in Arthurean legend, and was described by Malory in the 1600s as being the cup from which Jesus drank at the last supper, but the idea of the cup/cauldron was introduced into the Arthurian legend by Chretian de Troyes four centuries earlier, with no such associations.

The cauldron is seen again, as it boils and bubbles in the first act of Macbeth. The three Wird sisters of Shakespeare's play are the Anglo-Saxon Wyrd, or the Triple Goddess of the Moon who dwell in a dark cave, by a pool. The individual names of the Wyrd have been lost to us, but they might not be unlike those of the Triple Goddess of the Norse, known collectively as the Norns, and individually as Skuld, Urdr, and Verdandi. To the Greeks they were the Moirae; Clothe, Lachesis, and Atropos, and to the Romans, the Parcae; Nona, Decima, and Morte. (I have mentioned this in our other books, but it bears repeating here.) They all are spinners, or one spins the thread of life, one weaves its pattern, and one cuts the thread of life at death. They are past,

A group of cauldrons at Flying Witch Farm. The fireback behind the andirons is a copy of a seventeenth century one depicting the Three Fates.

present, and future; birth, death, and rebirth; Maiden, Mother, and Crone. If there can be any doubt that the three Wird sisters of Shakespeare are the Triple Goddess in her aspects as The Fates, recall that they describe for Macbeth his past, his present, and his future, and it is they who predict,

> *"When the hurley-burley's done*
> *When the battles lost and won."*

And so, the cauldron, as a magickal tool of the Craft, is a symbol of the Triple Goddess, and is an object used for scrying, for both looking into the future, and for clairvoyance or clear vision, to learn what is taking place at the present time in far-distant locations.

The traditional cauldron has a globous belly, a neck narrower than the mouth, three legs, and is of iron. When it is to be used, it is filled with water to form a deep and limitless pool for gazing into. A silver coin might be dropped into the water to act as a focal point, or the deep black water may be used to capture a reflection of the silver Moon Herself.

An old tradition warns that one should never bargain when shopping for ritual tools or magickal objects, but by performing a variation of the charm given in the section on finding books, it is very likely that when the perfect cup or athame is found the price will be affordable. A friend was recently on a quest for a cauldron. When he found the perfect one at an antique mall it was marked $2700, but the over-anxious dealer ran up to him and said, "I could let you have it for $13.00!" He considered this a sign from the Goddess whose symbol is the cauldron and whose sacred number is 13.

The Witches' broom, or besom, has a history that is as ancient as the cauldrons; no one can say how old that is. Like the wand, it is associated with the world tree. The traditional besom is made of three kinds of wood, the brush is of birch, the handle of ash, and the two bound together with willow. Birch is the tree of rebirth, willow, the tree of death; and ash, the Tree of Life or the world tree. Just as the shaman's drum, the rim of which is an offshoot of the world tree, is often called the "Shaman's horse," so the Witches' besom is sometimes called the Faerie's horse. It is upon this besom that the Crone rides to the spirit realms at Halloween, and it is upon this Faerie horse that the Witch might ride to an altered state in an ecstatic round dance. It is possible that this besom is also associated with the hobby horse, which is a remnant of ancient cults that worshiped the White Goddess in the form of a white horse. To the Celts, this horse Goddess was known as Rhianon. She was called Epona by the Romans, and the Greeks associated the sacred horse with Demeter. In England today there are still as many as eight "chalk horses" scraped into the landscape on an enormous scale, in her honor, and it is this Goddess who is represented by the hobby horse in the traditional Yuletide mummers parade, so realistically reenacted in the now classic film, "Wicker Man." And there can be little doubt that it was upon her broad back that Arthur and his knights in shining armor rode out in quest of the Grail.

The functions of the besom in ritual are many and varied. For one thing, the besom is a symbol of purification and is used to magickally cleanse the Circle or ritual area prior to a rite, but only after it has been cleansed physically by vacuum cleaner or dust mop. It is also a symbol of masculinity or femininity, depending upon which way it is turned; brush upwards it is a female or Goddess symbol (besom having become a derogatory slang word for woman in England), handle upward it represents the God or male principle. In the latter case it is sometimes used as a staff alone, without the brush. This is the "Stang" of some Anglo/Saxon traditions mentioned earlier, and interestingly in some cases, this staff or stang of ash is "shod with iron" by having a nail driven into its lower end, which is obviously another remnant of Horse Goddess worship. Finally, the besom is a symbol of the union of the God (ash), with the Goddess (birch). The besom is also used in ritual dancing and for inducing astral projection.

Some of the most personal tools are articles of personal jewelry. As important as many of the tools on the altar, jewelry is often taken for granted, though most Pagans and Wiccans seem to have an instinctive affinity for jewelry. In fact it is often possible to pick out the Pagans in a crowd by the amount of jewelry worn, even if the pieces are not obviously symbolic.

One of the earliest references to jewelry in a Pagan context is of course the myth of Ishtar and her descent into the Underworld. In this myth, the Goddess is described as wearing necklaces, bracelets, earrings, anklets, a girdle of jewels, and a crown. The myth describes her descent into the realm of the dead, and as she passes through each of the seven gates, her articles of jewelry are returned to her. Detailed sculptures of Ishtar, or Astarte, show all of her jewelry, but stylized ones often show seven necklaces.

A similar tale is told among the Germanic peoples. In this mythology the Goddess had to spend one night with each of four dwarfs in order to obtain the magickal necklace, Brisingamen. This necklace gave the Goddess the power over life and death. The four dwarfs represent the four directions and also preside over the Underworld. In the Faerie tale, Snow White, the symbolism of which I discussed in detail in *Ancient Ways,* the Goddess spends an unspecified amount of time with seven dwarfs until she is tricked into eating a poisoned apple by the Queen, who has become the Crone. In Germanic Paganism, as in most Paganism, the Circle is actually recognized as being a sphere, and as such it has not four, but seven directions; North, South, East, West, Above, Below, and Center.

From Celtic pre-history there are many famous sculptures that show this magickal necklace. One done in relief in silver depicts the God, sitting in the "lotus position," holding a snake which forms a circle around him. Upon his head is an antlered headdress and about his neck is a magickal necklace or torque. Another sculpture is a sandstone menhir from St-Sernin-sur-Rance, France. It is highly stylized, but is clearly intended to be a woman. She has about her hips a cord or girdle, and about her neck are seven necklaces.

With this wealth of history and tradition it is little wonder that most Pagans and Witches wear necklaces as a regular part of their ritual tools. Many on the Path today wear a Pentagram as proudly as a Christian wears a cross, but the pentagram is not the only symbol that is appropriate as magickal jewelry. There are many symbols suitable for many paths. My own preference is a bronze Sun wheel on a cord, which is a popular symbol throughout ancient Europe. There is the ankh for those on an Egyptian path, the torque for those of the Celtic tradition, and for any who have an affinity for Native American, there are "fetish" necklaces or, a porcupine quill "medicine wheel," which is, again, the Sun wheel, and has basically all of the same meanings as its European counterpart. The magick necklace need not be any of these obviously symbolic ones either, but any piece of jewelry for which one has strong feelings. Some traditions use silver bracelets engraved with magickal inscriptions instead.

These pieces of magickal jewelry can be worn as amulets or as storehouses of magickal power generated during the sabbat rites, or they may be thought of as dwelling places for familiar spirits (which will be discussed at greater length in a later chapter). In any case such magickal jewelry is always worn during sabbat rites and esbats and rituals, in almost every tradition.

There are two final ritual objects to be discussed. These are the cord and the scourge. Cords have an ancient history and one that has been entwined with magick since the first cord was spun. Once the ancient Goddess first spun the thread of Life and the first midwife cut a navel cord to give an infant independent life, cords have been used to bind and to release, to unite and to measure, and to encircle and protect, and to do all of this magickally.

Some traditions use cords of various colors for various purposes, while others simply use a cord as a belt tied around the waist. The cord might have several knots tied in it at specific intervals for various magickal reasons or it might simply have a knot tied in each end to keep it from unraveling. It may be nine feet in length, so that when folded in half and looped over a stake in the ground it can be used as a compass to draw the nine-foot magick Circle, or it might be four and a half feet in length to accomplish the same purpose without being doubled, or it might be the length of its owner from head to foot.

The cord which equals its owner's height has its origins in a very old Witchcraft Initiation tradition called "Taking the Measure." This tradition was carried out in various ways, including measuring the one about to be initiated with a ruler or yardstick and the measure was recorded in the coven's Book of Shadows, or the priest or priestess, acting as God or Goddess, would put their hand upon the head of the postulant and say something like "give to me all that is beneath my hand," or the person being initiated would be measured against a cord and the cord cut to their exact height. This cord was then kept by the coven and was a way of saying that the initiate agreed to give their entire "self" to the Old Ones. It has been said that during the persecution times the coven kept the cord, and should the initiate leave the coven and threaten her fellow Witches with disclosure, the cord would be buried and as the cord rotted in the ground, so would the betrayer be punished in a like manner. While this might be true, the act of cutting a cord is symbolic of birth. An Initiation has always been thought of as a rebirth and so the cord would probably have been treated in the same way as the birth cord was in that particular tradition.

Closely related to the cord is the scourge, which in many cases is made of cords, often nine in number, knotted at the ends. One of the most controversial aspects of the Gardnerian tradition, the scourge and its use in the Initiation rituals is a remnant of an ancient and far more vigorous form of punishment referred to as the Ordeal, but is generally abandoned by other traditions.

The ritualized blood-letting described in the previous chapter is, in all likelihood, a modified version itself of an ordeal designed to induce a "near-death experience" during the training of a shaman in ancient times.

In the mythology of the Norse and Anglo-Saxon, the very shamanic God Odin (Woton) underwent several such ordeals. In one he sacrificed an eye in exchange for one sip from the Well of Mimr in order to gain the gift of prophecy, and in another he hung crucified by his ashen spear on the Tree of Life for nine days and nights until he received the secrets of the runes.

In today's society such ordeals are all but forgotten, but within the Catholic church, when a boy or girl comes of age, and joins the church of their own free will, the rite of Confirmation includes a ritual slap which is a remnant of the ancient "ordeal of pain." Many who have been confirmed Catholic, however, may feel that the ritualized "slap in the face" seems intended more to humiliate or subordinate, than to initiate.

Other ordeals of pain that are sometimes undergone today, prior to an Initiation, are piercing (usually of ears) and tattooing (both discussed in the previous chapter). The latter, in some cases were used to form a link between the initiate and a particular spirit or divinity, and may be the origin of the infamous "devil's mark," that the good Christian Witch-hunters took such great pleasure in trying to discover.

In ancient cultures as far apart as the Nazca in Peru and the Minoan in the Mediterranean, there are labyrinths which seem to wind into a central chamber and out again, while in Denmark and England there are spiral paths of stone or earth. The ancient ritual "Troy Dance" seems to suggest that to tread the spiral path into the center of the labyrinth and out again was to reenact the cycle of birth, death, and rebirth. Since an initiation is a rebirth, perhaps those ancient labyrinths which have never revealed their secrets were once the place where ancient initiation rituals took place. Perhaps the six young men and six young woman sent from Sparta every year to the chamber of the Minatour deep within the labyrinth on the island of Knossus were not victims of sacrifice, but initiates into a secret priesthood. After all, six young men and six young women, presided over by a priest or a priestess, is a perfect coven of 13.

Today such "ordeals of terror" are recalled in acts like the haunted house tours arranged for Halloween entertainment, or amusement park houses of horrors, where not only does one tread a labyrinth, but where unknown terrors lurk around every corner. If one wishes to undergo an ordeal of terror prior to an Initiation, and to reap the benefits of confronting one's own fears, it is easy enough to arrange one. Taking a guided tour through a cave, a ride in the elevator of a skyscraper, a flight on an airplane, or handling someone's pet snake or rat, whatever one fears doing the most (within reason and with proper safety precautions, of course), can be an initiatory ordeal of terror, if entered into for that purpose, and with perfect love for and trust in the Gods.

When a new name has been chosen, when the necessary tools have been acquired and the Book of Shadows is begun, when the year and a day have all but come to an end, there is but one final preparation. That is, to withdraw from the mundane world for a period of isolation.

Ideally this period of about 24 hours should be spent in darkness and in meditation, and with moderate fasting. When this period of isolation has ended, then just prior to the rite a ritual bath is taken, with the water containing purifying and cleansing herbs, and sea salt. If possible, the bath might be taken by candlelight. Finally, the postulant will don the ritual robes and arrive at the place of initiation.

If one is being initiated into an existing coven or tradition, then in all likelihood that group will already have an Initiation ritual. However, if this is not the case, the following is an Initiation ritual based on traditional Wicca.

The priest (if the postulant is a woman) and the coveners have already made the final preparations. There will be on the altar, aside from the usual ritual tools, a nine-foot red cord, a blindfold of black, if possible, a vial of anointing oil (see chapter six for formula), the priest's white-handled knife, and the personal tools of the postulant, which had previously been given to the priest for this ritual, along with the postulant's Book of Shadows.

The Circle will have been cast, leaving an opening in the East, and the opening rites performed. This will probably be a Full Moon Esbat, and at a point in the ritual just prior to the Blessing of the Cakes and Wine, a covenor (of the opposite sex of the postulant if possible) will go to her, blindfold her with the blindfold, and tie her hands together with the red cord. The postulant, thus bound, is led by a covener to the opening in the East of the Circle where she is met by the priest, who challenges her with words such as:

> *You who stand, at the boundary between the world of men*
> *and the realms of the Spirits —*
> *How do you come to this Circle?*

The postulant answers;

> *With perfect love and perfect trust.*

The priest then kisses the postulant and bids her enter, while the covener who has brought her here now gently pushes her into the Circle and then ritually closes the opening in it.

The priest takes the postulant and leads her widdershins around the Circle, spiraling to the center as the coveners chant:

> *Eko Eko Azarack*
> *Eko Eko Zomelak* (or some other such traditional chant)

When priest and postulant suddenly stop before the altar at the center of the Circle, the chanting stops, and the priest demands to know:

> *By what name do you*
> *Stand before the Gods?*

To this the postulant replies by giving her new Craft name. Then the priest asks:

> (Craft name) *are you prepared to undergo an ordeal*
> *(or have you undergone an ordeal) to prove your faith?*

The postulant replies;

> *Yes*

(At this point, in a Gardnerian tradition, the postulant would be scourged, first three times, then seven times, then nine times, and finally 21 times, but many other traditions today waive this ordeal.)

The priest then continues:

> (Craft name), *do you swear to keep the secrets which*
> *will be revealed to you this night within this Circle?*

The postulant will answer appropriately and the priest continues;

> *Do you promise to honor and defend the Mighty Ones*
> *whom you will come to know in our Ancient faith?*

Again the postulant answers appropriately, and the priest continues:

And do you swear to assist and defend
your sisters and brothers in the faith?

Once again the postulant answers appropriately, and the priest then asks the postulant to repeat after him:

I, (Craft name), before the ancient Goddess
And her beloved consort,
Do solemnly swear
To keep the secrets of the Craft
And to honor the Lord and Lady always
And I understand full well
That should I betray this oath
I shall be shunned by my sisters and brothers in the faith
And the mighty Gods themselves
Shall turn their backs upon me.

This having been said, the priest lays his hands on the shoulders of the postulant and, focusing his energy on the transformation that is taking place, says:

Now you shall be as one reborn.

And he removes the blindfold from her eyes, saying:

Now will you see the world
For the first time.
As it truly is
A place of Magick,
Beloved by the Gods.

And as he removes the bonds from her wrists he says;

Now do you leave behind
The death of your former life
Free from this night onward,
To walk the hidden path of the Ancient Ones.

And now the priest holds the red cord that had bound the postulant's wrists, so that one end of it touches the floor and, at the point which is in line with the top of her head he folds it and cuts it with the white-handled knife, saying:

Now do I take your measure.
Now do I cut the cord with which
You were bound in the mundane world,
And in so doing, I give you new life.

The priest hands the cord which is the postulant's measure to her, and she ties it about her waist saying;

With this cord which is my full measure
I am bound to none but the Mighty Gods!

The priest now leads the postulant doesil away from the altar, spiraling around the Circle, and as they go each covener greets her with a kiss (or a handshake). When the Circle has been completed, the priest and postulant circle again doesil, this time beginning at the Eastern point, saying something like the following:

Spirits of the East welcome our new sister (craft name)
Guide and protect her, and inspire her with ancient wisdom.

Spirits of the South, welcome our new sister (craft name)

Guide and protect her, and set her heart ablaze
with the joy of magick.

Spirits of the West, welcome our new sister (craft name)
Guide and protect her, and sooth her spirit
With intuitive knowledge of life eternal.

Spirits of the North welcome our new sister (craft name)
Guide and protect her, and nurture her with
Well-being in the physical world.

Now the priest and postulant return to the altar at the center of the Circle, and the priest continues:

Shining Spirits of the upper reaches
Welcome our new sister and show her
The ladder that leads to higher realms
And shimmering places of enchantment.

Shadowy Spirits of the Underworld,
Welcome our new sister,
And show her the way between the worlds
To the places of the ancestors.

Finally, the priest takes up the cup of salted water, saying:

(Postulant's Craft name)
Here do you stand at the hub of the wheel
Before the altar of the Ancient Ones.
In their names and before these witnesses
Do I anoint you.

Then making a symbolic mark upon her forehead with the water, he says:

> *In the name of the Lady* (Coven's name for the Goddess)
> *Do I anoint you.*

Then, taking up the wine and making a mark on her forehead with some of it on his finger, he says:

> *In the name of the Lord* (coven's God name)
> *Do I anoint you.*

And finally the priest takes up the vial of oil, and touching his finger to it, he anoints the postulant on the forehead saying:

> *Lady* (coven name) *and Lord* (coven name)
> *In your names do I anoint* (Craft name)

Priest and Initiate then turn to the altar and the priest continues:

> (Goddess name) *and* (God name)
> *Here before you stands* (Craft name),
> *An initiated one.*
> *From this night forward*
> *Shall she know and honor you*
> *By your true names.*

This might be followed by the priest explaining to the new initiate the magickal purposes of the various tools upon the altar and whatever magickal secrets the coven may possess.

The ritual ends with the initiate consecrating her ritual tools and signing her Craft name, along with her height (her full measure), in her own Book of Shadows.

For the solitary practitioner, the following rite is a basic one which may be altered to fit any traditions.

At the center of the area that will be the Circle, an altar is arranged that contains all of the tools that the postulant has gathered. There too will be two candles, one representing the Goddess and one representing the God. If statues or objects representing the Gods are also present, these might be placed next to the appropriate candles. There is a cord on the altar, and a vial of anointing oil. The Circle is cast with the finger as has been done previously. The postulant sits or kneels quietly before the altar in darkness for a few moments, contemplating the vows that are about to be taken, then lights the first candle, the Goddess candle, saying words like:

> *O ancient Goddess* (name),
> *By this name, and many others*
> *Shall you be known to me.*
> *From this night onward*

Will you illuminate my life
So that I will see, as one reborn.
And from this night onward
Will I serve at your altar.
And when I your child call upon you
By the name (Goddess name),
I ask you will respond.

The postulant then lights the God candle, saying words like:

Beloved Lord (name)
By this name and others
Shall you be known to me.
From this night onward
Will you illuminate my life
So that I will see as one reborn.
And from this night onward
Will I serve at your altar
And when I call upon you
By the name (God name)
I ask you will respond.

The postulant then stands before the altar, disrobes, and takes up the cord:

O, ancient Lady (name) *and beloved Lord* (name)
Here do I stand before you, naked and alone.
I offer unto you all that I have
Which is naught but myself.
And by the name (chosen craft name)
Shall I be known unto you.
And as a sign that I am reborn
A child of (Goddess name) *and* (God name)
Do I, (Craft name) *take my measure.*

Holding the cord so it touches the floor at the postulants feet, and folding it at a point in line with the top of the head,

And cut the cord of my rebirth!

Cutting it through with the white-handled knife, the postulant then ties a knot in each end of the cord and ties the cord about her waist saying as she does so:

As this cord was cut this night
To give me (Craft name) *new life,*
So it is tied to bind my life to the Gods.
So mote it be.

The postulant, now an initiate, then takes up the athame, consecrates it in the four elements present on the altar and in the names of the Gods. It is now a tool of great power with which the postulant, for the first time, casts a magick Circle, saying something like:

> *Spirits of the North, Spirits of the East*
> *Spirits of the South, Spirits of the West*
> *By your power and protection is this Circle blessed,*
> *That it may be a place between the worlds,*
> *Where mortals and spirits meet*
> *And the mighty Gods themselves.*

The initiate might then dance ecstatically around the Circle until ready to stop. The initiate then takes the plate of cakes and consecrates them in the name of the God and Goddess, and does likewise with the cup of wine.

After partaking of the cake and wine is the traditional time for the performance of magick, and the most appropriate magick for the initiate to perform at this time is the consecration of all other tools, amulets, etc. Finally, the initiate might take up the vial of oil, consecrating it in each of the four elements and in the names of the God and Goddess, and then saying words like the following, anoint herself:

> *In honor of the covenant I have made*
> *With the Mighty Gods this night,*
> *I anoint myself with this oil*
> *Consecrated in their names.*

The 13 points to be anointed are the soles of both feet, both knees, the genitals, base of the spine, the navel, both breasts, the heart, the lips, the two eyes, and the forehead.

Then, before ending the rite, the initiate may open the Book of Shadows to the title page and record her Craft name, her full measure, and the date (in Wiccan terms) of her initiation.

Then the rite is ended.

Like all of Nature at the time of the Vernal Equinox, when we are initiated we are reborn. As initiated Pagans or Wiccans, we know that all of Nature is a manifestation of the Gods and we know therefore that we, as a part of Nature, are each of us also a manifestation of the Gods. To know and to accept this is to be forever changed. The initiate knows that our every thought and every act, performed completely of free will, is an expression of our relationship with the creative forces. Nature is not, as the new religions believe, what we are here to rise above. Nature is what we are here to joyfully act within. The initiate, then, acts with responsibility, for we are now conscious participants in the creative process of evolution, and in the life of the world.

Chapter Four

Handfasting

Handfasting

The May sun climbs higher in the morning sky, setting droplets of dew to shimmering like jewels in the sweet green grass. Beneath the leafy canopy of trees filled with bird songs greeting the day, the dappled sunlight dances in celebration of life's beauty. Everywhere there are flowers! Green and brownstriped Jack-in-the-pulpits rise tall above the nodding yellow heads and mottled leaves of adder's tongue; and like tiny laundry on a line, rows of Dutchman's breeches dangle from their stems. The pure white buds of bloodroot, still enfolded in downy leaves, push upward to blossom briefly before their petals are blown away by a breeze. Dappled like the forest floor, a fawn stirs in its grassy nest, and ferns unroll their fronds.

Everywhere the Spirits of Nature, the Faerie folk, dance and celebrate. Life in all its youth and beauty, and deep in the forest, hidden from the eyes of the mundane world, beneath a bower of hawthorn blossoms, pink and white, the Lady, crowned with a chaplet of flowers, has wed the Lord of the Greenwood.

Beltane, the feast of the Sacred Marriage, stands across the Wheel of the Year from Samhain, the Feast of the Dead and the beginning of the new year in many traditions; and it is at Samhain, a time for divining the future, that many a maiden employed many a method to divine the identity of her "True Love." Here is a partial list.

* Go to a well at midnight on All Hallows Eve and gaze into it and the face of your true love is sure to appear.

* Peel an apple so that the peel remains in one continuous piece on All Hallows Eye and toss the peel over your left shoulder. The peel is sure to form the initial of your true love.

* On All Hallows Eve, cut an apple into nine equal portions. By the light of the moon eat eight of the pieces and toss the ninth over

Jumping the Broom

your left shoulder. Then turn quickly and you are sure to glimpse the face of your true love.

◆ Holding a hand mirror on All Hallows Eve, gaze into it, looking over your left shoulder. You are sure to see the face of your own true love.

◆ Name a hazelnut for each man in your life and on All Hallows Eve place them in a row before the hearth fire. The first to jump is sure to be the name of your true love.

While such magickal operations might reveal to a young woman, or man for that matter, the identity of a future marriage partner, how many ever do find their Own True Love, and what does that mean anyway?

There are many who believe, and I am among them, that everyone has a soul mate, one who has been our "other half" or divine twin since time began and with whom we will be reunited. Once reunited we remain together until the end of time, and probably, in some future incarnation, become one single individual. He is her "knight in shining armor," she is the Grail of his Quest.

A collection of antique turn-of-the-century Halloween post cards depicting methods of learning the identity of your Own True Love.

I first met my own true love during the Peasants' Revolt in 14th-century England. As I stood on the gallows our eyes met, just seconds before that lifetime ended. We came together again in 18th-century Pennsylvania where we raised a family in a log cabin until the French and Indian War put an end to our life together. A few lifetimes later we were born just a few blocks away from one another in New York City. When our families moved us to the suburbs six years later we were again within walking distance from each other. We finally followed our own life paths, which were bound to meet, and we have been together ever since.

If you have not yet found your own true love, here is a charm to help attract him or her to you. On a Friday, a day sacred to the Goddess of Love, during the waxing Moon, take a piece of pink or light red fabric, cotton, silk or satin, but not synthetic, and fold it in half so that you can cut out two identical heart shapes about two by three inches. Place the two hearts face to face and stitch them together, leaving a one-inch opening in the seam. Turn the little heart pouch right-side-out.

In a small bowl, blend together dried red or pink rose petals, dried lady's mantle leaves, whole almonds, garlic cloves, apple seeds, and Southernwood. Enchant the herbs as you blend them in the moonlight with words such as:

A charm to attract your Own True Love.

Bring my True Love unto me
As I will so mote it be.

Repeat the chant six times, then stuff the little heart with the herbs, stitch up the opening in the seam and attach a pink or red cord to the charm, so that it can be worn about the neck. The charm could be embellished with decorative stitching around the edge. A few herbs that could be substituted for those mentioned above are:

Basil	Heartsease (Johnny jump-ups)	
White or pink beans	Maidenhair fern	
Jasmine flowers	Meadowsweet	Male fern
Violets	Myrtle	Rosemary

Two other herbs that are strongly associated with the Goddess of Love are Myrtle and Yarrow.

Here is a candle spell that might be used in conjunction with the previous charm.

On a Friday night when the Moon is waxing to full, take a pink, red or white candle and anoint it with Love Oil. (To make Love Oil, warm about ¼ cup of olive oil in a small pan and pour it over fresh or dried rose petals, or a combination of rose petals, violets, and basil. Let the oil stand until the following night, then pour it through muslin to filter it. Keep the oil tightly corked in an amethyst-colored glass bottle.) Anoint the candle with the Oil of Love and cast a Circle of rose petals. Stand in the center of the Circle and light the candle, saying something like:

Magick candle burning bright
Be a beacon in the night.
Guide my own True Love to me
As I will so mote it be.

Then carry the candle to the Northern point of the Circle and hold it high, saying:

If my True Love dwells to the north
Magick candle bring him forth.

Then carry the candle to the East and exclaim;

If in the east my True Love be,
Candle draw him unto me.

Holding the candle high at the Southern point, call out:

If in the south does my love reside
Bring him swiftly to my side.

And finally, holding the candle high at the Western point:

And if my True Love lives in the west
Call him to me, I request.

Watch for a sign at each of the points. This will usually be something like the flame of the candle flickering in an unusual way, but it is just as likely to be a rattle of a window, a shooting star, or the strange behavior of the cat. Note the direction you were addressing when the sign occurred. Then, complete the Circle by returning to the North. Hold the candle high once more, then carry it to the center of the Circle saying:

Here at the crossroads do I stand.
So shall my True Love cross my path.

Then, without extinguishing the candle, carry it to a window in your home that faces in the direction that you were addressing when the sign was given, and repeat the words;

Magick candle burning bright
Be a beacon in the night.
Guide my own True Love to me.
As I will so mote it be.

Allow the candle to burn for about an hour before you extinguish it. Then each night for the next five nights (six nights in all), light the candle again and repeat the enchantment, leaving the candle to burn for at least an hour each time, or one-sixth of the candle.

During this period, and until the next New Moon, pay particular attention to your dreams, especially those of a romantic nature, and follow up any clues, such as visiting the site where such a dream took place. Also, during this period follow any impulse to go places or do things if at all possible. Sometimes Love has to be met halfway.

When your own true love has entered your life, you might be tempted to try a love potion on your mate, but this is not advisable for two reasons. The first of these is that most of the concoctions traditionally called "love potions" are actually aphrodisiacs, or believed to be so, and many of these contain ingredients which can be dangerous. Besides, good health, a relaxed environment, and an active imagination are all the aphrodisiacs a skilled Witch really needs.

The second reason that love potions are not advisable is that those potions which contain an ingredient intended to bind an individual to you magickally are considered manipulative. Any magick that is done to cause a person to act according to anything but their own free will is manipulative, and considered by some a form of "black magick." Besides, there could be no pleasure in being loved by someone because they are compelled to love you, and do not love you for yourself. The secret ingredient in love potions of this type, of course, is a few drops of your own blood.

The whole issue of manipulative magick raises some very interesting questions. "When does magick cease to be helpful and begin to be manipulative?" "What are our obligations as the workers of magick, and as its victims?"

Magick is manipulative whenever it is worked for the purpose of causing a specific individual to act against their own will. For example, a charm or spell to attract a lover is one thing, but the same charm or spell performed to influence a certain person to be attracted to you, when they haven't been before, is manipulative. However, the basis of all magick is the mind. Aleister Crowley defined magick as, "causing change to occur in accordance with one's will." By applying one's will, whether through simple concentration on a desire, or through the performance of magickal acts, or through simply accomplishing the desired effect physically, when the goal has been achieved magick has been worked. We are all constantly being influenced by others on every level of consciousness, intentionally or unintentionally. We are affected telepathically by those who love us and by those who envy or despise us, living or discarnate. We are affected by political, social, and religious propaganda, and we are influenced by television commercials, as well as by those who anoint and name images made in our likeness. The process begins the instant a nurse pins a pink or a blue bow on our cradle, and it continues throughout our lives. Witches tend to be more aware of this than others, which is why many of us came to find the Old Ways in the first place. We have a clearer understanding of our own goals and desires, so are able to recognize influences which would turn us away from our purpose. Knowing this, we are able to joyfully apply the Wiccan rede, "an it harm none, do what ye will!"

Still, when your own true love has entered your life, a toast is in order, and there are some drinks which, while they do not contain the "Dust of Broken Hearts," or other such ingredients, are in their own right, love potions. One such drink is apple cider, made from a fruit sacred to the Goddess of Love. It might be spiced with cinnamon and cloves, themselves ingredients in love charms. For a similar drink with an alcoholic content, fresh-pressed apple juice can be fermented into a lovely sweet wine which is delicious served mulled, with spices added.

Another appropriate drink is tomato juice, since tomatoes are also called "Love Apples," and were once a forbidden fruit. A pinch of basil to promote understanding and sympathy, and a dash of tabasco or hot sauce in proportion to the passion of the relationship might be added. For an alcoholic drink, vodka is a traditional addition. Drops of blood in this "Bloody Mary" are optional, but if they are used it must be from both partners, and with the full knowledge of both.

Now toast one another and pledge your love, and begin to make plans for a Handfasting.

Beltane is the celebration of the Sacred Marriage, as it has been down through the ages, a celebration of the union of the God and the Goddess, of male and female, of spirit and matter. It has been celebrated by the priestesses of Ishtar in the wedding chambers atop the ziggurats of ancient Sumer, and by ecstatic dancers around the Maypole, the venerated phallus image entwined with ribbons and adorned with flowers, as it was symbolically plunged into the sacred wells of the Earth Mother.

This celebration of the Sacred Marriage at Beltane is the celebration of one of the most basic beliefs upon which Wicca, and most traditional Pagan religions are based—the belief that, as all of Nature is a manifestation of the Gods, and that since all of nature operates on the law of polarities, so must it be with the Gods. Everything in nature has its counterpart, its complement, that which makes it complete. Where there is male, there also must be female. Where there is dark, so must there also be light, because just as we are blind in total darkness, so are we blinded by total illumination. To see, we must have light and shadow. Where there is heat, there must also be cold, as either extreme will cause death.

In any pair of complements in nature, one is positive and one is negative; that is, one generates energy and one receives it. The energy flows from one to the other, from positive to negative, until perfect balance is attained.

There is no cold, only the absence of heat, there is no darkness, only the absence of light, but this concept of positive and negative has been greatly misunderstood. New Agers explain unpleasant situations as the result of "negative energy," but energy, by its very nature, is positive and cannot be negative. Unpleasant situations are simply the result of the absence of energy, or energy used for negative purposes. In the first millennium before the current era (B.C.E.), the Persian philosopher Zarathustra extrapolated that "since everything in nature has its opposite, then good must be opposed by evil," but this philosophy is based on a falsehood. Everything in nature does not have its opposite, that which will annihilate it. Everything in nature has its complement, that which makes it whole, or complete, which causes perfect balance and harmony. Good and evil are simply value judgments and do not exist in nature; only balance and harmony do.

It is this perfect balance between the polarities which is celebrated as the Sacred Marriage of the God and the Goddess at Beltane. It is the same Sacred Marriage that is celebrated whenever a couple, heterosexual or gay, is united by Handfasting. Every bride is a reflection of the Goddess on her wedding day, every groom, the God.

It has been traditional from early times for a bride to wear white on her wedding day. This is, for followers of the new religions, to express the physical virginity of the bride on her wedding day, but to Pagans it expresses her association with the Maiden aspect of the Goddess, and this is an entirely different matter. The Maiden is the Goddess of Love, Beauty, and Fertility. Like Ishtar, she may have had many lovers, but she is still young, and beautiful, and full of potential life. The Goddess Diana requested of the Gods that she be an eternal virgin, yet other stories of her mythology tell of her seductions and her lovers, and this is perfectly natural because, as Goddess of the Moon, she ever renewed her virginity, ever became new again.

The passage from physical virginity to the shedding of one's virginity is a rite unto itself and does not necessarily have anything at all to do with Handfasting or the wedding night. In some cultures, a girl's physical virginity was done away with at the time of her birth. In our own ancient cultural past it is very possible that when a girl came of age, her virginity was removed for her by the tribal priest, who, having called the God down upon himself, acted as and for Him. Such a priest would, in all probability, be a highly skilled lover, making the event a pleasurable and positive experience for the girl, who was already prepared for it intellectually, emotionally, and spiritually. Of course, in such a culture a young man's first sexual experience might also be with a woman who served as priestess to the Goddess of Fertility. In mythology, children of such unions are called "heroes" or demigods, but this is not the same as those Gods who are born as the result of the union between a God and a mortal woman. The latter is a mythological way of expressing the union of Spirit and Matter.

This right of priests, priest/kings, and feudal lords to relieve a girl of her virginity carried over into the current era, and there are supposedly historical references to kings and lords claiming the right to take a woman on her wedding night. This act, having completely lost its spiritual significance, became simply, royal rape.

For the young adult about to have her or his first sexual experience, in our present hypocritical and contradictory society, there are no rites to celebrate the passage, except the experience itself. This experience is usually a spontaneous one with little or no preparation, but for that rare individual who has chosen the Ancient Path prior to their first sexual experience and who has given the event thought and planning, it can be more. To prepare for the rite, first prepare the area where it is to take place. Without putting too much emphasis on ritual, cleanse the area with a sprinkling of salted water and a censing with incense. Light the area with candles, pink or red, which may have been anointed with rose oil. Then take a cleansing bath in salted water, infused with purifying and fragrant herbs. When the bath is finished, pat dry, and by candlelight gaze at your own reflection in a full-length mirror (if possible). When the proper frame of mind has been achieved, intone words such as:

Ancient Goddess, I, your daughter (or son) (name)
Am about to offer up my childish innocence.
Through the magick of your love
May it be with honor and with joy.
Through my body may my partner
Know the ecstacy which is union with you,
And through the body of (name), *my partner*
May I know the bliss of union
With him who is your consort, our Lord.

(A few words, naturally, would need to be altered in the case of a young man.)

Meditate on this for a few moments before donning the garments chosen for the occasion. Then join your lover and embrace. For the sexually skilled Witch, every time is as the first time.

And so, the traditional white wedding gown, for the Pagan or Wiccan woman, represents not a state of physical virginity so valued by the followers of new religions, but her identity with the Goddess in her aspect as the Maiden, Goddess of Love, Beauty, and Fertility, and the Goddess of the Moon, who by ever renewing herself remains the eternal virgin.

As the bride is the Goddess on the day of her handfasting, so the groom is the Lord of the Greenwood. As she is the eternal and self-renewing Maiden, he is the son of the Great Mother who must die to be reborn. He is the resurrected son of Nature, the God of the Waxing Sun, who will generate the energy, and she is the Grail that will receive it. It is he who will provide the spark of spirit that will animate the body of flesh that only she can provide. As the bride is the Moon Goddess, the groom is the Sun God; as he is the Sky Father, she is the Earth Mother. They complement one another, and make each other whole.

Just as the bride is a reflection of the Goddess on the day of her handfasting, and the groom is that of the God, so too are other members of the party living representatives of aspects of divinity. Not the least of these is the mother of the groom.

The bride's mother-in-law plays the part of Venus, Goddess of Love and Beauty, in the myth of Cupid and Psyche. In this myth the maiden Psyche had grown so beautiful and worthy of admiration that mortal men, awed by her beauty, began neglecting the worship of Venus. This so angered the Goddess of Love that she instructed her son Cupid, the God of Love, whose Greek counterpart is Eros, to cause Psyche to fall in love with some loathsome creature. Cupid intended to carry out his mother's will, but when he beheld the beauty of the maiden Psyche, it was he who was struck with Love. He carried Psyche away to a palace in a distant land where they dwelt in bliss for a time, but Venus found them and, still angry, sent Psyche into the Underworld to do her a favor, and bring back a box containing some of the beauty of Proserpina, whom the Greeks called Persephone. Venus knew that Psyche's curiosity would cause her to open the box, and when she did she was overcome by the black fumes of the Underworld which caused her to fall into a death-like sleep. Cupid found his beloved in this state and revived her. He then brought her to the Father of the Gods who, at the request of Cupid, granted Psyche immortality. Then, in the sight of the Gods, the couple were wed, and Jupiter/Zeus ordered that Venus be reconciled with her daughter-in-law.

As the mother of the groom is the Goddess in her aspect as the vengeful and jealous Venus, who must be reconciled with the Maiden, and Mother Goddess who seeks to be reunited with her child/consort, then the mother of the bride is certainly Demeter, the sorrowful mother whose daughter Persephone is the bride of Hades. Persephone must leave her mother to dwell in her husband's realm, thereby separating the Two Who Are One.

Since Beltane is the celebration of the Sacred Marriage, the entire month of May was set aside for the Gods, and in ancient times it was considered unlucky for mortals to marry during the month of May. Instead, the following month, June, was considered the best month for mortal marriages. June is named for the Goddess Juno, who, as the Roman counterpart of the Greek Goddess Hera, is the Queen of the Heavens. She is the wife of Jupiter, Father of the Gods, and she is the patroness of all women from the moment of their birth to the instant of their death. Juno has many aspects. As Juno Virginnalis she is the protectress of maidens, and as Juno Matrona she is the protectress of mothers. As Juno Natalis she is the Goddess of Birth, and the women of Rome made offerings to her on their own birthdays. As Juno Jugalis she is the Goddess of Weddings and of Marriage, and so it has become a tradition, passed down to us through the ages, from ancient Pagan Roman times and possibly before, that the month of June is the traditional month for marriage.

Moon and June and honeymoon have rhymed in more than one sappy love song, and that is because the June wedding has connections not only with the Greco/Roman-Mediterranean traditions, but with the Anglo-Saxon as well. According to the lunar calendar of the ancient Anglo-Saxons, the month that followed the spectacular blossoming of flowers in May was called the Mead Moon. Mead is a sacred drink made of fermented honey, and many magickal properties have been attributed to it. After the abundance of pollen and nectar gathered by bees from the blossoms of May, beehives fairly overflowed with honey, which could be gathered to make the sacred drink. And so the lunar month in June came to be known as the Mead Moon, or the Honey Moon.

Honey also has other links with magick. In Italian Witchcraft, sacred sabbat cakes are almost always sweetened with honey. Like certain species of birds, honey bees are harbingers of spring, foraging for food whenever the temperature rises to about 60 degrees. A single queen bee lays enough eggs to produce many hives full of bees, and it is only the queen that lays the eggs and creates new life. Therefore, the honey bee is a symbol of, and sacred to, the Goddess. The famous statue of Artemis at Ephesus has a row of honey bees among the many sacred animals which adorn the multi-breasted figure of the Goddess, and for these reasons too, a traditional Pysanky design is the honey bee, so stylized as to look like a geometric arrangement of flowers.

Bees also produce wax, and they produce it in perfectly geometric, six-sided cells. Six, of course, is a number sacred to the Goddess of Love, Beauty, and Fertility. It is also a number that is the basis of most Pennsylvania German "hex" signs, "hex" being the German word for witch, but also the Greek word for the number six. Both the Catholic church and many ceremonial magicians use only beeswax candles in their rituals, and of course it is the same beeswax that is used to inscribe the magickal eggs called Pysanky.

Down through the centuries, the connection between human fertility and the fertility of crops, between the union of a man and a woman, and the union of the Spirits of Nature has been a close one. So much so, that rituals performed to promote the fertility of crops and the rebirth of nature employed human symbols and plant symbols almost interchangeably. In Russia, a part of an ancient May Day ritual transferred to Eastertime was to bundle birch twigs into the form of a woman, dress this figure as a bride, and eventually throw her into a running stream or river, in a symbolic union of the Female elements of Nature with the Male elements, those of death and resurrection. In Germany on May Eve, which is called in that country, Walpurgisnacht (because, in an attempt to Christianize this blatantly Pagan celebration, it was said to be named for the Christian bishop Walpurgis), a tree called a Walbur tree was danced around by a man called the Walbur. He was clothed from head to foot in sheaves of grain, in such a way that the heads of grain formed a crown upon his head. He was then led in procession through the village streets, which were lined with branches of birch; symbolizing, again, the feminine element of Nature, the Goddess. Elsewhere in Germany, school children on May Eve, or during Easter week, would go into the greenwood and cover one of the boys among them with green leaves. This Little Leaf Man is led in a procession which includes one or two little girls, carrying a basket which they fill with gifts of sweets and cakes gathered as they go from door to door. In Alsace, a little girl dressed as a bride is led from door to door by a procession of children who beg treats, blessing those who are generous, and cursing those who are not with the failure of crops and farm animals. So the fertility of Nature itself is somehow linked, not only with the Sacred Marriage of the God and Goddess which is reflected in the marriages of men and women, but also with their representatives as little children, and this ancient custom is still carried on today with the tradition of the flower girl strewing petals in the path of the bride, and her (the flower girl's) consort, the little ring bearer. Here the magick obviously works both ways. Children present at a marriage insures children in a marriage, while the union of a man and a woman insures the fertility of Nature and the eternal rebirth of Nature as symbolized by the children.

The close association between the union of a man and a woman, and the flowering and fertility of Nature is evident, too, in the traditional abundance of flowers at a wedding. Even at a typical church wedding, in the midst of dark December or of frozen February, there is usually a profusion of flowers; not just blossoms of the season, but a wide variety of flowers in a rainbow of colors; roses and gladiolas, carnations and lillies. There are flowers on the altar and flowers at the end of each pew, the bridesmaids and the maid of honor carry bouquets of flowers, and the flower girl carries a basket of blossoms or petals. And of course, the bride carries her bouquet of purest white, while the groom wears a boutonniere of a flower or two with a leaf of fern, a vestigal symbol of his association with the Lord of the Greenwood.

At the wedding feast which follows there are flowers on every table and even the wedding cake will be adorned with flowers of icing or sugar.

In many ancient cultures, rain and water are practically synonymous with fertility. In India a bridegroom sprinkled his bride with water, using a tool resembling a comb or a rake, in order to insure fertility. We can find this connection still apparent in another traditional marriage ritual that takes place prior to the wedding, the bridal shower. The two most popular symbols employed for bridal shower decorations, the watering can and the umbrella, and of course, the name of the event itself, make no sense at all when considered in a modern context, but to the Pagan the ancient symbolism is obvious: water = rain = fertility.

But the tradition of the June wedding, the bridal shower, the flower girl, and the ring bearer, are not the only wedding traditions that are still carried on today as they were in Pagan times. There are many others.

The wedding ring, itself a perfect circle symbolizing the Goddess, dates to Roman times and was placed then, as now, on the traditional ring finger, because it was believed that an artery ran from the ring finger directly to the heart, which was believed to be the seat of love and affection. Interestingly, to those familiar with the Yogic system of chakras, the astral centers located somewhat along the spinal column and associated with various organs, which both receive and generate psychic energy, it is the chakra located in the area of the heart that is believed to be the chakra of unselfish love.

A turn of the century May Queen or bridal crown,
made of silk, paper, and painted cotton.

The wedding procession, which today is limited to a short stroll from the front door of the church or chapel to the altar, was, in earlier times and smaller communities, one that began at the home of the bride and proceeded through the village from house to house, ending at the site where the ceremony was to take place, or from the site of the ceremony, back to the bride's home. The bride and groom may have ridden in a horse-drawn cart at the head of the procession, followed by the villagers. In Eastern European countries, the procession also includes a trip to the village well, since all of life's passages are seen as involving water, or the crossing of it.

In some cultures today, the bride and groom go about from one table of guests to another after the wedding feast, with a pillowcase into which guests are expected to drop gifts of money. This tradition is probably one closely related to the previous one of the wedding procession. In Pagan times the magickal energy generated by a bride and groom on their wedding night, like any ritually performed Great Rite, was believed to have a powerful effect on the fertility of crops, and so, like the King and Queen of the May who went about the village, begging gifts at farmhouse doors, blessing those who were generous, and blighting those who were not, the bride and groom who proceeded through their village in a horse-drawn cart adorned with flowers, no doubt were showered with gifts by villagers who hoped to received some of the couple's magick.

One strange tradition that may have to remain a mystery is that a bride is supposed to wear, or carry "something old, something new, something borrowed, and something blue." The rhyme itself comes from the old English. According to one source, the borrowed object was a garter loaned by a woman who was happily married, so that by sympathetic magick, marital happiness would be transferred to the bride. While this might be true, it is more likely that the intention was to transfer fertility magick, and, as we Wiccans know, the garter, which figures in another wedding tradition, has other meanings as well, which will be discussed shortly. Another source claims that the borrowed object might be a gold coin loaned to insure good fortune in the marriage, but anyone familiar with the ways of magick knows that to borrow a coin and then return it is not good magick for material gain, so the gold coin is probably the "something old." The "something new" is usually the bride's dress which, one of these sources tells us, was white for protection, and the "something blue," the "color of the Moon" was worn for added protection. Another source explains that the "something blue" was in the form of small lengths of blue ribbon lightly stitched to the bridal gown for protection, and which were to be taken by young bachelors for good luck in marriage. The bit of blue ribbon was sometimes tied to the garter. If all of this sounds a bit jumbled, it is only because the sources mentioned here were looking at these remnants of the Old Faith from outside the magick Circle, but they did preserve enough information for us to reconstruct the original, if perhaps not the *only* original meaning of the old English rhyme, which might have been something like this:

Something Old—an old gold coin to insure good fortune in the marriage.

Something New—a new dress signifying the new life about to begin. This dress would be white, signifying the maiden aspect of the Triple Goddess, and the Moon itself and its relevance to fertility.

Something Borrowed—an item probably borrowed from an older married woman, one who had had several children, in order to transmit to the bride the magick of her fertility and ease of delivery.

Something Blue—might have been bits of blue ribbon but whatever it was, the color blue has been considered a color of protection in many cultures since ancient times.

One wedding tradition which really seems to have Wiccan significance is the garter. It is the garter which today is usually the "something blue." As every Wiccan knows, the garter is the symbol of the Witch Priestess. Before there were pantyhose, or garter belts, or even the satin and lace and elastic garters worn by brides today, garters were usually of leather with a buckle, and looked a lot like a dog collar. Many an illustration in an old Faery tale book shows a Faery godmother wearing such a device, sometimes just below the knee. Traditionally, when a woman has become the priestess of a coven, she wears a garter as the symbol of her position, and should the coven grow and be subdivided, she is entitled to add a buckle for each new coven. At the risk of repeating myself (and every other writer on the subject) the following story must be retold for the benefit of any new readers.

It is said that the Royal Order of the Garter was begun by King Edward III of England, after he rescued one of the royal ladies of the court when she dropped her garter on the dance floor. Rather than trying to hide the fact that she was a priestess of the Old Faith, he held her garter high and announced to all the court, "Evil to him who thinks evil." King Edward, as head of the Royal Order of the Garter, wore a robe embroidered with 169, or 13 times 13, garters. It is very difficult to deny the Wiccan symbolism here.

However, the traditional Witch garter is red, symbolizing the Mother aspect of the Triple Goddess, not blue like the traditional wedding garter. This suggests several things. First, that if the garter is the borrowed object, it was borrowed to transmit fertility magick. Second, that if the garter was not borrowed, but belonged to the bride, then possibly the garter was originally thrown, not to the bachelors at the wedding feast, but to the maidens as a way of selecting a new priestess for the coven as the bride stepped down, since in some traditions only a maiden can be priestess.

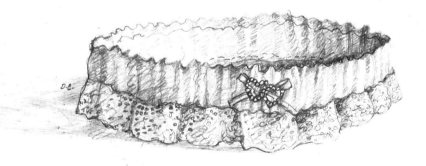

The Bride's Garter.

Eventually, the bits of blue ribbon which were originally attached to the bride's gown, to be snatched by bachelors as she danced by, were then tied to the garter, and finally, when all of the original meanings of the customs were lost, the garter itself became entirely blue, and is today tossed to the bachelors at the wedding feast. The specific type of good luck that the blue garter or ribbon was believed to impart to the bachelor was a faithful wife when he did marry, and this probably has something to do with the term "True Blue."

Still, the Old Ways were not entirely forgotten. Something still had to be tossed to the maidens at the wedding feast, and today it is the bridal bouquet, reminding us again that the bride, by sympathetic magick, is not only passing on the happiness of the union of a husband and wife, but also the association of that union with the fertility of vegetation.

To bring sweetness to the marriage, some brides have carried a packet of sugar in one of their bridal gloves, and indeed, one source tells us that the "something borrowed" might have been a lump of sugar for this very purpose. Traditionally, there is no shortage of sweets at a wedding feast. One of the most popular at an Italian wedding is *confetti*, roasted almonds in a pure white sugar shell. These are usually tied up in a little white net bag, adorned with a sprig of artificial lily-of-the-valley, and a tin or aluminum wedding ring, and then presented in a clear or white plastic container, in the shape of a heart, dove, shoe, swan, or something similar. These charming gifts are given as favors to each of the guests at the wedding feast.

The word "confetti" means sweet or candy, but it is likely that the original intention was not to insure sweetness in the marriage but, once again, fertility, since the almond is the symbol of Attis, the Phrygian God of Death and Rebirth, or Resurrection. Attis, whose worship became very widespread in Rome, was born when his mother placed an almond on her lap to admire its perfect symmetry and beauty. The almond vanished and in due time Attis was born. The great Goddess Cybele loved him for his youth and beauty, but when he was forced to wed another he killed himself by self-mutilation. Cybele demanded of the Gods that he be restored to life, and it was granted, but only for half of every year. It is the cult of Attis that, at the time of the Vernal Equinox, held week-long revels known as the Rites of Spring, which ended with great joy and shouts of "He is risen!" The cult of Attis may have been condemned by Christian Rome and the Rites of Spring banned, but the shouts of his worshippers have echoed down through the centuries and been repeated by followers of the new god, and his symbol, as god of fertility and rebirth, continues to be a traditional part of Mediterranean wedding customs, as sweet today as it was in the days of Pagan Rome.

One of the many euphemisms for getting married is "Tying the Knot." Another is "Getting Hitched," which literally means tying one thing to another, such as a horse to a post, which brings us back to "Tying the Knot." The knot referred to is the "Love Knot" or "True Lovers Knot."

I recall many years ago seeing a troupe of Mexican folk dancers perform something called the Love Knot Dance. It was performed by several couples, who each danced together in a close circle. On the ground was a ribbon—about twelve feet long and about four inches wide. It lay doubled, and as the pairs danced around it the women manipulated it with their feet so that by the end of the dance they had tied it into a Love Knot which they then held up for all to see.

The old English folk tune "Barbara Allen" tells us of the hard-hearted Barbara and her rejected suitor, Sweet William, who eventually died of a broken heart. When he was "dead and laid in grave," Barbara Allen realized what she had done and, after making her own "final preparations," she simply pined away and died, and;

> Out of Sweet William's grave there grew a rose
> Out of Barbara Allen's a briar.
> They grew and grew, in the old church yard
> Till they could grow no higher.
> At the end they formed a True Lovers Knot,
> And the rose grew 'round the briar.

An assortment of confetti containers.

The point of all this is that Sweet William was able to do in death what he was not able to do in life, wed the hard-hearted Barbara Allen, and it also reminds us, once again, of the close association between vegetation and the union of a man and a woman.

A Love Knot or True Lovers Knot is one of the first we ever learn to tie in our shoelaces, and it is possible that once such a knot was actually tied as a part of a Handfasting ritual.

The magick of the True Lovers Knot lies in the fact that when it is pulled one way the knot tightens and becomes stronger, but when pulled the other way, it is the easiest knot of all to untie.

Aside from the sweets already mentioned, another, the most traditional at a wedding, is the wedding cake, and it too has an ancient history. A cake is simply a type of sweetened bread, and bread is a product of sacred grain. Both grain and bread are associated with the Goddess. In fact, the word "lady" comes from an old Anglo-Saxon word meaning "kneader of bread." From ancient Sumer to the countries of Eastern Europe, the act of baking bread was a sacred one and miniature terra-cotta shrines have been found in Old Europe which contain bread ovens and scenes of bread baking. In ancient Sumer, bread was being baked in hundreds of shapes for various purposes and there were many different recipes.

To the Pagan eye, today's multi-tiered wedding cake topped with a tiny plastic bride and groom bears a stunning resemblance to those ancient temples in the land between the two rivers, the ziggurats of Mesopotamia atop which stood the marriage chambers of the Gods. But the cake alone is only a part of the Pagan symbolism still in use at almost every wedding. The actual ritual is the cutting of the cake. It is the groom who, with the bride's hand upon his, cuts the cake with a knife, or in some military weddings, his sword, The fertility symbolism here is obvious, and in so doing he also seems to recreate, at least in action, a Pagan blessing of the cake.

But no wedding is complete without wine. Even the Bible, which I do not consider an absolute authority, attests to the pre-Christian tradition of wine at a wedding. Today's champagne is the meade of yesterday, but whether the wine is meade or champagne, Burgundy or Chianti, it is the symbol of Spirit, of the Male Principle, of the God. Even before the cult of Lord Dionysus, joyful God of the Vine and of Resurrection, the ability of wine to produce an altered state of consciousness, a sense of warmth and well-being, and to promote good health and long life, probably caused it to be considered a sacred drink.

And so, the traditional wedding rituals of the wine or champagne toast and the cutting of the cake seem to be a reenactment of rites ancient and once sacred, and when the vows have been exchanged and the newlywed couple leaves the church or chapel, or city hall, there is still another ancient fertility

A TRUE
LOVERS KNOT

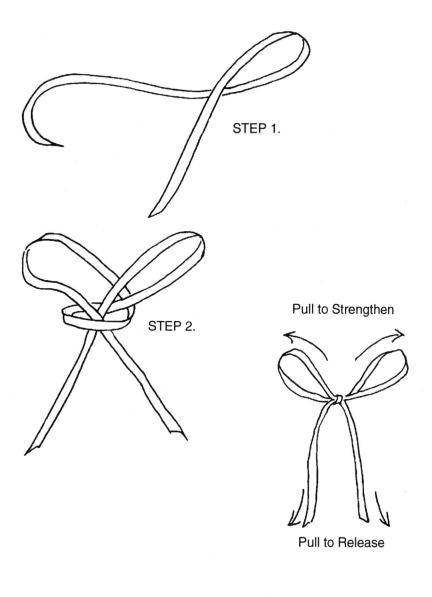

STEP 1.

STEP 2.

Pull to Strengthen

Pull to Release

rite to be performed. The couple is showered with grains of rice. In ancient times, no doubt grains such as wheat or barley were thrown to insure fertility. Rice, like wheat, corn, oats, and barley is a cereal grain, but since the industrial revolution, or at least the end of the last century, when the local village grist mills fell into disuse and grain was shipped directly to industrial flour mills and bakeries, rice became the only grain still easily available as a whole grain.

When the vows have been exchanged and the knot has been tied, when the rice has been thrown, when the cakes and wine have been distributed among the wedding guests, when the garter and the bouquet have been caught and the "something borrowed" has been returned, the bride and groom slip quietly away to change into street clothes and begin the honeymoon that marks the ending of an old way of life and the beginning of a new one. When they arrive at their destination there is yet another magickal act to perform. Traditionally, at this point, the groom carries the bride over the threshold, signifying that they have crossed over into their new life united as one. To the mundane mind, the threshold is simply a board nailed to the floor to mark the separation between one room and another, but to the Pagan it is a magickal place between the worlds, and much much more. The name "threshold" tells us that this simple piece of wood was probably once nailed to the edge of the threshing floor to prevent even the least bit of precious grain from being lost. So sacred was this floor upon which grain was threshed, that, when King David entered Judea, his first act was to purchase a threshing floor upon which to build his temple. One of the titles of Demeter is "She of the Threshing Floor," and it was upon the threshing floor that the Goddess Cerridwen, in the form of a black hen, swallowed the grain of wheat that Gwion Bach had shape-shifted into, so that she could give birth to the Magician Taliesin.

It is possible that in ancient times when Paganism was the world religion, the threshold that a newlywed couple crossed over, as one, was actually the entrance to the threshing floor, that sacred place of magick and fertility, and that they spent their first night here so that the magick of their union might be imparted to the grain harvest and that of the grain to their marriage. This reminds us of the close connection between human and vegetable fertility.

When we consider all of the traditions that come together to make up the traditional wedding of today; something old, something new, something borrowed, something blue, the cakes and wine, the garter and bouquet, and the showering with grain, we can see an entire collection of ancient rites—the meanings of which have been forgotten, but which have survived probably thousands of years. We can now perform these rites at our own Pagan and Wiccan Handfastings and we can restore to them the power and the magick that these sacred acts once held.

Just as traditional as the wedding cake and the garter is the age-old custom of giving wedding gifts to the newlywed couple.

On certain islands in the South Pacific, a powerful magickal charm is given to a couple about to be married. Deep down on the floor of the Pacific ocean grow remarkable creatures called glass sponges. These animals are made up, not of soft spongin like other sponges, but of spicules of silica, or glass. They are very beautiful, shaped somewhat like drinking horns, with covered tops, looking as though made of white crinoline or fine netting. The inner space of these creatures is sometimes entered by a species of tiny shrimp in their larval stage. These shrimp are always a male and a female, and, as they grow, they become entrapped in their lovely house of glass, where they live happily ever after as husband and wife. Glass sponges that contain a pair of these shrimp are given as gifts the the newlywed couple, to insure a long-lasting marriage.

While a microwave oven or the keys to a new Mercedes might be fine gifts for those married outside the Craft, for the Wiccan or Pagan couple who have just been handfasted, gifts with magickal properties are also appropriate, and these sometimes require a bit of imagination, as well as Craftsmanship.

One such traditional magickal gift is Poppets. These small magickal figures are versions of the Voodoo doll. They are actually a pair of small cloth dolls made to represent the bride and groom, and stuffed with all sorts of magickal things. The final product can be as simple or as finely detailed as the maker's desire and talent permits.

To begin such a pair of dolls, fold a piece of thin cotton fabric of a color resembling flesh tones in half and draw one outline for the bride and one outline for the groom. These need only be as detailed as a gingerbread-boy cookie cutter and about six or eight inches in height. Next, cut the cloth in half so that each figure is on a separate folded piece of cloth. Now draw with pencil or pen, facial and other physical features on each figure. Again, this may be as simple or as detailed as you wish, and this is not just a matter of talent and ability. Sometimes a simple primitive statement is more magickally powerful than a fussy and realistically detailed one.

No matter how well drawn the features of the couple are, they can be magickally reinforced by adding their names and astrological signs, and whatever other symbols you wish to. Now, unfold the cloth and place it on an embroidery hoop, and embroider all that you have just drawn, using colored thread wherever appropriate. For example, embroider the astrological sign in the correct astrological color.

When all of the embroidery is finished, fold the fabric as before and cut out each figure, allowing a quarter inch for a seam all the way around. Then place the two cut-out pieces of each figure face to face and stitch them together, using a simple small running stitch, leaving an opening at the top of the head about two inches wide. Turn the figures right side out and stuff them with magickal herbs, stones, crystals, amulets, and talismens, all expressing the blessings you wish for them in their marriage.

To do this, on a Friday, during a Waxing Moon, take a small bowl and blend together some of the following herbs:

For Happiness:

Five Finger Grass	Valerian
Basil	Costmary
Meadowsweet	Agrimony

For Health:

Eucalyptus	Allheal
Mint	Sage
Comfrey	Chamomile

For Fertility (if the couple intends to have children):

Cyclamen	Motherswort
Mistletoe (with berries)	Mandrake root
Hazelnuts	Cinnamon bark

For Good Fortune:

Hyssop	Bayberry
Coltsfoot	Yellow dock

For Love:

Elecampane	Apple (seeds or blossoms)
Cloves	Myrtle
Rose petals	Yarrow

For Protection:

Garlic	Bergamot
Hawthorne	Ash
Rue	St. Johnswort

Put one good handful of an herb from each category that you wish to give the couple a magickal gift from, and as you place the herb in the bowl, state aloud;

Meadowsweet do I add for Happiness!
(or some similar affirmation)

When all the herbs you have selected have been placed in the bowl blend them together thoroughly, chanting words such as:

MAKING A POPPET

1. Cut two identical pieces

   Embroider face and features onone side

2. Place two pieces face to face

3. Stitch pieces together

   Leave an opening

4. Turn right-side-out

   Stuff with herbs

   Add yarn hair to close top

Herbs of Venus, Moon, and Sun
Now the Magick has begun.
By leaf and root and bark of tree,
As I will so mote it be!

Chant and blend, chant and blend, until you feel the power of the herbs in your fingertips. When this is done, if there is not enough herb mixture to really fill the poppets, add some straw or sawdust or cotton, or any benign but organic filler. Now stuff the poppets, being careful to share the mixture equally between the two. Then other magickal gifts might be added; rose quartz crystals for love, almonds for fertility, runes such as ᛒ for the brides poppet and ᛉ for the groom's, inscribed with red ink to give them life on bits of parchment or staves of ash—the possibilities are endless. Just be sure that the magickal properties with which you endow the poppets are ones the couple really wants.

When the poppets both are finished, stitch the tops of the heads closed, using thread that duplicates the couple's hair colors, and perhaps a pattern of stitches that resemble their hair styles.

To enhance the charm even more, the poppets might be dressed appropriately, a simple grey flannel suit for him if he is a businessman, or blue denim if he is a farmer. Tools of their trades might also be added, a cardboard palette for the artist, a book or pencil for the writer.

When all the finishing touches have been added, the poppets are to be bound together. Traditionally, this is done by placing them face to face and winding a length of pink or red ribbon around both of them and finally tying the ends of the ribbon together in a True Lovers Knot while intoning:

Herb and poppets with ribbons round,
May (bride's and groom's names) *by Love be bound.*

Wrap the pair of poppets in a piece of white linen and present them to the couple, along with a list of the wishes you included in the charm (love, health, prosperity, etc.). The couple might want to keep this wonderful charm in some secret place, such as under their bed, or in a magickal cabinet.

Another magickal gift suitable for the newly handfasted couple is a cross-stitch sampler. Traditional old samplers usually have a short verse or bit of Bible text, but this can be replaced by a few lines of text recording the names of the couple and the date and place of the Handfasting, and perhaps the name of the priest and/or priestess who joined them, and whatever other information seems pertinent, much like a Pennsylvania German marriage certificate "frakture." The text might be surrounded by a stylized version of the couple rendered in cross-stitch, along with symbolic blessings such as a deer representing the horned god, stalks of corn for the Goddess, a house that the couple might desire and perhaps small figures representing children.

Hearts, doves and Love Knots would also be appropriate; but aside from the symbolism incorporated into the design, the magick of the cross-stitch sampler is in the cross-stitch. Each tiny stitch is the Rune X which has a double meaning. It is on one hand the symbol of the energy exchanged between a man and a woman, and at the same time it means "Wedding Gift," so every stitch of a sampler of this kind is a blessing in itself.

Whenever producing a magickal work of this kind, a quilt or a sampler, it is not always easy to work within a circle, but the gift can be imbued with magick by beginning it in a circle, and by stating with the very first stitch, "with this knot, the charms begun." Then meditate for a few moments, each time you take it up to work on it, on the purpose of the magick, and when it is complete, with the last stitch announce, "with this knot the magick's bound!"

For a couple who plans to, or wishes to, have children, there are many fertility charms that would make fine magickal Handfasting gifts. Among the people of Old Europe, magickal eggs inscribed with symbolic designs of birds or roosters are given to insure fertility. And there is one traditional Ukrainian egg inscribed so that the entire egg is a pregnant woman with her hands on her belly—symbol of fertility and new life. This egg reminds one at once of the wooden Russian dolls that open to reveal a smaller doll inside, which also contains a smaller doll and so on. These dolls almost certainly originated as fertility charms themselves. In the countries of the Mediterranean, many of the same charms used as protection against "maloccia," or the evil eye, are also used as fertility charms. These include the *manu in cornu* charm for men and the *manu in fica* charm for women, both described in the first chapter, and "the horn" mentioned in the second chapter. All three of these charms are traditionally made of red coral, which has magickal properties of its own.

Acorns, almonds, and hazelnuts are all fertility charms, especially for men, and among the traditional herbal charms are the Mandrake root shaped like a man or a woman, either naturally formed or carved to help the resemblance. High John, or John the Conqueror root is also a traditional fertility charm, and it is probably the fact that this little blackish-brown bulb-like root comes from a bog plant related to St. Johnswort that gives it its magickal power.

Damiana and southernwood are both herbs believed to be aphrodisiacs and to have fertility magick.

The palm tree is a symbol of male fertility almost everywhere it grows, and the berries of our own native saw palmetto are believed to be effective for male potency. The enormous nut of the coco de mer palm, which grows only in the Seychelle Islands, was considered a powerful fertility charm, while figs and pomegranates are symbols of female fertility.

Of course, not every couple joins in Handfasting just for the purpose of reproducing, and since the greatest single problem endangering the planet—our Mother, the Earth—is overpopulation, then having a large or even a medium-sized family is no longer a wise choice. In order to prevent unwanted pregnancies, our Pagan ancestors used to place an egg pierced with thorns under their marriage bed. Happily, today there are much more reliable methods for making every child a wanted child.

One of life's passages that sometimes occurs at about the same time that a couple is handfasted is moving into a new home. It might be a new house or old, or it might simply be a larger apartment. In any case, the move into a new home is very symbolic of a new phase of life about to begin, whether one has handfasted or not, and is one of the most exciting of life's changes. Here is a new environment in which one will live, work magick, and carry out plans, hopes, and dreams, possibly for the rest of their lives. Such an important change should certainly be marked and celebrated magickally.

A house blessing ritual has several purposes. One is to cleanse and purify the living quarters, and to attune ourselves with them; and another is to introduce ourselves to the house spirits and gain their friendship and their help. Often, when a house is being built, a coin is placed in the foundation, and many builders, when constructing a house, leave a branch of green leaves, or a small evergreen tree at the highest peak of the framework. This tree branch, like the last sheaf of wheat, is left standing as a place for the spirit, in this case the spirits of the trees cut to build the house, to which to retreat. In Old Europe, when a house was built, offerings of eggs and wheat were sometimes placed in the walls as gifts to the house spirits.

If you are building a new home, or having one built, do leave offerings of coins, crystals, or herbs in the foundation or within the walls, but if you are moving into an already existing dwelling, such offerings can be hung over doorways or tucked away in corners. Before beginning a house blessing ritual the house should be cleansed, first on a mundane level—scrubbing and vacuuming—then on a more spiritual level, to banish any negative influences left by the previous residents. Enter each room first with a bowl of salted water, to which such purifying herbs as rue, vervane, hyssop, or wormwood have been added. Sprinkle this purifying potion in each room with words like:

> Be gone unfriendly spirits,
> Return from whence you came.

Sweep each room with the besom, repeating the same phrase. Enter each room again with a stick of purifying incense, repeating the same phrase, and finally enter each room with the Athame, drawing a banishing pentagram or similar symbol.

A major exorcism is not really necessary, and sometimes spirits that were hostile to former residents might be friendly to new residents who are friendly to them. Once you feel psychically that the house is cleansed, the blessing can begin.

On the altar there might be a bowl of cream or ale, some bread or cakes, a bright shiny penny for each room or section of the house, and a bell with the sweetest, clearest sound you can find. To begin the ritual, if at all possible, cast a Circle around the house, but, if that isn't possible, sprinkle a circle of salt around the dwelling. If that is not possible, as in the case of an apartment, cast a Circle indoors according to your ways, and, at the same time, visualize the athame creating a neon blue circle around the entire dwelling. Invite the Lord and Lady, and the Spirits of the Four Directions to enter and protect the Circle cast within your new home and around it.

Then, take up the bell and ring a single, clear note, saying something like:

> *Spirits of this house, friendly spirits,*
> *Be welcome here!*

Ringing the bell again,

> *Kindly ones, friendly ones, helpful ones,*
> *Dwell among us here!*

Ringing the bell again,

> *Shining bright ones of above,*
> *Shadowy ones of below,*
> *Join us in our rites and in our lives!*

Ringing the bell again,

> *Dance friendly spirits with us now,*
> *The joyous round!*

Slowly begin dancing around the Circle doesil, ringing the bell and being aware of friendly presences. When the time to end the dance is felt, return to the altar and hold up the pennies in the palm of your hand saying something like;

> *Before the Lord and Lady,*
> *And in their presence*
> *Do I offer these gifts*
> *As tokens of my friendship.*

Still ringing the bell as feelings dictate, leave the altar (remember, the Circle is cast around the entire dwelling), and taking the pennies, hide one in some secret place in each room of the house.

Then, returning to the altar, bless the cakes and the cream in the name of the Lord and Lady. Then hold them high and state something like:

These cakes and this cream,
Blessed in the sacred names,
Do I leave for your pleasure,
Spirits of this house.
It is my wish and my desire
That you reside here with us,
In love and in peace.
And that if you choose to do so,
That you will give a sign.

(This sign will probably not be given immediately.) Ring the bell again and close the rite according to your ways, but continue to celebrate with cheerful music.

Aside from inviting the friendship and protection of the spirits of the house there are many magickal herbs which also give protection to a home. Most of these are well known: rowan, rue, St. Johnswort, and mistletoe. Four-leafed clovers have been placed in the foundations of houses for luck, and if it's too late to do that, under a carpet will work as well. A four-leaf clover, a rare find, is a natural Sun wheel, but there is a similar, closely related charm that can work as well. Bay leaves are sacred to the Sun and if one is placed in each of the four corners of a house, an apartment, or a room, they form an effective, and aromatic, Sun wheel which will encircle the dwelling space with protection and fill it with radiant energy.

There are several gifts that are traditional to give to a couple or to an individual when they move into a new home. In my family, it has been customary to always give a living plant as a house gift. A living plant is the gift of life. Salt is another traditional house gift. Salt is used for purification and is vital to good health. It is also a symbol of the element of Earth, and brings with it the blessings of the Earth, wealth and agricultural success. In some traditions a broom is a customary gift for the new home. In Eastern Europe, when a young woman was wed, she was given a crown of pure white eggs which were later taken from her and exchanged for a broom. The broom is a symbol of domesticity, since it is used to keep the house clean, and it can do so on several levels, including the mundane and the spiritual. Once a house has been blessed, the broom should always be used in such a way that it sweeps in from doorways, never out, because to sweep outward at a doorway is to sweep good fortune away.

Finally, if the newly handfasted couple has moved into their own house, in a suburban or rural situation, one of the most magickal of gifts, if it is feasible, is a pair of shade trees; oak, maple, or ash. These trees, when planted to

A wreath of eggs by Myque Molotzak, like those once worn
by Ukrainian maidens about to be wed.

the south of the house, can provide benefits for centuries to come. In colonial days and long before that, when almost all houses were built facing south to take advantage of the Sun's warmth, a pair of shade trees planted in front of the house were called Bride and Groom trees. In summer the shade from their foliage provided a natural air conditioning for the house, and in winter the trees shed their leaves and allowed the Sun to warm the house, and all within. Today, the same two trees, now full grown, can help to reduce fuel bills summer and winter, as well as helping to replace a small part of the forests of this planet that have been destroyed. Perhaps the Druids foresaw this, since, in ancient times, certain pairs of Sacred Oaks were named Og and Magog—Lord and Lady, Bride and Groom.

"Until death do us part," has been the traditional wedding vow until recently, when some couples began writing their own, sometimes very specific vows, but, for the Wiccan or Pagan about to be handfasted, the term of their union is expected to be much longer than that. Being a spiritual bonding, Handfasting is believed to unite a couple for all of their future incarnations, and for all of those periods in between, unless otherwise specified. This is in keeping with the tradition that we will "Merry meet, merry part, and merry meet again," or the belief and desire that we will be born again at the same time, and in the same place as those we love, so that we can "meet and remember, and love again." For anyone who has found their Own True Love it could not be any other way.

But people do grow, and change, and sometimes grow apart, and while a Wiccan or a Pagan Handfasting may not be legally binding unless the priest/ess is also a minister, it is spiritually binding. In order to avoid repeating the mistake of an unhappy union or an incompatible relationship in many lifetimes to come, when the marriage has failed it is best to perform a handparting ritual as soon as possible, and if there is to be a long and unpleasant divorce process, a handparting should be performed while the relationship is still a friendly one.

To perform a handparting, a priest or priestess does not need to be present, just the couple once handfasted, who now sincerely wish to go their separate ways. The ritual is best performed during the waning moon, and the True Lovers Knot formed at the Handfasting is the only object necessary. (If there is no such knot one may be made prior to the rite and consecrated in the sacred names, representing the union about to be dissolved.) Here is a simple handparting rite.

With the True Lovers Knot on the altar, the couple should cast the circle according to their ways, then state something like the following;

> Lord and Lady,
> Spirits of the Four Directions,
> We have come together
> In this Circle
> Cast in your honor,
> So that in your sight and with your blessings
> We may undo that which has been done.

The couple might then walk hand-in-hand to the East, then slowly widdershins around the Circle, finally returning to the altar. There they might turn to face one another saying something like:

> (name of the partner),
> I bid you Merry part and fond farewell,
> And as your path and mine
> Now turn in separate ways,
> I wish you Blessed be!

After a final kiss each partner will take one end of the True Lovers Knot, and, while gazing at one another, gently pull to untie the knot while "feeling" any last bits of malice slip away. Then the rite is ended, and the ribbon that was the Love Knot returned to Nature—dropped into running water or hung in a hawthorn tree as a sincere wish to release one another.

But for the couple who are about to be handfasted, who have both found their Own True Love, this rite is not a part of their reality.

As the day of the handfasting approaches, when the Mead Moon is waxing to full and the scent of roses and honeysuckle fills the warm dry air and new-mown hay perfumes the nights, all is made ready for the two who will be joined as one.

The Circle, having previously been cast and consecrated by the priest/ess, might be decorated with seasonal flowers or fruit, which need not be white. A small table to serve as an altar should be placed at the center of the Circle and adorned with the same symbols of the season, and perhaps a pair of candles. There should also be a small plate of cakes and a cup of wine, the rings, if there are to be any, and a 2-foot length of 1/4-inch-wide ribbon in pink, white, red, or whatever color is symbolic to the couple about to be joined.

The four Elements should be placed at their respective quarters—an earthenware bowl of soil or salt at the North, incense, a feather or a medicine fan at the East, a red candle, lit, at the South, and a glass or silver bowl of water in the West. If there are to be attendants, two men and two women are ideal, and they could stand at the quarters holding the elements, the men at the North and the South, the women at the East and West. If there are no attendants, the elements might be placed on four small tables or on trays.

Finally, when the Circle is in readiness, a broom, or a Witches' Besom if the couple is Wiccan, should be placed nearby where it will be easily reached, and placed across the threshold in the East at the end of the ritual.

When the time for the ceremony arrives, and the guests have assembled around the Circle, it is time for the bride and groom to enter.

In ancient times, a bride was often brought to her husband's village in a cart bedecked with garlands of flowers, and accompanied by a priest and a procession of family and village members. This actually is a reenactment of a religious rite performed at the Vernal Equinox when the Goddess herself was brought into the village in the form of a statue or other representation, drawn in a cart.

While a cart is not always the way a Pagan bride will enter the Marriage Circle today, one way she will probably *not* enter the Circle is by being escorted by her father, to be handed over to her husband like a piece of merchandise to be passed from one man to another. Regardless of the means of transportation, the bride and groom might enter the Circle together, side by side, preceded by attendants and followed by family members who will wait outside the Circle. Traditionally the bride and groom will enter the Circle from the East, holding hands.

The priest/ess will greet them at the altar with words like:

> Welcome (bride's name) *and* (groom's name) *to this Circle*
> *Cast as a place where you will be joined in Spirit.*

The couple then follows the priest/ess to the North Quarter. The priest/ess takes up the bowl of salt, and holding it aloft, says words like:

> *Spirits of the North whose element is Earth,*
> *Give your blessings to* (bride's name) *and* (groom's name)
> *Who are about to be handfasted.*

Sprinkling them with salt, the priest/ess continues:

> *And grant to their union your gifts of stability,*
> *Strength and fertility.*

The couple meditates for a moment on these gifts and then gives thanks to the spirits of the North.

The couple then follows the priest/ess to the East Quarter. The priest/ess takes up the symbol of the element, and holding it high, says words like:

> *Spirits of the East whose element is Air*
> *Give your blessings to* (bride's name) *and* (groom's name)
> *Who are about to be handfasted.*

Then, censing or fanning them, continues:

> *And grant their union your gifts of*
> *Wisdom and understanding.*

The couple meditates for a moment on these gifts and then gives thanks to the Spirits of the East.

The couple then follows the priest/ess to the South where she takes up the red candle, and holding it aloft, says words like:

> *Spirits of the South whose element is Fire,*
> *Give your blessings to* (bride's name) *and* (groom's name)
> *Who are about to be handfasted.*

Then holding the candle above the couple, the priest/ess continues:

> *And grant their union your gifts of Love,*
> *Passion and creativity.*

The couple meditates on these gifts for a moment, then gives thanks to the Spirits of the South.

Now the couple follows the priest/ess to the West Quarter where she takes up the bowl of water and asks:

> *Spirits of the West whose element is Water*
> *Give your blessings to* (bride's name) *and* (groom's name),
> *Who are about to be handfasted.*

Then sprinkling the couple, she continues:

> *And grant to their union your gifts of*
> *Intuition and Inspiration.*

Finally, the couple follows the priest/ess back to the altar at the center of the Circle. The couple and priest/ess face each other across the altar. The priestess speaks words like:

> *Now do we stand at the center of the Circle*
> *Where all things meet their opposites;*
> *Male and Female*
> *Darkness and Light*
> *Spirit and Matter*
> *God and Goddess*
> *That which makes each whole and complete.*
> *Just as you two* (bride's name) *and* (groom's name)
> *Are about to join as one.*

Priest/ess holds up plate of cakes.

> *As a symbol of this* (bride's name) *do I offer these cakes*
> *Which represent the Goddess.*

The bride accepts the plate of cakes from the priestess and (gently, without mashing it all over his face) feeds one to the groom.
The priest/ess continues:

> *From this day, and through this union* (groom's name)
> *Shall you know the Goddess through* (bride's name).

The priestess takes up the cup of wine.

> *Likewise, as a symbol of this, do I offer this wine*
> *Which represents the God.*

The groom accepts the cup and passes it to the bride who takes a sip of the wine and returns the cup to the groom.

> *From this day and through this union* (bride's name)
> *Shall you know the God through* (groom's name).

Facing each other, bride and groom now join right hands as the priest/ess takes up the ribbon and loosely ties their hands together with it forming a "True Lovers Knot." The priest/ess may say words like:

> *Now as I tie this True Lovers Knot*
> *You two are joined as one.*
> *Gentle are the bonds of this union.*
> *Pull one way and the bonds are strengthened.*
> *Pull the other and they are loosened.*
> *Now may you speak your vows.*

Now the bride and groom exchange the vows that they have written and agreed to beforehand.

Then, with the help of the priest/ess, the bride and groom slip their hands out of the Lovers Knot without untying it. The priest/ess hands the knot to the bride, saying something like:

> *Through this rite, within this Circle*
> *You two have been joined in Spirit.*
> *Keep this knot as a token of your spiritual bonds,*
> *And as a visible symbol of these bonds*
> *Shall you wear these rings.*
> (Bride and groom exchange rings.)

Now (if the priest/ess is a certified minister recognized by the government) she or he might make the traditional pronouncement:

> *By the power vested in me by the State of _____ etc., etc.*

As soon as the pronouncement is over, bride and groom kiss, then walk to the Eastern Quarter and, with arms about each other's waists, jump the broom.

When the Mead Moon has ended and the two, now united, begin a new life, there are many changes that will come to pass, and many challenges to be met. There are Rites of Passage that still lie ahead, but never again must one be faced entirely alone.

Chapter Five
Midlife

Midlife

The hay-scented breezes of late June ripple through a field of ripening wheat, revealing the presence of the Lady of the Grain. Overhead a hawk slowly circles round the Sun, which seems to stand still at the zenith of the Midsummer sky, while below Pagans dance around the Midsummer fire, leaping and rejoicing, on this the longest day of the year. St. Johnswort, rue, and blue vervain add their herbal magick to the sabbat fire, and branches of oak and ash, and rowan tree.

On another hilltop, in another time, the sacred mistletoe was gathered in the sacred grove, and the Oak King of the Waxing Sun was vanquished by the Holly King. Once again today, Pagans gather on hilltops and around bonfires as we have down through the sunlit centuries, to celebrate with the Lord of Light at the height of his glory. Behind us are the blossoms and the beauty and the promise of spring, while still ahead are the ripe fruits, the sweet wine, and the golden grain of the harvest.

Like the Sun on Midsummer day, when we have reached the midpoint of our lives, we may pause for a moment to reflect upon the memories of our youth, those magick moments that seem to have happened only yesterday, and then look to the rich harvest of the future that lies in the years ahead. Like the Roman God Janus, from this hilltop of our lives we may look in two directions, both backward at our past and forward at our future, and from this vantage point may we enjoy the views.

There comes a point when we can review our life since we came of age, not in terms of years, but in terms of decades. In our teens (one), we became individuals, entities separate from our parents. Numerologically, ten is equal to the number one, the number of the single unit, the self.

In our twenties (two) most of us entered into the partnership of marriage, and became part of the duality, the polarity, and the give and take of the number two.

Using the skills that have been developed.

By the thirties, many have started families and the two have become three, a number of completeness, of perfection and of the Goddess. The thirties are years of happiness.

Four is the number of hard work, of the four directions, of the Earth Plane and of square and solid foundations. Our forties seem to be the decade in which we reach the peak of our careers, when we can begin to plan and save for the future and establish the business upon which the rest of our lives are based.

Like the number five, our fifties are a decade of change, activity, and for some, whose families have grown up and left home, a decade for travel. Many have changed from parents to grandparents, and for women it is the time for the "change of life," or menopause.

Six is the number of beauty, peace, and harmony. For many this is the decade in which we retire, to enjoy rest and relaxation and the rich rewards of our life's labor.

Our seventies are the years in which we, as Pagans, must acknowledge our own mortality and begin to contemplate the spiritual side of life and prepare for our passage into it, which is in keeping with the mystical number seven.

Eight is the number of executive power, when we have earned the right, through years of experience, to join the council of the elders, provided that we have learned to apply the lessons of that experience.

Nine is the number of a cycle completed, and, for those fortunate few of us who may reach the decade of our nineties, the cycle of our lives must be just about complete.

But from our vantage point at midlife, the decade of our nineties and the frailties of old age are as distant and as obscure as the carefree play-filled days of our childhood.

It is hard to know precisely when midlife occurs, because the aging process is a gradual one, and we are not usually privileged to know exactly how many will be the number of our years, and so the date at which one celebrates the passage into the middle years is usually an arbitrary one, but one rich in Pagan history and tradition. As we usually come of age in our 13th year, we just as traditionally enter midlife at three times 13 years, or at age 39. This applies equally to both men and women. (Though the legendary midlife crisis often occurs a year or two later.)

As each year contains 13 lunar months, 13 years contain 13 times 13 lunar months, or 169. Thirty-nine years contain three times as many lunar months. The Sun God, as the legendary King Arthur, died in his 39th year, slain by his own son Mordred, whose mother was Arthur's sister Morgana. As the Sun God, Arthur died at the height of his power, before it began to wane. In another tale of Arthur, that of Culhwch and Olwan, there were

39 magickal tasks to be performed, suggesting 39 years, or turnings, of the Sun wheel.

The magickal number 39 abounds in legends and folktales and is usually a clue that the tale pertains to a Moon Goddess or a Sun God, the moon goddess of threes and 13s, the Sun God of the Waxing Sun at the zenith of its reign.

But unlike the Sun God who is vanquished at the height of his glory by the god of the waning year, or killed by his own son, we are neither killed nor vanquished. We simply pass quietly from one phase of life to another. Behind us is our youth and somewhere in the distant future our old age, but for now it is a time of equilibrium, a time of balance and of power, a time to be savored and enjoyed. It is a passage to be celebrated!

Since at this time of life most of us indulge in the practice of reviewing our lives anyway, this is a good time to review the past 39 or 40 years in magickal terms; not the magickal skills we have acquired and developed over the years but the mundane events of our lives as seen in magickal terms. Ancient people viewed themselves and told their tales in such terms where everyday life was closely bound to magick and mystery, and so today when the bonds between mundane life and magick seem at times to be nonexistent, for those of us on a magickal path it is all the more important to do so.

The legend of a life might begin with words like;

> Once upon a time, when the world was a bit younger than it is today, in a year when the world was at peace and the Sun was in the sign of Pisces, during a great blizzard was I born.

or,

> I, Robert, son of Richard the builder, whose father was Richard the Elder, was born in the city of Brotherly Love on the night that the Wolf Moon was full.

and so on.

A woman, of course, would wish to list the matrilinear side of her ancestry, especially.

Schooling could be described in terms like:

> After I had learned the arts of writing and mathematics in the village of my birth, and had come of age, I went to the distant city of _____ to study the arts of law, etc.

Military service might be expressed in the terms of a warrior. Illnesses and diseases might be written of as monsters defeated, dragons slain, or demons overcome.

All of the prominent personalities in our lives might be viewed as aspects of divinity (which, in fact, they are), or various characters of mythology, or archetypes from the Tarot. The goals of our life can be seen as the objects of a quest, and the fortuitous meetings and synchronistic happenings that led to the achievement of those goals can be viewed as divine intervention, or magick.

When the legend that is your life has been written down and brought up to date, remember it can never be considered finished until the final passage, or even long after that; it need only be a few paragraphs to a few pages long. It is then that the various stages and episodes of one's life can be seen in archetypical terms that have occurred and recurred in the mythologies and legends of many different traditions. Furthermore, we can choose which myths to which we prefer to compare our own life, and in so doing determine our future to some degree.

However, the purpose for this exercise is not to predict the outcome of our lives, but to review the past unto the present for two reasons. The first of these is that once the superficial has been discarded, and the unimportant details scraped away, our lives have been more meaningful and successful than we, especially at this age, usually give ourselves credit. And the second reason, not really so different from the first, is to see for ourselves how truly magickal our lives have been when viewed in the proper light. One of the greatest secrets of magick is to see it in everything, because all that is, is a manifestation of the Gods.

It might not be an easy task for us to write the legend of our own life for several reasons. Often, when a person is about to enter midlife, there is a great deal of negativity. There is a tendency to review our lives in terms of the goals that have not been achieved; but by looking at our lives in magickal terms, we can put the past where it belongs, behind us, recognize the positive magick that has taken place up to the present, and then get on with our lives and work toward the future.

It might be tempting to ask others close to us to write the legend for us, but while the input of those close to us might be encouraging and possibly more positive than our modesty would allow us to be, no one knows the magick of our lives as we do ourselves. On the other hand, most of us would be embarrassed by sounding egotistical, and so it might be helpful to consult with close family or coven members who might be more objective in recognizing the magickal archetypes represented by the people and events of our lives.

Still, it will be up to us in the end to write the legend of our life from a magickal perspective. If it were not for this magickal viewpoint, then the *Iliad* and the *Odyssey* of Homer would just be the stories of a man who went to war and then went back home.

This is a time when we may take stock of our worldly possessions and realize that we have all that we need, and most of the things we ever wished for. This applies to things magickal, as well as to things mundane. Up until now we have been adding to our magickal knowledge, something we will continue to do throughout the days of our lives, but we will also be discarding ideas that didn't work and rejecting concepts that do not fit comfortably with what we have come to know. Until now we have been adding to our herb closet, accumulating new magickal tools, and embellishing our rituals with bits and pieces gathered from here and there. As we enter our middle years we might begin to feel a magickal house cleaning is in order. Herbs that didn't perform the magick attributed to them in some herbal or dusty grimoire might find themselves consigned to the compost heap. The athame that was given to you at your initiation, the one with the gorgeous Celtic knot design on the handle, is still as beautiful as it is powerful, but your taste is now more classical, not so "middle ages." And the Beltane rites that you have added to over the years now seem uncohesive and redundant, and the marginal notes detract from the original beauty of your Book of Shadows. All of these feelings are signs of intellectual and spiritual growth, and indicate a readiness for a new phase of life to begin.

As such, all of the herbs, charms, and tools that have been accumulated over the years since initiation might be examined, and those that no longer seem to belong, or which seem to simply be outgrown, might be set aside.

If there are herbs of which to dispose, they might be gathered together and sorted out according to the element to which they belong. This information can be found in a good magickal herbal such as Culpepper's or Cunningham's. These herbs will then be discarded according to their elements, as this is the magickal way of doing so, especially if they were gathered magickally.

Herbs that are associated with the element of Water then, might be disposed of by being thrown into running water. Those associated with Fire, obviously, can be burned, which should be done outdoors since some might be toxic, and even if they are not, it can get pretty smokey. A word of warning—most herbs smell "illegal" when burned, so try not to burn your burnett downwind of your neighborhood narcotics officer. Herbs associated with the element of Earth should be buried, and those under the element of Air can be tossed from a high place, a hilltop or high rise window, and scattered to the Four Winds.

Each of these herbs might be enchanted as they are being returned to their elements with words like:

> *Herb of Air*
> *Return from whence ye came.*

Tools which have been consecrated, and which are not biodegradable are quite a bit more complicated to dispose of.

To begin with, each piece must be deconsecrated, but if you have a new tool that will replace the old one, why not transfer the power of the old one into the new. If, for example, a new athame has been found that suits your more mature taste than the one chosen at the time of your initiation, here is a simple rite.

Cast a Circle according to your ways, using the old athame. Then take up the new one from the altar and consecrate it in the four elements and in the names of the Lord and Lady. Replace the new athame on the Altar and again take up the old one holding it high with both hands. Visualize it pulsing with energy, the blade glowing. Recall to mind the magick it has performed. Then intone words such as:

> *Athame!*
> *Tool of Power!*
> *You who have served me*
> *Both long and well,*
> *The time has come*
> *For us to merry part.*
> *Yet one more magickal act*
> *Would I ask of you now.*
> *That you transfer your power*
> *To this new blade.*

Once again visualize the blade glowing with power. Then point the blade of the old athame at that of the new one. See the energy drain from the old blade into the new. Feel the knife lose its power as your hands relax their grip, and see the bright new blade shine with magickal energy.

Now take up a bowl of salted water and wash the old athame with the purifying bath, while intoning words such as:

> *Tool of Power,*
> *You who have served me*
> *Both long and well,*
> *As I consecrated you once*
> *With this purifying potion*
> *Now do I release you*
> *From your bonds of magick*
> *And return you to*
> *The mundane worlds*

You no longer are a tool of power
Old friend, merry part.
As I will, so mote it be!

Similar rituals might be performed for any working tool or altar article that is being replaced. There are other objects, remnants of charms worked or spells woven, stumps of candles, little bags of this or that, objects still filled with energy that, if grounded, might undo the spell, or if buried might be transformed. An ancient tradition was to keep a box, sometimes called a reliquary, to hold such objects, such relics of magick once made. Such a box will eventually become something like a battery charger, and when a charm or a spell calls for putting something "in a secret place," the reliquary would be a perfect place in which old charms and spells that have worked can lend some of their power to new ones. Such a box is also a perfect place to keep old tools that have been deconsecrated.

If you have found that over the years you have accumulated quite a number of magickal leftovers, then a container such as a reliquary might become the object of a quest. The only requirements are that the box be large enough to contain all that you already have, as well as all that you are likely to produce in the future. For the average Witch a box the size of a small chest is sufficient. The style of such a chest is not important. What is important is that it, like all magickal tools, appeals to your magickal self and stimulates in you that certain energy that makes magick happen. The other requirement is that the box has the magickal ability to contain magickal energy. There are several ways to achieve this. One method is that the box be equipped with encircling bands. These may be an original part of the box, such as bands of wood, iron, or bronze, or they may be added to it, such as bands of color, a carved Rune Row, or a traditional Pysanky design. This will act like the magick Circle to contain the magick within. Another method is to line the box with something that will insulate it magickally. Lead is a type of insulator, but we are talking about magick, not plutonium. Still, just as lead is not a good insulator, copper is. While it is true that copper is an excellent conductor of electricity and heat, it is a very good insulator of magickal energy, provided that one side is polished, and that the polished side faces into the box. The reason for this is that copper is sacred to the Goddess and was the material of which Her symbol, the mirror, was first made. The same effect could be achieved by lining the box with actual pieces of mirror, or even aluminum foil, using the same principle as baking potatoes. That is, that the shiny side faces inward, reflecting the energy back inside the reliquary where it can be reabsorbed by the magick charms.

At some point in our middle years we might recognize the fact that one of the joys of our youth that is now lost to us is the joy of discovering new knowledge. In our youth there were so many new things to learn. Every book was a treasure chest of new ideas. This seemed especially true for those of us who found the Old Religion during the consciousness-raising, mind-expanding days of the 1960s. But as we enter our middle years we begin to realize that there is really nothing new under the Midsummer Sun. There are just an infinite number of variations on a small handful of ancient themes. So our youthful joy of new discovery has not really been lost, it has simply become the quiet pleasure of deeper understanding. As students we carried our notebooks everywhere, jotting down each individual piece of information, but now we can file all of these pieces under a small handful of separate headings. This is the difference between knowledge and wisdom. Knowledge is the awareness of the hundreds of thousands of different genus and species of life upon this planet, but wisdom is the awareness of the oneness of all life.

Nowhere does this shift of awareness become more evident to the middle-aged Wiccan than in our Book of Shadows, these books now worn with years of use, and blessed with wax and wine. Perhaps the actual moment when we reach the midpoint of our spiritual life is when we look at our Book of Shadows, and say to ourselves, "This book really needs to be redone!"

Like so many things in the Old Religion, this process is very likely to take a year and a day. If you are planning to re-do your Book, begin with the next Sabbat to be celebrated. Gather as much material as possible about the traditions surrounding the Sabbat and take notes on all of the traditions, invocations, and rites that appeal to you. Eliminate anything from your old Book of Shadows that no longer fits with your own tradition, for whatever reason, whether it is too much like ceremonial magic, too New Age, or just too wordy. Make an outline of all of the elements you wish to include in your ritual, and be sure to write a paragraph at the beginning specifying everything you will need for the ritual. Each sabbat rite in our own Book of Shadows begins with something like:

> "The Circle is adorned with Summer flowers. On the
> hearth is a bundle of Oak and Fir for the Midsummer fire,
> and a bundle of Magickal Herbs. Above the altar hangs a
> Sun Wheel of Rowan and Vine and last year's Sun Wheel
> is on the hearth. On the altar are amulets of protection to
> be consecrated in the smoke of the Sabbat fire."

A paragraph such as this is not merely a checklist for the preparations just prior to the sabbat rites, but for a week or two before the sabbat as well. This paragraph insures that never again will the Circle be broken because one of the most important elements of the ritual was forgotten.

Under the eaves in the attic, an old trunk holds all that remains
of spells cast and charms that have worked their magick.

Once all of the elements of the rite have been carefully selected and arranged in the most reasonable order, all that is left to do is the wording of the ritual itself. This is why it is important to create the ritual as the time of the sabbat approaches. Surround yourself with symbols of the season and become familiar with the sabbat traditions. Be filled with the spirit of the season, and let the words of the ritual flow through you onto the page.

Continue this process around the wheel of the year and in a year and a day, when the final sabbat has been celebrated, the new Book of Shadows will be complete.

Then, at the next New Moon or sabbat gathering, consecrate the new book and offer the old one on the sabbat fire, or place it in the reliquary.

As we enter our middle years, we also enter the period of our lives when for most of us our earning power is at its peak. Just as we have acquired certain occult skills as we have matured, so have we acquired and refined our professional skills. So also have others in our chosen field of endeavors, and the competition is stiff; but now that there are children's college tuitions for which to pay, along with the mortgage, the middle-aged Pagan or Wiccan has magick to call upon, as well as professional skills, in order to earn the extra money needed to pay the ordinary expenses of living and set aside a little extra for the future.

Nowhere are there more confused feelings than where money, magick, and spirituality come together, but there is really no reason for this. Money has been called "the root of all evil," but this is not true. It is human greed, if anything, that is evil where money is concerned, not money itself. On the contrary, within a spiritual context, money can be an expression of love, respect, and admiration. Money is the reward for the craftsman who has perfected his craft. It is the symbol of appreciation given by the buyer of the craftsman's product.

Once money is seen in this light, and not as something evil and corrupt, and in direct conflict with spirituality, then a major obstacle to earning will have been overcome. Furthermore, if the work that you do is in accordance with the Old Ways, then money earned through this work might be seen as rewards from the Gods through the channels of karma. This is true as long as the law "And it harm none," can be applied.

Still, no matter how noble our careers might be in the mundane world, earning enough is not always easy. Sometimes a little magick is necessary.

The dried, powdered roots of yellow dock have for a long time been considered effective for attracting good fortune into the home. Simply brew a potion by sprinkling some of the powdered root into water and bringing it to a boil. Boil it for a few minutes and then allow the amber, acrid-smelling liquid to cool. Then, on a night of the Waxing Moon, anoint the door knobs and thresholds of all of the entrances to the home, while chanting words like:

*Good fortune
Enter here!*

Another herb that has fortune-increasing powers is coltsfoot. The old Latin name for coltsfoot, *filius ante pater*, meaning "the son comes before the father," comes from the fact that the bright yellow dandelion like blossoms and seed heads appear long before the foliage of the plant itself. It is the leaves, large and dark green above and downy gray beneath, that are the parts used. Gather the leaves as the Wart Moon is waxing to full, and hang them in a cool, dark place to dry. Then each month when the Moon is New, take a few of the dollars earned in the previous weeks, place them in a small box and sprinkle them with some of the dried herb while chanting

*Coltsfoot grant this boone,
Money grow like the Moon!*

When the Moon is waxing to full the money may be put in a special savings account, or left in the box to be added to month after month, but it is not to be spent. The purpose of this spell is to accumulate a large sum of money. Repeat the charm on a monthly basis and whenever new money is available to be laid away. It will eventually become obvious that the money in the box,

Coltsfoot growing at the back of the herb garden.

or account, is growing at an increasing rite. This money should be saved until you reach your goal.

Things green or gold such as yellow dock, or the yellow flowers and green leaves of coltsfoot, are often associated with good fortune. This is as true of candles as it is of herbs, as yellow is the color of the precious metal of the Sun and green is the color of Nature and of growth.

Here is a candle charm to be performed during the waxing moon. In the center of the altar place a gold or yellow candle which has been anointed with a commercially prepared increase oil, or one prepared at home using herbs such as those mentioned above. The candle might also be inscribed with such Runes as ᚠ or ᚾ or symbols such as $. Surround this candle with six green ones which have been similarly anointed with oil and inscribed with Runes.

If these candles are of Bayberry, all the better. Surround this with 13 bright, shiny coins. Gold ones would be perfect, but if you had them you wouldn't need to be doing this charm, would you? Bright, shiny new pennies will do. Light the gold candle first, then the six green ones in a sunwise order. Gaze at the flames and chant slowly and rhythmically, words like;

> *Candle of gold*
> *With candles round*
> *The money comes*
> *By magick bound.*

Chant this once, then six times, then 13 times, while holding an image in the eye of the mind, of hands exchanging money for the wares you make or the services that you provide professionally. When the chanting is finished, extinguish the candles in the same order in which they were lit. Gather up the pennies the same way and put them in your pocket. Spend one of the pennies each time you make a purchase and be sure to have spent them, all but one, by the dark of the Moon.

On the New Moon toss the last penny over the threshold into your home, then hide it in a secret place near where it fell and keep it there as a charm of increase.

Repeat this charm as often as possible, always at the full of the moon. It does not work very quickly, but it does work very well.

Meanwhile, remember that the Gods help those who help themselves, so while this spell is being worked it is the wise Witch who is busy improving professional skills and techniques in order to enhance the magick.

For those of us who found the Old Ways early in our lives, by the time we enter our middle years our magickal skills have become highly developed. By now we can create appropriate rituals for the sabbat rites, rituals which open us to the realities of the spirit world and which charge our psy-

A Spell for Increase.

chic batteries so that we can perform acts of magick and of healing, and by this point in our lives we understand the basics of magick and can devise a charm or a spell for just about any purpose. The well-rounded Witch has many psychic skills at her disposal. She can look into the future at will and read the past. She can intuit the truth about others while respecting their right to privacy and she can read the past and present from inanimate objects when necessary. She can know of events taking place at a distance and control many of the events taking place in her immediate surroundings; and just about every Witch has one or two skills which she has worked hard at developing since initiation. These may include the casting of runes or reading the Tarot, contacting the spirits of deceased loved ones, or psychic healing; or they may be more objective skills such as the blending of magickal oils or incense, the embroidery of ancient designs on altar cloths, or the telling of ancient tales. Whatever the skills may be that we have mastered, the midpoint of our lives is a good time to do two things. One of these is to go back to our first source of information on the subject, the first book we ever read on the Tarot, the first interpretation of the runes we ever explored. This can accomplish two things. One will be to affirm the skills that we have worked so hard to acquire, and the other is to reveal some bits of wisdom that perhaps we did not understand at the time, but which now, in the light of experience, can open vistas of understanding.

The other thing we might do at this point in our life is to begin developing another skill, one entirely different than those we have already acquired, and we have the rest of our life in which to perfect it.

One day when our children have come of age, when we look in the mirror and recognize the face of our own mother or father looking back at us through the glass, sometime between our 39th and 40th birthday, there will probably be a moment when we recognize the fact that we are entering our middle years. For women, most of us reach our sexual peak at this time of life, a condition which will last for years into the future; while men, whose sexual peak passed with their 20th birthday, now have the confidence and assurance of a successful career which does much for their hormone levels. This is a time to celebrate one of life's most unsung passages, the achievement of our greatest power, where we will remain for many years to come.

To celebrate this passage into midlife, what could be more appropriate than a traditional birthday party?

There is an old saying, "that life begins at forty," and in a sense, a new life does begin, as is the case with every rite of passage. In recent years it has become a tradition to wear black, decorate with black, and give gifts of black at a 40th birthday, suggesting that turning 40 is the same as being dead and a 40th birthday is really a funeral. The idea here is an attempt at humor, but on another level the concept is quite profound. In order for life to begin anew at 40, there must first be a death. Without death there can be no rebirth, no resurrection.

One old birthday tradition which suggests the idea of an ordeal, and therefore the symbolic death prior to rebirth, is the birthday spanking. This birthday beating includes one stroke for each year, and one for good luck. If this doesn't sound enough like a ritual, then consider one way that the birthday spanking was administered. In an old birthday tradition called "The Old Mill," all of the boys and girls in the village stood in a row, each one facing the back of the boy or girl ahead of them, and all with their legs spread wide to form a tunnel. The boy or girl celebrating a birthday would then crawl through the tunnel of legs from front to back, being spanked by each boy or girl as he or she crawled along.

This is a universal symbol of birth and rebirth, and more than one so-called "primitive" tribe still uses this very ritual as a part of a coming of age rite of passage. There is also a traditional Witch dance which is called, among other things, "The Old Mill," which involves activity quite similar to this old birthday custom.

Following the traditional birthday spanking is another old tradition, the ritual of the birthday cake. This custom, which possibly began in ancient Sumer, and which may have acquired its current form in medieval Vienna, is a three-part ceremony which has several elements a Witch might recognize. First, the cake is ritually carried into the darkened room, its candles ablaze, while the assembly sings a not-so-ancient tune expressing their fondness and their wishes for the happiness of the celebrant. Second, as all eyes gaze at the flaming candles, the celebrant makes a silent wish (expressing the power of secrecy), and at last blows out the candles (sabbat fire), breathing life into his or her wish and leaving the room in smokey darkness. Finally, following this the lights are turned on again, and the birthday child ritually makes the first cut in the cake, which is then cut and served to all present.

While games and entertainment which are not ancient in origin may be a major part of today's birthday parties, there is one more tradition which is very old and mentioned in more than one folk or Faerie tale. That is the cus-

Horus Amulet.

tom of giving birthday gifts. Almost anything is an appropriate birthday gift, usually, but for someone who is about to enter midlife there are some things which might be special.

As has already been stated, this is a time when we can look backward at our past and forward to our future. What could state this more clearly than a scrapbook filled with photos, of life's passages already made, of sabbats celebrated and year wheels turned, of coveners and clansmen merry met and merry parted with, of all the magickal moments of our lives, and another scrapbook, this time with pages still blank, for all the seasons yet to come and all the magick still to be made.

Sun symbols are also appropriate at this time of life, especially for men, expressing as they do the life force and the energy of the Sun in all its radiant splendor. The Rune ⚡ is just as perfect an expression of this. The Egyptian Horus as a charm, or his symbol, the hawk, also express this idea. A lion is an appropriate masculine symbol of the Sun, while the Egyptian lioness Goddess Sekmet, sister of Bast, is a fine feminine Sun symbol, and of course, anything of gold or bronze is a symbol of the Sun. A gold charm bracelet, while far beyond the means of most of us, would certainly be a perfect gift for a woman about to enter mid-life.

As the Sun at its height of power symbolizes the man in his middle years, so does the Moon in its fullness symbolize the woman at midlife. While many feel that a woman is associated with the Full Moon and the mother aspect of the Goddess as soon as she conceives, most ancient mythology associates the New and Waxing Moon with youth, fertility, and the bringing forth of new life. Just as the Corn Maiden presides over the planting of the fields, it is the Corn Mother who reigns at the harvest when the grain has reached the fullness of its maturity. The Maiden and Waxing Moon represent potential life, the Mother and the Moon at full represent that potential realized, and it is this mother aspect of the Triple Goddess of the Moon with which a woman begins to identify as she enters her middle years. This is also reflected in the fullness and roundness of a more mature figure that was once lithe and lean. For a woman at this passage, symbols of the Full Moon and things of silver are the perfect gifts.

There is another tool popular among the Pennsylvania German traditions of magick. That is the Hex stick. The Hex stick is the magician's staff, but with a twist—literally. A Hex stick is a naturally spiralled length of wood, usually of maple, and it occurs when a vine, usually honeysuckle, grows around a maple sapling. As the maple grows, the vine tightens its grip, causing the maple to grow in a spiral shape. Sometimes the vine kills the maple, sometimes the maple breaks the vine and continues to grow into a very thick spiral shape. Whichever the case may be, a Hex stick is the object of a quest, just as is the Stang in some British traditions, and the "shaman's horse" in

A Witching Stick and the horsetails that are traditionally used to polish it.

most shamanic traditions. Once found, the Hex stick is stripped of its bark and polished. This polishing was once done with a bundle of Horsetails, a primitive plant with a rough texture that was once used as sandpaper and scouring pads. The secret of the Hex stick is in the number of twists in the spiral. For a new initiate, a stick with a single twist is traditional. For the advanced practitioner, a staff of three spirals is more powerful, and for the Hexenmeister a staff of five or more twists is reserved. For any Wiccan or Pagan about to enter midlife, a staff of three twists, representing three times 13 years, is a wonderful and powerful gift, regardless of their tradition.

Among the people of Eastern Europe, especially the Ukraine, the magickal eggs known as Pysanky are made, or more correctly, written, since the symbols used in their designs form an ancient language for many more occasions than the Vernal Equinox. Among these sacred and talismanic eggs are a series of designs which are called, in order: The Princess, The Queen, and The Old Woman. These three ancient designs represent the three stages of a woman's life, Maiden, Mother, and Crone.

The first of these, the Princess, is an abstract design which seems to be at once an ear of corn, an egg and a hen, all of which represent potential life. The second design, the Queen, seems to be more obviously a long-necked bird. With its tail spread, wings upraised, and a crown upon its head, it is, in all likelihood, the sacred crane which is one representation of the Goddess in this part of the world. The third design, the Old Woman, seems to be a stylized representation of a spider, albeit missing a pair of legs. This image calls to mind Arachne, and the Goddess as the spinner of the thread of life, the weaver of the web of life, and she who cuts the thread at the end of life.

These three designs seem to be summed up in a fourth design known as the Great Goddess. In this symbolic representation, the figure has two pairs of upraised arms, which seem to represent the New Moon rising, and immediately recall to mind figures of Astarte from Mycenae, with upraised arms and striped mantle, the Goddess as Maiden. The figure also wears the crown of the Queen and Mother, and has the three pairs of arms and/or legs of the Old Spider Woman. All four of these designs, whether they are written on eggs or embroidered on clothing, date back uncounted centuries before Christianity became the official religion of the land, and all are appropriate gifts for the many passages of a woman's life.

Every woman, at some point in her middle years, comes to the end of her child-bearing days. For some it happens when they are in their fifties, for some, in the late thirties, but for most, menopause begins sometime in their mid-forties, and the process is a gradual one. The symptoms and variations of menopause, and the length of time it takes, are endless in variation, but according to the medical profession, a woman's risk of becoming pregnant is over when she has not had a period for one full year.

FOUR TRADITIONAL DESIGNS

The Princess

The Queen

The Old Woman

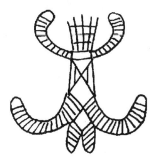

The Great Goddess

Naturally, if the woman is a Witch, then she enters a new stage of life when she has not had a period for a year and a day. As accustomed as we woman are to marking dates on calendars in red ink, this gives us plenty of time to contemplate the meaning of this transition. On the one hand the days of our youth and the magick of our ability to bring forth new life will have come to an end, but on the other hand we are finally free of the burden of child-bearing and the risk of pregnancy. We can begin to turn our attention toward ourselves without the interference of the ebb and flow of hormones playing havoc with our emotions and coloring our views of reality. No longer will our blood flow so that we may give new life. No longer will our happiness wax and wane with the moon. That mystery has been revealed to us and it is now time to move on. When a year and a day has come to pass and not a drop of blood has flowed, it is time to celebrate this most intense of passages. The following is a simple rite designed for a woman to perform alone. If it is altered to be a group rite, it is for women only, as this is one of Woman's Mysteries.

After sunset, cast a Circle and light the candles at the four quarters. On the altar, or at the center of the Circle, have a small hand mirror and a comb, and two red candles lit. After the Circle has been cast, take up one red candle, light it, and hold it high, saying something like:

> *Ancient Goddess, Mother of all Life*
> *I (Craft name), your daughter, stand at a threshold.*
> *Behind me are my childbearing years, and ahead*
> *Is a door through which I cannot see.*
> *At your altar, Lady (name) do I offer to serve you,*
> *That I may follow in your ways.*

Now carry the candle to the East point.

> *Spirits of the East, whose element is Air,*
> *Through your magick was I able*
> *To bring forth new life*
> *As does the Sun when it rises in the East.*

Then going to the Southern point, raise high the candle, saying something like:

> *Spirits of the South, whose element is Fire*
> *Through your magick was I able*
> *To make a tiny spark*
> *Into the flame of life*
> *Warm and bright*
> *As the sun at Midsummer.*

Going to the Western point again, raise the candle and intone something like:

> *Spirits of the West, whose element is Water*
> *Through your magick was I able*
> *To open wide the gates*
> *Letting the birth waters flow*
> *Uniting Spirit and matter*
> *Just as they part where*
> *The Sun sets in the West.*

And finally, going to the point in the North, and raising the candle high, say something like:

> *Spirits of the North whose element is Earth*
> *Through your magick was I able*
> *To feed and nurture the flesh of new life*
> *Giving growth and strength*
> *Just as our mother nurtures us*
> *Like the new born Sun at Yule.*

Then returning to the East, gaze at the candle for a few moments, meditating, before saying words like:

> *But the Wheel has turned*
> *Once and a day*
> *Since my blood has flowed.*
> *My time for giving new life has ended*
> *Behind me are the days of flesh*
> *Ahead are the days of Spirit.*

Extinguish the red candle and return it to the altar, taking up the second candle. Carry it, unlit, to the Eastern point and hold it high, saying something like:

> *May this be the day of my rebirth,*
> *Freed from the burdens of the past!*
> *Now do I light this candle*
> (taking flame from the quarter candle)
> *As a sign of my new life,*
> *As the morning Sun at Beltane,*
> *Spirits of the East, now may I receive*
> *Your gifts of clear thinking and inspiration.*

Going to the South, meditate for a moment before saying something like:

Spirits if the South, behold I am born anew
Now may I receive your gifts
Of creativity and energy.
Let this candle be a symbol
Warm and bright
Like the noonday Sun at Lammas.

Going to the West, meditate again before saying something like:

Spirits of the West, behold I am reborn.
May I now receive your gifts
Of intuition and of knowledge of the Spirit World.
May this candle symbolize these gifts
As promised at the Samhain Sunset.

And then going to the North, meditate for a moment before saying words like:

Spirits of the North, behold my new beginning
Now may I receive your gifts
Of strength and solidity.
And let this candle be a symbol of these gifts
Burning steadily in the darkness of an Imbolc night.

Carrying the candle back to the altar, place it so that its flame illuminates your face. Take up the hand mirror and gazing at your reflection, begin to slowly comb your hair, while chanting mentally or softly aloud:

Behold my true self
Changing, yet unchanged.

When finished take up the candle again and intone words like:

Ancient Goddess, Queen of the night
Keeper of the Dark Mystenes,
I, your daughter (Craft name), *stand before your altar*
Changing yet unchanged,
That I may follow in your ways.

Feel the gifts of the four directions and of the elements as they mingle and flow through you, and if you feel so moved, dance around the Circle until the rite is ended. So mote it be!

As we enter midlife, when our children have come of age and our parents have retired from their life's work to join the elders and enjoy the rewards of their labors, when the sunny days of our lives have reached a zenith, and our grandparents have crossed beyond the veil, we must pause and

A Woman's Celebration of Midlife.

mark the occasion. With solemnity and rejoicing we must savor the time and remember it well.

The following is a brief rite designed to celebrate the passage into midlife for a man. An almost identical rite might be performed for a woman, and the necessary changes are mentioned later.

The purpose of the rite is to acknowledge the positive aspects of this transition so that this period of life can be enjoyed. In a world in which most spend the first half of their lives worrying about the future, and the second half regretting the past, it is the Wise Ones who live for, and enjoy the present. That is what this passage is about. Ideally, the rite would be followed by an old fashioned surprise birthday party.

The subject of the rite will be asked to wait outside the ritual area for an extended length of time. On the altar are a pair of gold candles, one to the left and one to the right. There may be a bowl containing grain such as wheat on the one side, representing youth and fertility, and a loaf of bread on the other side, representing the reaping of the harvest. Above the altar might be a solar symbol such as a Sun wheel (for a woman, a lunar symbol such as a silver disc or a round mirror). There should also be symbols or photos of the man's accomplishments and victories placed about the altar or Circle, and there should be a chair of honor placed in the North, facing South, and upon it a wreath of laurel leaves. When the Circle has been cast and consecrated, a door has been left open in the South. Coveners holding sprigs of mistletoe (or St. Johnswort or other herb sacred to the Sun or Moon for a woman) might line up on both sides of the doorway, and as the subject of the rite is led into the Circle, strike him with the sprays of herb.

When the subject has passed through this ordeal he is met at the altar by the priest and priestess. The priestess proclaims:

> All hail him whom we honor this night!
> (Craft name) who has passed through
> The trials of his youth
> To arrive victorious at this gate!

Then the priest, lighting one gold candle, says something like:

> This gold taper do I light
> Colored like the waxing Sun
> Of the Oak King.
> May it be a reminder
> Of the golden days of your youth.
> May its radiance remind us also
> Of the promise of a sunrise
> (Craft name) this taper is lit in your honor!

The priestess lights the second candle speaking words like:

> This taper of gold do I light
> Colored like the waning Sun
> Of the Holly King
> May it be a reminder
> Of the golden days that lie ahead.
> And may it remind us too,
> Of the glory of the sunset.
> (Craft name) this taper is lit in your honor!

The priest and priestess carrying the candles, now may lead the subject doesil around the Circle as the coveners greet him with hugs and handshakes, until he comes to the chair (throne) upon which he is told to be seated. The candles of gold shall be placed on either side. Then raising the laurel wreath, the priestess might say something like:

> (Subject's Craft name) this wreath of laurel,
> The crown of heroes,
> Do I place upon your head
> As a sign of the honor
> We have for you this night!
> Now listen to the legend.

The priest or an appointed covener will then read aloud the legend of the subject's life thus far, with respect, ending with words like:

The legend continues.

At this point the two gold candles, altar candles, quarter candles, and any other lights might suddenly be extinguished, and a birthday cake ablaze with candles of its own be brought in.

When the wish has been made and the candles blown out, the Circle might be struck and the Spirits of the Four Directions thanked and dismissed, and a traditional birthday party celebrated.

If the rite is for a woman, the candles should be three, one white, one red, and one black. As they are lit words like the following might be said;

> *Lighting the white candle*
> *This taper of white do I light,*
> *A symbol of the Waxing Moon.*
> *May it be a reminder*
> *Of the radiant days of youth*
> *And may its flame remind us*
> *Of the Goddess ever renewed.*

A man celebrates Midlife.

Lighting the black candle:

This taper of black do I light
A symbol of the waning Moon.
May it be a reminder
Of the mysteries that lie ahead
And may its flame be a symbol
Of the light brought forth from darkness.

Then lighting the red candle:

This candle of red do I light
Symbol of the Moon at full.
Red is the color of life
The flame is the fire of life
May this taper represent
The fullness of your life
And the time which is now!

A crown of laurel might be replaced by one of Artemesia for a woman and the rest of the rite could be the same, as given above.

If the rite is being performed by a solitary, the parts of the priest, priestess, and subject will all be performed by the individual but other than that no changes are really necessary. Of course, it's a bit difficult to give yourself a surprise party, but a few close friends of like mind might be invited following the rite, so that the event will truly be a celebration.

In the long warm days that lie ahead we will gradually leave our youth behind us to cheerfully watch the youth and growth of a new generation. In the light and warmth of the Midsummer of our lives we will play and work with new-found power and success. We will savor the sunny days and hay-scented nights of our lives and bask on the beaches of our summer vacations.

As the light of the Midsummer Sun begins to wane, the days grow warmer still. We will feast on the fruits of our labors and reap the rewards of hard work. The warm, humid days buzz with the songs of cicadas, while high overhead a hawk circles, and silently the grain grows ripe and grapes darken on the vine.

Chapter Six
Priestess & Priesthood

Priestess and Priesthood

The dry, breezy days of June stretch into the hot, humid days of late summer, endlessly lush and green. In the afternoons, cows gather under trees to chew quietly in the shade, while grazing sheep grow fat. In the fields the corn grows tall and ripe, and golden acres of wheat wave when the Lady is in the grain. The weather vane squeals rustily, turning in its socket to point at storm clouds on the horizon. As we prepare to celebrate the Lammas feast, amid the rolls of distant thunder the reaper whets his blade.

When the sacred grain has been gathered, when it has been threshed by the flail, and winnowed to separate the wheat from the chaff, when it has been ground to a fine flour between the stones of a mill, then mixed with water and perhaps other ingredients, and baked in an oven, then the sacred loaf will be broken and shared at the Lammas feast. So sacred is this ancient process and the grain which it involves, that it was once presided over by priestesses. As time passed and the meaning of the sacred loaf was lost, the sacrifice of the grain was still honored as a ritual act and the reaper of the last standing grain was honored for a year.

Today, there are those of us who hear the ancient voices and recall the promise made at Eleusis, who recognize the Lady in the grain and hope to see the ancient rites, with their reverence for all life, restored. Those people are today's Pagans, and those among us who preside over the ancient rites are our priests and priestesses.

Prior to the age of agriculture and its child, civilization, when people still lived in the small groups of hunter/gatherer societies, or were pastoral nomads who drove their flocks to greener pastures, those who presided over spiritual matters and magickal rites were the shamans of the tribe.

These earliest of Pagan priests, the shamans, performed a vital task in a culture which understood that all of nature is a manifestation of the divine creative impulse, and therefore everything in Nature has a spirit. When early man, in the eternal quest for food, went from eating the flesh of animals left

Bestowing the Horned Crown.

by other predators to becoming a predator himself, it was necessary that some member of the tribe contact the spirits of the hunted animals in order to maintain the balance and the harmony of the web of life.

It was the shaman who filled this position. It was he who entered the spirit world, through ecstatic dance, chant, drumming, or the use of trance-inducing herbs, in order to learn what acts needed to be performed, not only to prevent the animal spirits' vengeance, but to insure their fertility as well, so that the cycle of birth, death, and rebirth could be repeated and the drama of the hunt be played again.

This was the first religion, begun when the world was young, when the veil between the world of men and that of nature spirits was always thin, and when the affairs of mortals and those of the mighty Gods were more closely intertwined than they sometimes seem to be today.

As the roaming herds of bison, deer, and wild horses became the domesticated herds of cattle and sheep, and the spiritual web that connects all life began to be forgotten, shamanic rites to insure the fertility of the flock continued to be performed.

When agriculture gave birth to civilization and the hunting of animals was no longer necessary, the ancient reverence for the victim of the sacrifice was transferred from the animal slain in the hunt to the grain cut down at the harvest. In one of the first great civilizations on earth, that of ancient Egypt, representations of the pharaoh, living god, and priest/king, hold two symbols which show the ancient and sacred connection between the old ways and the new, the shepherd's crook and the harvester's flail.

In the few remaining hunter/gatherer societies today, it is the men who hunt and the woman who gather. There is no reason to expect that the hunter/gatherer societies of 30,000 years ago were arranged differently. It was men who dealt with the making of weapons, the hunting and butchering of animals for food, and the magickal rites which appeased the spirits of the hunted animals and insured their rebirth and return, so that the cycle might be repeated. No doubt the rites performed for animals were also performed for deceased members of the clan, so that they too would be reborn, into the same tribe, among their own family members, to love again those who were loved before.

But in this same society, life depended not so much on the occasional game brought back by hunters, as on the fruits of the earth, the wild grains, berries, vegetables, and nuts that were daily gathered by women. These women also had the power to bring forth new life so that the tribe might continue, and this power was magickally associated with the cycles of the Moon, as she waxed and waned in the ancient sky, dividing the year into months and months into weeks. So while the shamans of the tribe performed the hunting magick, and the rites of the spirit world and burials, it was in all likelihood a woman, probably a midwife, who presided over the rites of childbirth, the keeping of time, the harvesting of the fruits of the earth, and eventually the planting of crops. While these ancient priests and priestesses both worked within their own areas of expertise, they most certainly must have worked together, each contributing to the well-being of the community; he working with the magick of the Spirit Father and the Horned God, she with the magick of the Earth Mother and the Moon Goddess.

As civilization grew and life became more complicated, the simple Mother Goddess and Father God were divided and subdivided into deities that presided over every minute aspect of life, but in the end, all gods are one God, all goddesses one Goddess. To the ancient Sumerians they were known as Ishtar and Tamuz, to the Egyptians, Isis and Osiris, to the Phrygians, Cybele and Attis, and to the Greeks, Gaia and Uranus. As cultures evolved, new ideas replaced old ones, as Cronos replaced his father Uranus, and as cultures declined and gave birth to other cultures which, in turn grew and declined, the Old Gods gave birth to new ones as Rhea and Cronos gave birth to Zeus and Demeter.

Zeus, father of the Gods, did indeed father quite a pantheon, and among these gods is Dionysus, one of the most recent of the Greek Gods; the peak of his worship dating to about the eighth century before the current era. Dionysus, who changed a ship's mast into grapevines and sea water into wine, is the God of the Vine, of wine and of joy, and his temples were the theaters of ancient Greece. In his mythology is the reminder of his ancient origins and his oneness with the old shamanic gods of precivilization. According to his myth, the Meanads which followed and served him on the night of his festival, Lupercalia (Feb. 15), would chase after a fawn or goat in a wild hunt, tear the living animal to pieces, and feed on its raw flesh. In memory of this at his festival, the priests of Dionysus, the goatskin-clad Luperci, would strike barren women with goatskin thongs in a fertility rite that no doubt had its origins in the far distant past.

Like Ishtar, and other goddesses and gods who came before and after him, Dionysus descended into the underworld, the realm of the dead, and returned, defying and defeating death; and in so doing, like the ancient horned one honored by the shamans, he became a god of resurrection and of rebirth. While the consort of Dionysus is Ariadne (Arrianrod, Aradia) he is frequently associated with Demeter the Greek Goddess of the Grain. When her daughter Persephone was taken by Hades to live with him in the underworld because he loved her, she was so saddened that she caused the earth to become barren until her daughter was returned to her. In the village of Eleusis, where the Mother Goddess Demeter and her daughter Persephone were reunited, the great Goddess gave to the world the sacred knowledge of the planting of grain, the wisdom with which to bring about civilization, and to those initiated into her mysteries, she gave the joy of life that comes with the certain knowledge that death is not an end.

What occurred when one was initiated into the Eleusian mysteries is not known, because no initiate ever revealed that secret which he was sworn to keep. There are only clues from which practitioners of true magick may deduce some of the rituals that might have taken place.

But regardless of the rites that may have taken place, regardless of the fact that Demeter and her daughter Persephone were known as the two who are one, and that Dionysus had Ariadne for his consort, even the ancient Greeks considered Demeter and Dionysus as something of a pair. This association between the Goddess of the Grain and the God of the Vine tells us of the sacred relationship between bread and wine. The fact that the priests of Dionysus, the Luperci, wore the skins of goats as the symbol of their priesthood, and that the mythical followers of the God of the Vine, the Meanads, went into the primal wilderness to hunt the wild goats and fawns, suggests that the cult of Dionysus was actually the civilized echo of a religious tradition far more ancient, and that the sacred wine was a substitute for sacrificial blood and its association with the shamanic world of the spirit. Such transferences can probably be found in the mythologies of other traditions; for example, the Mead of Inspiration sought (and found) by Odin.

Arthurian scholars tell us that the original French term "Graal," first used in the Legends of Arthur in the eleventh century, comes from the Latin word *gradalis,* meaning a bowl, or a cauldron that cannot be emptied. The word "sangreal," then, would mean "holy grail." In *Witchcraft: A Tradition Renewed,* Valiente and Jones tell us that sangreal means not holy grail, but sang (blood) and real (royal) or royal blood, and refers to the blood of the sacrificed priest/king. This is a very enlightening insight which does not eliminate the former interpretation, but enhances it!

The profound significance of the cup of wine and the loaf of bread was not lost on the founders of the new religion. One of the most sacred parts of Christian ritual, certainly of the Catholic mass, is the consecration of the host (blessing of the bread) and Communion. This rite is performed in remembrance of the first (Christian) communion performed at the Last Supper, when the priest/king Jesus took up the bread and said "This is my body," and taking up the cup of wine said, "This is my blood," and in doing so, eliminated the Goddess of the Grain.

But the Goddess of the Grain, the Ancient Mother, cannot be eliminated. She continues to be. She is a part of all life. Now that Pagans are free to practice the Old Religion as our ancestors did, the Ancient Goddess and Her consort/son are revered once again. Their symbols are everywhere in our rites; the cup and the athame, the cakes and wine, the corn dolly, and the horned crown, and whosoever performs rites in their honor are their priestesses and priests.

One of the more important elements of most traditional Pagan and Wiccan sabbat rites today is the Blessing of the Cakes and Wine. When this is done in a coven gathering it is performed by a priestess and/or a priest, and when it is done by a solitary practitioner, that individual is a priest or priestess.

Presiding over the sacrifice of the sabbat was not the only duty of the priestess or the priest in ancient times. The real purpose, in fact, was to insure the well-being of the community, in whatever way was necessary. Conducting the proper sabbat rites was one way. Another was the ability to control the weather. If there was too much rain, or not enough, and the crops failed, it was the priest or priestess who was to blame. The methods of con-

Ariadne—the Sleeping Goddess.

trolling the weather were many. One way to cause rain, from the Cherokee, is a perfect example of homeopathic magick. When rain was needed, the shaman and other members of the tribe danced in the dry fields, chanting invocations, and sprinkling the parched earth with a branch dipped in a bowl of water.

A Scottish method for bringing rain was to dip a length of cloth in a bowl of water, then, strike it three times upon a stone while chanting:

> *I knok this rag upon this stane,*
> *To raise the wind in our Lords name:*
> *It shall not lie till I please again!*

(Since we do not have the charm for ending the storm, it would not be advisable to use this particular charm to raise one.)

Among the Pennsylvania German folk, there is a Hex sign for rain making which includes a teardrop design. This teardrop symbol is usually combined with a Sun symbol to insure a balance of rain and sunshine, but when rain is desperately needed, a Hex sign of just rain symbols is painted and hung. This rain Hex is usually made, sold, or given with the strict warning that it be taken in as soon as the rain begins, but there is a local legend of a Hexenmeister who painted and hung such a Hex sign to help alleviate the drought of the summer of 1955. The rains came, but the Hexenmeister failed to take down the Hex sign. The result was one of the most devastating floods ever to hit the Delaware valley.

Another method of controlling the weather was to tie the wind with knots. This charm was usually made by Weather Witches for sailors. If the sailors' ship was becalmed, he would untie the first knot for a gentle breeze. To untie the second knot would bring a strong wind, but to untie the third knot would be to unleash a tempest.

A similar charm was given to Ulysses by Poseidon. The Sea God gave to the hero all of the foul winds tied up in a leather pouch, so that Ulysses would have clear sailing, but one night his crew, curious and somewhat rebellious, opened the pouch, releasing the tempest and sending the ship and all aboard her on one of the greatest adventures ever told.

Where there is no wind to tie up, there are Witches who have the ability to "whistle up the wind." By imitating the sounds and motions of the storm bringing wind, these women could control the weather. Needless to say, what was once the activity of priestesses and priests later became the secret knowledge of wise women, cunning men, and those who were to be persecuted as Witches. This is probably what lies behind the country folk saying:

> *Crowing hens*
> *And whistling women*
> *Will come to a no-good end.*

Today, weather control (or at least influence), is still a part of a Witch's basic training in many traditions. One of the simplest exercises a student is given is to sit outdoors, with a good view of the sky. Enter a meditative state, and then select a cloud, a small one at first. The point of the exercise is to make the cloud move closer or further away, regardless of wind direction, or to make it dissipate.

Now here I have to tell a personal story, because it is both relevant and amusing. Many years ago, when Dan first planted our vineyard of 125 vines, a very close friend of ours planted a very serious vineyard of 700 vines. A few days later he had to go away on an extended business trip and asked us to look after his vines for him, which we were happy to do. But a few dry days became weeks of drought, and while Dan was able to water our vines by hand, our friend's vines were beginning to show signs of suffering, and there was no way we could water the entire vineyard by hand. Finally we decided to conjure up some rain. Each afternoon we would work together visualizing a great storm cloud coming up over the hill and giving both vineyards the drenching they desperately needed. For three days we focused our energies on bringing rain, and then, on the morning of the fourth day, there was a knock at our door. It was a very psychic friend who lived a mile up the road. "What's wrong?" he asked, looking very worried, "For three nights I've had this dream. I keep seeing a big dark cloud over your house!" I'll never forget the puzzled look on his face when we both burst out laughing. When we regained our composure we explained, confirming his dream. Later that day we had a cloudburst, not exactly the flood of 1955, but enough to save the vineyards and to alter the weather pattern, ending the drought.

When it was discovered that water could be found underground in almost limitless supplies, and irrigation lessened dependency on weather, a new facet to the priests' or Witches' abilities was added—the ability to find underground water sources by the magickal process known as divining, or dowsing. One of the earliest tools used to perform this act is the "divining rod." Today water dowsing is done with such devices as the pendulum or a pair of L rods, but the original divining rod was a simple forked stick. Simple maybe, but powerfully symbolic. The forked stick or branch usually has two "handles" and a "pointer." I once saw a New England Witches' divining rod from the early 1700s, and the "pointer" was almost exactly the same length as the two handles. The result was an object of three equal arms, each separated by about the same angle, a perfect symbol of the Three-Formed Goddess. At the same time, if this divining rod is stood upright it is a symbolic representation of the Horned God, and divining rods are traditionally made of magickal hazelwood.

Another function of the priestess and priest was to foretell the future for the welfare of the community, to predict attacks by enemies, the failure of crops, or the shortage of game, and also to divine what might be done about it. The methods were many, but probably all of them originated from the art of reading omens. When our race understood its relationship with Nature there must have been a keen awareness of it, and anything out of the ordinary was immediately noted. Sometimes these extraordinary occurrences indicated natural events such as the coming of a storm, or a severe winter, but other times such omens might have indicated other kinds of events. It was the tribal shaman, or wise woman, then, who, with shamanic vision was able to recognize the true meaning of the omen and advise the members of the community. Frequently, it was the flight patterns of birds that were read as omens. It was birds that brought the springtime when they flew north, and it was birds that left the land to the barrenness of winter when they flew south again. Birds, especially wading birds like herons and cranes, were believed to be messengers of the gods, and from the patterns they formed by their migratory flights or the foot prints they left on the banks of the primordial swamp, many a sacred alphabet originated.

Those who could interpret the sacred script or read the runic messages were the tribal priests and priestesses, but there were other methods too, to foretell the future. Among these was scrying. That is, to gaze into some object in which images of the future would appear. These objects included the crystal ball, the polished blade, the Witches' mirror (described in *Ancient Ways*), or the cauldron filled with water. Gazing into the latter was sometimes facilitated by dropping a silver coin into the velvety black depths of the water, to act as a focal point. But the coin of silver, metal of the Moon, is more than a focal point. It actually replicates a reflection of the Moon herself. In ancient times, gazing at the Moon was believed to bring about an altered state of consciousness in which one could see into the Land of Faerie, and it probably still does. Scrying was one of the practices banned by the Synod of Exeter in 1287, as being "dishonorable to God."

All of the above methods involve either intervention from the world of Nature Spirits, messengers of the gods, who arrange what appears to be the random selection of anything from runes to yarrow sticks, or actually entering the realm of the spirits of Nature and the deceased through scrying, with or without the aid of ecstatic dance or psychoactive herbs. There were also methods of communicating with the spirits of the deceased, and of the ancestors directly, either through a direct contact, such as mediumship, or what is today called channeling, or through the use of some device through which the spirit might give messages. These devices, such as the Ouija board, the pendulum board, or the wine glass, are probably much more popular today than their prototypes might have been in ancient times. Among so-called "more primitive" people, direct spirit contact, such as that demonstrated by practitioners of Voodoo or the shamanistic Buddhists of Bali and Java, is still fairly common. Whatever the method employed, necromancy, contacting the spirits of the deceased, or of Nature, for the purpose of learning the future, was not done for any purpose except the welfare of the community. When the community was threatened by those who would impose foreign rule and a foreign religion, naturally all of these methods were employed for the welfare of the Pagan community and used against its enemies. The fact that these methods were condemned, under penalty of death in some cases, seems to be testimony to their effectiveness.

Today, most covens or groups have among their members a variety of talents to draw upon. There are usually an astrologer, a Tarot reader, one who is attuned to spirits of the deceased, another to Nature Spirits, a healer, or one who has shamanic vision. There is almost always someone with the necessary talent to deal with any situation.

One more function of priest and priestess, since ancient times and into recent times, is the reenactment of the Sacred Marriage. From the rites performed in the sacred marriage chamber atop the ziggurat of Babylon, to the Mediterranean ritual known as Benevento, and the "Great Rite"' of Western Europe, sacred sexual union has been a part of Pagan religious ritual since before recorded history. No other aspect of Pagan practice has caused more controversy, nor precipitated more persecution. Nor has any other aspect of the Old Religion attracted so many, shall we say, less-than-spiritual seekers to the Craft.

The purpose of ritual sex is two-fold, and of two kinds. The first, and more sacred, rite is properly performed between a priestess and a priest after the Goddess has been drawn down upon her and the God has been drawn down upon him. Their sexual union represents, in powerful symbolic terms, the union of all polarities, of all the complements of which Nature is made, and of the creative impulse that created Nature. This one simple act, performed in a sacred context by two who have been touched by the Lord and Lady, is one of the most powerful rites that can be experienced.

The second kind of ritual sex is sexual union among the members of the coven, the village, or the community in general, such as the rites performed in cornfields by our European ancestors at planting time, or those performed by their ancestors who wore the skins and masks of animals, and who danced and frolicked and mated in imitation of the eternal cycle of birth, death, and rebirth. The purpose of this kind of sexual ritual is to generate and release a very powerful kind of magickal energy that can be used by nature to insure a plentiful harvest and increase herds and flocks. This is the kind of magick referred to in the rune recited by village youth in the May Day chant:

Don't tell the priest about our rites
For he would call it sin,
But we have been in the wood all nite
A'conjurin' Summer in!

The Great Rite, whether performed privately or within full view of a coven, whether performed actually, or symbolically as with the cup and athame, is one of the most magickal parts of the Craft, and to discuss it more explicitly is to profane it. It is the one aspect that has excited the enemies of our ancient faith to condemn us legally and to persecute us to near extinction for having "intercourse with the devil." (For anyone who has come this far in the Craft but doesn't know how to have sex, there are plenty of books in the appropriate sections of bookshops, but to discuss sex explicitly in a book about the Old Religion is unnecessary and puts us all at risk.)

In earlier times, no doubt, a person who showed signs of being especially gifted in the areas of clairvoyance, prophecy, or the healing arts was probably selected to be the priest or priestess of the village. In even more ancient, shamanic times, as in shamanic cultures today, there are some specific signs which indicate that a person has shamanic abilities. Primary among these is a birthmark. The pivot point of many a "Sword and Sorcerer" film, this birthmark is not necessarily a skin discoloration in a particular design; there are other marks as well, such as an extra toe or finger. Since shamanism within a tribe is sometimes hereditary, one family producing the shamans generation after generation, this might explain the symbolism of an hereditary birthmark or deformity. There are also physical episodes such as spells of unconsciousness or epileptic seizure which indicate shamanic abilities in some cultures. Other traditions look for signs of the transmigration of the shaman's spirit, a child born at the moment of the old shaman's death, followed, perhaps, by signs of recognition or ability on the part of the child.

And then there are external indications of shamanism, such as being struck by lightning. This is such an important sign of shamanism that lightning symbols are often painted or embroidered onto the shaman's ritual clothing. Lightning is a manifestation of electromagnetic energy, the same kind of energy that is generated when a woman brushes her long hair while gazing in a mirror, symbolic of the Goddess. It is also the same kind of energy that is generated when a quartz crystal is wound with copper wire, and possibly for this reason, the shaman's robe is also often decorated with quartz crystals. Whatever the link between electromagnetic and psychic awareness is, electromagnetism does enhance psychic ability, or supernatural (meaning above and beyond the mundane) awareness, and this is the function of the shaman.

As the shaman of the Russian steppe wears a robe that might be embroidered with symbols of lightning, festooned with ribbons, and hung with quartz crystals, so the shaman or medicine man of the Plains Indians of North America wears the skin and horns of the buffalo, the priests of the Hopi clans wear specific headdresses, body paint, and clothing, the Buddhist monks of Tibet wear robes dyed in rare saffron, and the priests of ancient Egypt wore the skins of leopards and shaved their heads. Even the priests and ministers of modern Christianity wear the black clothing and white collar of their calling or profession.

While today's Pagans and Wiccans are pretty much out of the closet, the priestesses and priests of the Old Religion do not consider themselves "authority figures," who need to wear special clothing in public to set themselves apart from, and above, all others. Still, there is a time and a place when it might be appropriate for priestess and priest to wear special attire relative to their priesthood.

While some traditions celebrate their sabbats and rites skyclad, in recognition of the fact that magickal energy radiates from every part of the human body, still others wear ritual robes that are worn for no other purpose except for magickal rites. Simply donning these robes helps to alter the mental state in preparation for the magickal rites that are about to begin. Traditionally, even those who wear ritual clothing are skyclad underneath, and barefoot. While this clothing might block some of the magickal energy, the majority of it radiates from the hands and from about the head, and that much energy is quite enough.

There are some who have theorized that the human race originally adapted to the climate perfectly without need for protective clothing, and that clothing evolved for magickal and religious reasons, not practical ones. It is also believed that the poet Sapho, who conducted a school for priestesses on the island of Lesbos in the Fifth century B.C.E., specifically taught her students the magickal traditions of clothing sacred statues with ritual clothing and ornaments.

This ancient magickal impulse is still carried out among women of the Catholic church who dress figures of the Infant of Prague in elaborate garments of silk brocade, embroidered with threads of silver and gold. It is also practiced in Thailand where the Jade Buddha is adorned with various gold crowns and garments at the beginning of the cool, hot, and rainy seasons. And it is still carried out by Pagans and Wiccans in a very symbolic way when we wrap an acorn-tipped wand with green ribbon at Imbolc, entwine a flower-crowned Maypole at Beltane, or adorn a fir tree with symbols of fruit at Yule.

If it is appropriate, in the deepest, most magickal parts of our mind, to adorn these symbols of our God and Goddess, then it must surely be appropriate that the living representatives of the Lord and the Lady, our priests and priestesses, be just as appropriately dressed, according to the season.

Ritual robes (unless the tradition is skyclad) can be used to help to draw and direct particular aspects of magickal energy. While the robe of the initiate need only be white or black, the robes of the priestess and priest who organize and direct the energy gathered and generated by the coven might be of colors specifically chosen for compatibility with the seasonal sabbat about to be celebrated.

Ritual robes are simple and inexpensive to make (and enough has been written about how to make them that there is no need to go into that here). An enterprising priest or priestess might consider making robes for the specific sabbats until there is a wardrobe of robes for the entire year wheel.

Beginning with Yule, the priestess might don a ceremonial robe of red, the color of the Goddess in her aspect as the Mother of the Divine Child. Since the only requirement for a ritual robe is that it be of a natural fiber, the robes of Yuletide might be of wool for warmth at this coldest time of year. For the priest who represents the Divine Child at Yule, a robe of white would be appropriate. It might be ornamented with a Sun wheel of gold, or with sprigs of holly and of oak. These might be embroidered, or they might be real leaves and sprigs stitched to the robe for the sabbat nite.

For Imbolc, the priestess might want to wear a robe of silver, gray, or white, representing the Goddess as she does this sabbat in Her aspect as the Maiden. This might be ornamented with the silver crescents of the New Moon. For the priest at Imbolc, a robe of deepest indigo dotted perhaps with tiny gold stars, representing as he does the Sky Father or the Spirit about to descend into matter.

For the Vernal Equinox, or Eostre, the priestess might select a robe of soft yellow-green, the green of new spring buds, if she is to represent the Green Goddess of Spring, or she might choose a robe of pink, the pink flush of the Eastern sky at sunrise, if she will represent the Goddess Eostre. For the priest a robe of leafy green will do, as he will represent the God of Nature and its resurrection.

At Beltane, the robe for the priestess is traditionally of purest white, as she will represent the Maiden at the Divine Marriage, and for the priest, the leafy green robe of the Lord of the Greenwood.

Gold is the color that is most appropriate for the robe of the priest at Midsummer, since he will represent the Sun God at the height of his power. The robe of the priestess might be the flame red of the Mother Goddess, touched by the Midsummer Sabbat fire.

At Lammas, the robes of both priestess and priest might be of red. The priestess representing the Corn Mother might have her red robe of Motherhood adorned with ears of golden wheat, while the priest wearing the red robe of the sacrificed god might also have ears of wheat as ornament, representing as he does the God of the Grain as well. Or, both priestess and priest might wear robes as gold as grain, since they represent the Corn Mother and her son, the Grain God.

At the Autumnal Equinox, the priestess might don the black robe of the Crone, since, in some traditions it is at this sabbat that the Crone is welcomed. Also at this sabbat the priest might choose a robe of mystical purple if he is to represent the sacrificed God of the Vine.

For the Samhain Sabbat, of course, both priestess and priest would wear the black robes of this, the darkest season, as on this night the priestess represents the Crone, keeper of the Dark Mysteries, while the priest is the representative of the Horned God of Death and that which comes after.

Wearing robes of various colors symbolic of the season helps to intensify the seasonal magick and can act as a focus for an entire group.

Aside from the traditional ceremonial robes which might be worn during rituals, there is magickal clothing that can be worn in everyday situations. While it is true that many of us are accused of dressing strangely as it is, with "too much" jewelry, or make-up, long flowing black garments or tattoos, most of us know why we tend to do this. It is simply because the crystals and gemstones, colors and designs with which we choose to adorn our clothing and our bodies are sources of magickal energy, and it is a kind of energy that we can draw on secretly. While others might find our attire interesting, exotic, or amusing, only we can simply close our eyes, even in a crowded or public place and let the energy flow.

Still, the majority of us do not usually go about in pointed hats, black capes, and pentagrams as large as chest protectors, and there are even some among us who for one reason or another seem to wear clothing out of the broom closet rather than a clothes closet, but even the most conservative dresser among us can, with a little thought and less talent, give ordinary street clothing a magickal touch. As an example, it is not the way of our tradition, a blend of Eastern European and Mediterranean, to wear the pentagram as symbol, but rather the more ancient Sun wheel. Recently, when a friend noticed the bronze Sun wheel I usually wear, she commented, "You could sit face to face with Billy Graham and he wouldn't notice that!"

Symbolic clothing begins with color, and the color of the clothing we wear dictates the kind of energy we will be enfolding ourselves in for the day. Black, of course, is every Witch's favorite. It is the color of mystery and of magick and it has the ability to absorb into itself and its wearer the power of light and of every other color. It is the color of the Crone and of Hecate.

Indigo is also a color of magick and of mystery. It is a color of the higher spirit realms, and acts as a channel between the spirit world and the one who wears indigo.

Blue is also a color of spirit. It is the color of the upperworld, of the Sky Father, and of the highest levels of consciousness, The one who wears pale to medium blue is clothed in the peace and serenity of spiritual consciousness, while the one who wears the intense electric blue of Uranus is charged with the mental energy of that planet, an energy that can cause static or the random spark of a live wire if not controlled wisely.

The shades of blue-green, from palest aquamarine through turquoise to the deepest bluish-green, are the watery colors of Neptune's realm. They are the colors of intuition and ecstacy, and the deeper shades are probably the color referred to by the Gaelic word *Glas*, which is used to name or describe various sacred places and sacred trees. The one who wears these shades is surrounded by the magick of mediumship and meditation.

Green is the color of Nature and of Nature Spirits. It is the color of growing things and of the vegetation upon which all life depends. At a time when a bountiful harvest meant a family's wealth, the color also came to mean fortune or financial gain. It might then be mere coincidence, or intentional magick that our paper currency is printed with green ink. But most importantly, from the yellow-green buds of daffodils to the deep dark greens of the tropical rain forest, green is the color of the spirits of Nature. At a time when there was a balance between the followers of the Old Religion and those of the new, when Pagan peasants rose up against their oppressive landlords in situations romanticized in such tales as those of Robin Hood, a shade of green known as Lincoln green, made of the woad of the Druids and lime, was worn by the peasants as a symbol of their unity with one another and with the old Gods of Nature and the Faerie-folk.

Purple is a mystical and a psychic color, combining as it does the blue or indigo of the spirit world with the physical vitality of red. Deep purple, like indigo, links its wearer with the higher spiritual planes, while pale violet enfolds us with spiritual purity. Bright purple gives us intense psychic energy that can result in nothing more than a "leaky head" if not used wisely.

Purple grades through magenta into red which is the color of physical vitality and energy. It is the color of life-giving blood. A clear, ruby red is the perfect color to wear when you didn't get enough sleep the night before. It is also the color to wear to attract attention, but it is not the color to wear when dieting because its magick stimulates the appetite for food as well as for sex. The one who wears red, especially a deep, rusty red, can cause others to see red in ways not anticipated, because this is the color of Mars, the God of War. The one who wears red adds physical energy and the magick of the Mother Goddess to all other kinds of magick.

As red pales into pink, it clothes us in the magick of romantic love, and deep or "hot" pink gives energy to the kind of playful magick that can end in lovemaking.

To wear a deep red like burgundy, which combines the physical vitality of red with the mystical qualities of deep blue or indigo, can elevate our consciousness like a sip of consecrated wine.

Yellow is the cheerful, life-giving color of the Sun. It gives the wearer the magick of the sacred fire, both warmth and light, and it attracts wealth, both the spiritual and the physical. It is also the color of wisdom and knowledge.

Yellow blends with red to create orange, the color of warmth and friendship. The one who wears shades of orange radiates the magick that can attract warm friendships, and relationships based on understanding.

The warm colors, yellow, orange, and red, blend and deepen into shades of brown, the colors of the earth. In fact, many of them are called earth colors, because the pigments used to make them actually come from the earth, pigments like ochre, sienna, and umber. These pigments were used in magickal rites as long ago as Paleolithic times, usually in association with the dead. Today such colors still have the power to link us magickally with earth spirits and with the ancestors. These are the colors to wear when grounding or centering is needed, and the stability of the earth. To cloth ourselves in shades of brown is to enfold ourselves in the protective arms of the Earth Mother.

White is the color of the Moon. It radiates energy, just as black absorbs it. White represents the pure, white light of Spirit, which is made up of the three primary rays of color, red, yellow, and blue. These three colors represent the three states of God-hood; being, consciousness, and bliss. It is from these three primary color rays that all other color rays proceed. The one who wears white wears the magick of all other colors combined.

Gray is a combination of black and white. It has the power to absorb energy as black does, and the power to radiate it like white, although the power of each is diminished by the other. The one who wears gray wears the power to balance and neutralize energy. Gray is the color representative of silver, the metal of the Moon, just as yellow is the color of gold, the metal of the Sun. To wear gray is to wear the magick of moonlight.

The patterns of a textile, as well as its color, also contain magick.

Plaids, composed as they are of vertical and horizontal lines which intersect at regular intervals, have the magickal effect of balancing opposites. A plaid of blues and browns unites the powers of earth and sky. A plaid of red and green combines the power of the animal and the vegetable kingdom, and one of black and white balances the polarities of dark and light, night and day, life and death, male and female.

While vertical stripes might make us look taller and thinner, horizontal stripes are actually encircling bands and can act like the magick Circle, containing the power within us, until we are ready to direct it or use it for our own purpose. If you come home from the office feeling "drained," try wearing something with encircling bands, or even a border design around the hem. Put on the garment and slowly circle sunwise, chanting something like this:

North and East, South and West
Round and round the circles blessed.

This chant can silently be repeated while a ring of blue-white light is being visualized, first around the hem of your skirt, then a protective sphere around you whenever you feel your energy is being tapped by another, or that you are being used.

Unfortunately, this works only for a skirt, and is of little use to anyone wearing a business suit.

The colors and patterns of clothing textiles are almost infinite in their variations, and the majority of them can be used for magickal purposes, but an even more powerful magick can be given to articles of clothing by personalizing them with artistic touches of our own. There are many methods and materials with which this can be done. Probably the first thing that comes to mind as a method of ornamenting clothing is embroidery. There are the stitches themselves that may have magickal power, the cross-stitch which is a solar cross, and the chain stitch which is a series of connecting circles, and then there are the threads.

There is the silky linen embroidery floss in all of the colors of a magickal rainbow. There is the magick of the spirally spun crewel yarn dyed in the mellow colors of ages past, and there is the enchanted handspun yarn dyed with the magick of nature's colors. There are also the metallic threads that flash the gold of the Sun and the silver of the Moon, the electric blue of Aquarius, and the copper of the Goddess of Love.

And then there are the designs to choose from. While pentagrams and crescent Moons might be a bit too obvious for many occasions, or for the workplace, there are more subtle designs. There are the spirals and the mazes of the Mediterranean, the intricate knots of the Celtic world, or the bands of triangular designs of Eastern Europe done in a special stitch like the embroidery of the Greek Islands.

The people of India added a new magickal material to embroidery when they invented mirror embroidery. Tiny mirrors stitched into floral or geometric designs add the magick of "return to sender" in the presence of negativity, and a garment embellished with mirror embroidery can be as protective as a suit of armor in a hostile environment.

But embroidery is not the only method of magickally embellishing clothing. One of the most versatile mediums for decorating fabrics is textile paint. These paints come in little kits containing the three primary colors, red, yellow, and blue, plus black and white. With these five pigments the experienced painter can produce any color, but even the inexperienced can achieve some pretty amazing results, and the traditional artwork from which magickal designs can be adapted are limitless. Symbols can be borrowed from pre-Columbian or Pueblo pottery by those on a Native American path, or from Greek vases or the ruins at Minos for those whose tradition is Mediterranean. We can wrap ourselves in the serenity and splendor of an Egyptian tomb painting done on white linen. We can wear the power of our totem animal translated from a painting on the wall of a sacred cave, or the totem animal might be rendered from the highly stylized designs of the Book of Kells, designs which are not, incidentally, purely Celtic, but a blend of Celtic and Anglo-Saxon.

The reason for wearing magickally embellished street clothing is two-fold. For one thing, the magick in the colors and symbols we wear, like the power stored in our crystals and amulets, is there to be drawn upon when-ever we need it. It is the special power of secrecy, hidden where it is most eas-ily seen. But it is also there for those who have the eyes to see, so that we may be recognized by those of a like mind, or so that we may recognize them.

Since the first Paleolithic shaman donned the antlered or horned skin of a hunted animal, and reenacted the mating, the chase, the kill, and the rebirth of that animal, two things were established: that sacred ritual was

An example of Greek Island Embroidery.

the symbolic acting out of the wheels of life, and that the headdress played an important part in establishing the relationship between the shaman or priest and the spiritual world.

As the shamans became priests, and the priests became priest/kings, the headdresses became crowns, and when religion and politics separated (if, indeed, they ever did), the crown lost its spiritual associations but was retained as a symbol of power. The kingly crowns that we know today are usually set with precious jewels, crystal forms of various minerals, which were once, no doubt, treasured for their magickal and occult properties, but which today are appreciated mostly for their monetary value, just as the jewel-headed scepter, symbol of royal rulership, was once probably the crystal-tipped magick wand of a Faerie. Today these objects are symbols of wealth and power to most, but for those who follow the hidden path, the jeweled crown and the crystal-tipped wand are spiritual tools that can link us with the creative forces of the universe. They are not the symbols of powerful persons who rule in the mundane world, but of priests and priestesses who can direct and manipulate magickal energy.

When the priests and priestesses of ancient Babylon wished to contact their God and Goddess, they wore the sacred headdress. When the priest of a Hopi clan wished to contact a certain Kachina, he wore the appropriate headdress. When our ancestors went about wearing the heads and skins of animals and imitating their movements, they were condemned by the church and punished.

Today many of us have returned to the Old Ways, and for us it is traditional that our priests and priestesses wear the crowns symbolic of our Lord and Lady, the horned crown of the Lord of Death and Resurrection, God of the Hunted and of that which is sacrificed, so that we may live, and the Crescent Moon Crown of our threefold Goddess; Maiden, Mother, and Crone.

As has already been mentioned in Chapter Three, the necklace is a basic part of every Pagan's wardrobe, male or female, but for a priestess or a priest it is even more important, representing as it does both the magick Circle and the wheel of the year. The most traditional type is the torque, which has an opening in the front and a hinge in the back, and which forms a perfect circle when closed. This is the necklace, Brisingamen, forged for the Goddess herself, in Germanic myth, and stolen by Loki. Again, this is not the only type of necklace that is appropriate for a priest or priestess. The Goddess Ishtar wore a necklace which she relinquished upon her descent into the underworld, and which was returned to her upon her return. The necklace is not described in detail in the ancient tablets, but her girdle, a chain or article of jewelry worn about the hips like a belt (or cord) is described as a girdle of birthstones. For this reason, Witches in some traditions wear a necklace of 13 stones of the Lunar months (rather than the 12 birthstones of the solar

Above, left: vest pockets are decorated with sheet metal goats, surrounded by brass studs. Above, right: naturally dyed handspun yarns render a design borrowed from a Ukrainian Eostre egg on a skirt. Below: horses from an ancient cave painting canter across a hand-painted skirt.

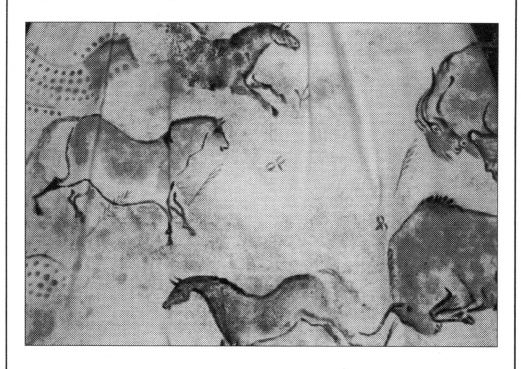

months). In certain African traditions, shamans wore a necklace of skulls made from the fingers and other bones of the shamans who preceded them, in the belief that these bones contained the power of the old shamans. Such necklaces were probably handed down and added to over the years. I have seen two such necklaces. The first was a string of small, crudely carved human skulls and bone penises. The second was a spectacular work of art: a choker of anatomically perfect skulls, graduated in size, the largest in the center being about three inches high, and between the carved bone skulls were perfect graduated spheres of clear gold and amber. Unfortunately, the necklace was being offered at a time when we couldn't afford to ask the price. Many years later we happened to find ourselves in the same antique shop, and I asked about the necklace and whatever happened to it. "Oh, one of our regular customers bought it. She's a Witch. A White Witch."

While all of the above-mentioned styles and materials for necklaces are, or have been, traditional, Witches today tend to wear whatever charms or amulets feel right. One style that is popular right now is a 24-inch chain, about one-quarter inch wide, to which a number of charms, amulets, pentagrams and crystals can be attached.

When the necklace has been found or obtained, it should be cleansed in salted water and consecrated in the four elements and in the sacred names.

This necklace, or amulet, symbol of a new priest or priestesshood, should be one entirely different from the one chosen at initiation.

Of all the articles symbolizing priestesshood, perhaps the garter is the most typical. Garters were worn in earlier times, just below the knee, to hold up hand-knit stockings. Long before the invention of elastic, these garters were usually of leather and the buckles that held them closed were sometimes jeweled. Sometimes the garter was just a length of ribbon tied in a bow. The garter was worn beneath the long skirt of a woman, hidden from view, but could easily be revealed with a swift gesture of the hand when necessary.

The traditional garter of a Witch is red, the color of the Goddess in her aspect as Mother, and for the priestess, it has a single buckle, but for the high priestess, one who has generated a number of covens, the garter traditionally is adorned with one buckle for each new coven. Since the maximum number for the traditional coven is 13, then perhaps the traditional number of daughter covens under one high priestess is also 13, adding up to 169 members all told, a number sacred to the Witches' Goddess, and this is apparently the meaning behind the story of the Royal Order of the Garter related in Chapter Four.

It is easy enough to make a Witches' Garter. All that is needed is a length of leather or ribbon about five-eighths inch in width and long enough to go around the leg, either just above or just below the knee, and a small ornamental buckle. Buckles ideal for the purpose can sometimes be obtained from those who supply accouterments to 17th- and 18th-century reenactors. If the garter is to be of leather, and the leather is untreated, it might be dyed with pomegranate skin, which would give the garter extra magick.

When the garter of red ribbon or of leather has been attached to the buckle and completed, it should be, like the necklace, consecrated in the four elements and in the sacred names, and with words like:

> *Garter, round as the Moon,*
> *Secret is your power.*
> *When you're bound about me,*
> *Will the Lady descend upon me.*
> *And with your magick,*
> *Will She be drawn down.*
> *And with your magick,*
> *Will the power be raised.*

Today there are many traditions, and many systems, and they have differing ideas concerning the passage from initiate to priesthood.

In more ancient times there was only the shaman and the community. There were probably no covens or degree systems, nor any need for them. The shaman was chosen by certain physical signs, mentioned earlier in this chapter, but almost always as well by a particular event, a moment of crisis such as a "near death experience" during which the shaman experienced that ecstatic state which was to be his or her entryway into the spirit world throughout his career.

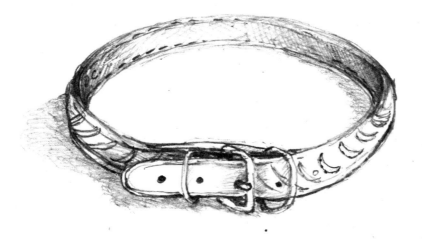

The Garter.

Later, the pre-Christian Pagans of ancient Greece, Rome, Gaul, and the Celtic countries needed no such degree systems. There were temples dedicated to various aspects of divinity where priests conducted sacred rites, and members of the community were free to come and go as they pleased.

Certainly, in classical times, a significant amount of study and training was required to become a priest, just as it was to become a shaman. There were also initiations into certain sects or cults, just as the youth of the shaman's community were initiated into the spiritual secrets of the group when they came of age. But it was not until the new religion gained enough military strength to attempt to convert all of Europe by force, shattering the Pagan communities and driving small groups of faithful practitioners into hiding, that a system of secret initiations and degree became necessary. This probably occurred during that mysterious era of human history known as the "Dark Ages," of which almost nothing is written or known. The Dark Ages, also known as the Middle Ages or Medieval Period, began about 500 C.E., with the fall of the Roman Empire, a time when almost all of the known world was still Pagan. Then the world was plunged into darkness, and when the lights came on again, 900 years later, at the dawning of the Renaissance in 1450, all of the known world was Christian. The church ruled everything.

This was the time of feudal systems, during which society was very clearly divided into ranks and degrees. It was the time of the Crusades, when the knights went off to the so-called "holy land" to reclaim sites sacred to Christianity that had been captured by the followers of Islam, just as sites sacred to our Pagan ancestors were taken over by the church. And it was a time, too, when the still-faithful Pagan who managed to escape the persecution of heretics conducted by the church, beginning in the ninth century, was beginning to incorporate into the Old Religion ideas and concepts, and symbols such as the pentagram, brought back by the Crusaders from the magicians and alchemists of places like Syria, Baghdad, and Persia.

So the secret initiations and the degree systems of modern Witchcraft probably originated in the medieval period, and may have originated as a means of protecting the Pagan community and its spiritual leaders at the time. The idea of a degree system, blended with the rigid ritual of ceremonial magick, seems to be the trademark of the medieval Witch, whose secret initiation into the Old Religion was a necessary precaution in a time of persecution.

Today, there are many traditions and systems. Among the Gardnerian traditions, or those based upon the Gardnerian, the first degree initiation into a coven is also an initiation into the priesthood, and acknowledges that one is qualified to conduct rituals as well as participate in them.

The Gardnerian second degree passage acknowledges an individual's right to conduct the rituals of a parent coven that has spawned daughter covens, and also to coordinate the activities of the daughter covens. The third degree initiation of the Gardnerian tradition acknowledges the right of the individual to practice the Craft on their own.

Other traditions have only two degrees. One of initiation, which acknowledges the right of an individual to participate in the sacred rights of tradition, within the Circle; and one of priesthood, which acknowledges the right of an individual to conduct the group or coven rights.

In either case, the priest or priestess is not considered the "leader" of the group or coven, only the conductor or coordinator of the rites performed by the group.

But what of the solitary? While there are some who say, "one cannot be a Witch alone," this was certainly not true of the shaman who was, in effect, a solitary working for the community; although sometimes members of the community acted as audience, or even orchestra, for the shaman.

And what of the self-initiated solitary practitioner? That question is most often and best answered with the question, "Who initiated the first priest or shaman?"

The self-initiated solitary practitioner becomes their own priest or priestess as soon as they dedicate themselves to the service of the Old Gods and perform their first ritual in Their honor. While the idea of a degree system is not of great importance to the solitary, there may come a time in their spiritual life when, either through study and practice, or through a mystical experience of some sort, a passage from one level of practice to another will need to be acknowledged ritually.

For the solitary practitioner or for one working within a coven or group, one sign of passage is the discarding of one's former Craft name and the taking of a new one. Taking a new name magickally reinforces the start of a new life. For the solitary, if the name is not "given" by dream or inspiration, it may be sought for in mythology or folklore. For one who is working with others, the name may be selected by the coven or group, with the consent of the one about to make the passage.

Like other passages, this one from initiate to priesthood, or high priesthood, should not occur before a year and a day. It should also be preceded by a period of isolation and meditation.

There may also be an ordeal, for which the Gardnerians have been greatly criticized for the use of the scourge, but this aspect of passage has been discussed in a previous chapter.

When the time has come for an initiate to make the passage into priesthood, when the new name has been chosen and a new amulet has been consecrated for the purpose, at a New Moon prior to a major sabbat—Lammas, the time of the sacrifice being most appropriate—a new priestess or priest might be crowned with the following rite.

The central altar will be adorned according to the season. Upon the altar will be a crown, symbol of priesthood; a silver crescent crown for a priestess, a crown of horns for a priest. If the initiate is a woman, there might also be a garter. Bread and wine or ale may also be present, and a small vial of anointing oil. (To prepare anointing oil, in a small pan heat, but do not boil, a small amount of pure olive oil. Add to this a few drops of rose oil or fresh or dried rose petals for the female element, a few drops of cinnamon oil or crushed cinnamon bark for the male element, and finely ground frankincense, a sacred element which acts as a link between Gods and mortals. Allow it to cool in moonlight, to be blessed by the Goddess, and to be warmed again in sunlight, to be blessed by the God, before filtering it. Place this oil in a dark glass bottle, imbue it with your own energy, and consecrate it in the sacred names. This oil will then be suitable for anointing both priests and priestesses.)

About the Circle are arranged eight small altars. Each of these altars represents a sabbat, and is placed on the circle at a point corresponding to that sabbat.

West	Autumn Equinox	A cup of wine
Northwest	Samhain	A skull or antlers and a cauldron
North	Yule	An unlit candle
Northeast	Imbolc	A wand and an ear of corn
East	Vernal Equinox	Three seeds and a bowl of earth
Southeast	Beltane	A wand and a wreath of flowers
South	Midsummer	A Sun wheel or wheel of some kind
Southwest	Lammas	A loaf of bread and a knife

When the Circle has been cast and consecrated, the priestess, if the one about to be crowned is a woman, will go to the initiate where she has been standing within the Circle and lead her to the priest at the altar.

The priest asks something like:

How do you come here?

and she answers something like:

I come as one initiated in the ways of the wise, to serve the ancient gods.

What then do you seek?

asks the priest, and she answers:

I seek to serve the Lord and Lady (using the names used by the tradition) *as their priestess.*

The priest continues;

> *Then* (old Craft name) *go to the Western gate.*
> *There, in that place of death*
> *Leave behind your name*
> *And begin your life anew.*
> *Serve our ancient Gods* (names)
> *In this Circle, cast in their honor,*
> *Which is the Circle of Time made manifest.*

The candidate goes to the Western Quarter where she kneels or sits in meditation as the coven drums, or chants something like;

> *Every ending is a new beginning*
> *The Circle is eternal!*

The chanting stops when the candidate ends her meditation. She will then perform a simple ritual at each of the small altars set up about the circle.

Lammas is the most appropriate time for this rite; however, if it is taking place at the time of another sabbat, then begin at the appropriate point on the Circle so that the ritual will conclude with the present sabbat.

The Horned Crown of a Priest.

The one about to be crowned might bless the wine at the West, sip it and pour a libation at the Northwest, light the candle at the North, and so on, sunwise around the Circle. This is actually something of a test, to be sure that the candidate understands the meaning of the sabbats and can create and conduct rituals according to ways of the coven's tradition. When the eight rituals have been completed, she returns to the priest at the center of the Circle. The Priest says something like:

> You have done well and served the Gods
> According to our ways
> By what name would you be known to them?

The candidate gives the name that has been chosen. The priest holds high the crown, saying:

> Behold this crown, symbol of our priestess.
> Should you accept it, know this
> It does not give you power
> Over others, nor set you aside.
>
> Yet, as you have not power over others
> Yours is a grave responsibility,
> For you are a vessel of the Lady.
>
> And you are Her representative
> In all of your acts and deeds.
> And if you reject this burden
> Then reject this crown also.
>
> But if you accept
> The weight of this crown,
> Know that many will be your trials,
> And many too, will be your rewards.

When the candidate has accepted the responsibilities of priestesshood, the priest places the crown upon her, and continues:

> Lady (new Craft name) *now before this coven*
> And within this Circle,
> With the Guardian Spirits
> Of the Four Directions
> As witnesses, do I anoint you.
>
> From this night onward
> When the Spirit of the Great Goddess
> Has been drawn down upon you (anointing her "third eye")
> You shall see with her eyes

Things unseen (anointing her lips)
You shall speak with her words
Things unknown (anointing her heart)
And you shall feel Her Spirit
And be unharmed.

The priest then takes up the necklace or amulet, and, placing it about the neck of the new priestess, says something like:

As a sign of your station
You shall wear this Torque
A symbol of the Goddess,
The sacred Circle, and the ever-turning wheel.

Then the coveners might dance around the new priestess and priest, chanting something like:

North, East, South, West
Earth, Air, Fire, Water

Now the original priestess steps forward and draws down the God upon the priest. He, in turn, draws down the Goddess upon the new priestess. The initiation would then be consummated with the Great Rite, whether it is performed actually or symbolically.

The Great Rite having been performed, the newly anointed priestess now symbolically sacrifices the God. Holding high the loaf, she then places it on the altar. Taking up her athame she states:

As he gave his power unto me
So do I give his power to this loaf.
Seed of his seed, sacred son
Of the Great Goddess,
Cut down in his prime
Lord of the harvest,
I send your spirit into this bread,
So that we may all partake
Of your sacrifice.

The new priestess then cuts or breaks the loaf, and distributes it among the coveners. She blesses the wine and does likewise.

The rite is ended.

The coveners gather around the new priestess, to congratulate her and bestow gifts upon her, to feast and make merry.

If the candidate is a man, of course, the rite might be very similar, except that the Crown of Horns would be used and the priestess would perform the rite. At the point when the Goddess is drawn down, she would be drawn down upon the priestess earlier in the rite, and the priestess would simply draw down the Lord upon the newly crowned priest prior to the Great Rite. Afterward, the new priest and the priestess would bless the cakes and wine as it is always done.

When a new priestess has been crowned for the purpose of forming a new coven, the original priestess might then become a high priestess. This rite of passage should be celebrated at the same time that it occurs, at the crowning of the new priestess. This might take place after the Blessing of the Cakes and Wine, with the presentation of the Garter.

When the cakes and wine have been distributed, and before the Circle has been banished, the original priestess may return to the altar, and taking up the garter, say something like:

> *Ancient Goddess and beloved God,*
> *Before this altar on this night of the (Barley) Moon,*
> *Was a new priestess crowned*
> *And dedicated to your service.*
> *As she has become like a daughter unto me,*
> *I am like a mother unto her.*
> *As a sign of her service to you,*
> *Will she wear this garter*
> *Which has been consecrated*
> *In your sacred names.*

The original priestess will then present the garter to the new priestess, or buckle it about her leg. The new priestess may then take up a new buckle, the loveliest she could find, and taking it to the altar, intone words like;

> *Lord and Lady, may my first ritual,*
> *As a priestess dedicated to your service*
> *Be to honor one who has shown me*
> *The mysteries of your ancient ways.*
> *May this buckle, blessed by the Elements*
> (as she passes it through the Earth, Air, Fire, and Water)
> *And consecrated in your names*
> *Lady (name) and Lord (name),*
> *Serve as a reminder of one*
> *Who has followed her, in the ways*
> *Of mystery and of magick,*
> *That will be her legacy.*
> *And may it also be an amulet of power*
> *To add to her own magickal power*
> *As High Priestess (new Craft name) at your altar*
> *Blessed be!*

The new high priestess will accept the buckle, adding it to her garter, and, thanking the new priestess, the Spirits of the Four Directions, and the Lord and Lady, she will then banish the Circle.

There is, however, no popular male counterpart to the tradition of the many-buckled garter as symbol of high priesthood, so I suggest that each coven or tradition begin one, such as the addition of a new pentacle or Sun wheel to the high priest's crown of horns for each daughter coven his coven has spawned.

There really is no need for a solitary practitioner to become a priest or priestess, since anyone who performs their own sabbat rituals is a priestess or a priest to the Gods they honor. Still, there comes a time in the life of a solitary when he or she can look back at the years they have spent on the path and realize how truly far they have come in their quest for knowledge and understanding, and in their service to the Gods of the Old Religion. Also, even though the solitary practitioner has no desire to work with a coven, or no coven to work with, most are in contact with a whole network of other Pagans and Wiccans who might need the services of a solitary priest or priestess on an occasion.

A Crown for a Priestess.

In order to be truly qualified to call oneself a solitary priestess or priest, what is necessary is a thorough understanding of the tradition you practice, as well as an understanding of the sabbats and how they relate to the mythology of that tradition. This, and a well-developed ability to create and perform rituals and rites, are all that are really necessary. This may take years, and is a process shortened for those who choose to study under the guidance of a priest, priestess, or coven, but for those who choose the solitary path, with only the Old Ones for guidance, the years spent will have been worth it. The decision that a promotion is in order is sometimes the result of a mystical experience, such as a dream or a vision in which the solitary sees him- or herself as being crowned or anointed on the spirit planes, or being invited to conduct a magickal rite there. As with other things in the life of a solitary, such an experience is not unlike the episodes in the life of a shaman.

When the time has come, when the signs have been given, and the solitary feels ready, a date should be selected. The night of the New Moon is always best for such rites, and, as with the Rite of Coven Priesthood, the time of Lammas when the priestesses and priests preside over the sacrifice of the harvest always seems appropriate. All that is necessary for the rite is a bottle of anointing oil, a crown or headband with a crescent moon ornamentation for a woman, or antlers, horns, or a Sun wheel for a man; and a garter as before if the rite is being performed by a woman. The solitary shall have selected a new name to reflect the new aspect of life that is about to begin.

When the altar is ready and the Circle has been cast, the solitary may sit, skyclad, before the altar. After a moment of meditation, the solitary may call upon the Gods with words like;

> *Lord and Lady,*
> *I call upon you this night*
> *To be present in this Circle*
> *God and Goddess*
> *I invite you to join with me*
> *In this place that is not a place*
> *Lord* (name) *and Lady* (name)
> *I call upon you to be present*
> *To witness what I am about to undertake.*
> (wait for a sign to be given)
> *For you, Lord and Lady*
> *Shall be my only witnesses.*
> *For* (number of) *years now*
> *Have I walked in your ways,*
> *Alone but for the light of your love.*
> *For* (number of) *years*

Have I served at your altar.
Now do I wish to dedicate myself,
Even further to your service,
I ask only that in your eyes
Will I be considered your priestess (or priest)
And as a sign of this, from this night on,
Shall I be known to you within this Circle as (new Craft name)
I anoint myself before your eyes
(anointing the forehead at the hairline)
As a sign of this intent.
May I always prove worthy
Of the task I undertake.
(anointing the soles of the feet)
And may I always have
Your blessings and your guidance
As I tread the solitary path
And the sacred Circle
Of your mysteries.
(taking up the crown)
I bestow upon myself
This crescent crown,
(or crown of horns)
Consecrated in your name
And ask that as I do
I shall be touched by your spirit.

If the solitary is a woman, she takes up the garter and buckles it about her leg, saying something like:

I bind this garter about my leg
As a symbol that I am bound to serve you.
And that its buckle shall,
Like me, be alone in that service.
Lord and Lady, God and Goddess (names)
All I ask is that a sign be given
That my priesthood is accepted
As I continue to serve at your altar.

Allow some time for meditation and for a sign to be given. When it has been given and received, and this can be on the mental as well as the physical plane, the newly anointed priestess or priest may want to dance around the circle until exhausted, then feast and make merry (as merry as a solitary gets, it's usually a more quiet kind of joy), until the Gods and guardians are thanked and the Circle banished.

When the harvest has been celebrated, when the golden grain has been gathered, and the consecrated bread has been distributed among those who tread the secret path of the wise, when the contents of the cup have been drunk and libations poured out upon the fertile earth, we who serve at the altars of the Ancient Gods shall know the power and the beauty and the mystery, long after the warm days of summer have passed and autumn's chill blows cold.

Chapter Seven
Elderhood

Elderhood

The late summer afternoons stretch into September evenings. In the fields, fat pumpkins ripen orange, some to be cut into the Jack-o-Lantern's fiery face, some to fill pie crusts for the harvest feast, and perhaps some to be magickally converted into coaches for the royal ball. In the meadow, goldenrod transforms the sea of green grass to a buttery yellow, and the fleeces of the grazing flocks of sheep grow warm and shaggy. In the vineyard, the clusters of grapes hang black and plump, waiting to be transformed into wine, or wither on the vine.

As shadows lengthen and dusk begins to gather, there is a familiar chill in the air. Deer in darker winter coats stir silently in the hedgerows. Indoors on these nights, in the warm yellow light of kitchens, grandparents tell their grandchildren the tales of wonder that were told to them by their grandparents when they, themselves, were children; and in the telling and retelling, recall once again that land of enchantment just beyond the edges of mundane reality. When we have reached the age when we may be relieved of the obligations of youth and midlife, we shall be free once again to explore this realm of wonder.

The transition from midlife to old age, for both men and women, is a gradual one. For women, the physical process called menopause will have been completed, and for a man this is a time when, had he been born a herd animal rather than a human, he might be driven from the herd, denied the right to mate and breed by a younger member of the flock, in all likelihood one of his own sons. Or he may have been killed by the younger male in the battle for dominance, as was Arthur by Mordred.

When we were children, we learned many things from our grandparents. Today, there are Pagans and Wiccans who can claim a hereditary tradition, one which was taught them, not by their mothers and fathers, but by their grandmothers and grandfathers. In a sense, a great number of us can

Telling the Old Tales.

claim a direct hereditary tradition, passed down to us orally from our grandparents. Many of these traditions may not be complete systems, but they are genuine relics, to be incorporated into systems made up of many bits and pieces. It should be the goal, for every one of us who is fortunate enough to still have grandparents living, and especially those who came from the "old country," to gather as much of this information, and even language, as possible, before the opportunity is lost forever.

As we come of age in our youth, we become the new generation to carry the banners of our clan. We still have parents, who are in their middle years, to comfort us and guide us, and we still have grandparents, who have become the elders, to love us and to teach us the old ways. As we enter our middle years, our parents move into elderhood and our grandparents pass beyond the veil to continue their guidance from the other side. Then, as we leave our middle years behind, it is we who are about to enter elderhood. It is we who are about to become the reservoir of tribal wisdom. No longer may we look to those older for wisdom or guidance, because they have all gone on. It is we who are about to become the elders; and our only guidance, besides the knowledge we have gained, will come from the world of spirit.

This passage celebrates the end of the time that our energies are turned outward toward physical activities, and marks the beginning of the time that we turn our energies inward, toward more spiritual activities. It is a time too, when our physical growth slows down, cells are not replaced as quickly, and, gradually, our physical bodies begin to separate from our spiritual bodies.

In the southernmost part of Ethiopia, there is a tribe that to this day still settles the matter of elderhood in a rather unique way. About every 30 years, (it used to be every seven or nine years) the Mursi tribe holds a large group Coming of Age rite. Every man of the tribe from age 15 to 45 is automatically promoted from boyhood to manhood. The main privilege that comes with the passage into manhood is the right to be heard in the discussion of important issues of the tribe. The privileges of elevated status are also transferred to the wives of those men who undergo the passage rites.

This rite of passage, called the Nitha by the Mursi, is presided over by the tribal Shaman. It begins with those about to be initiated being separated from the tribe. Tribal wisdom and knowledge are revealed, and the boys are given adult names, both individually and as a group, and there is a mock battle between the boys and those who became men at the last Nitha.

The finale of the rites is the slaughter of three oxen. Though this violates our law of "Harm None," the name Nitha means slaughter. The entrails of the slain oxen are then laid out in the shape of the Mursi's traditional territory, and wherever dark spots or blemishes appear, it indicates the places where the tribe's traditional enemies are likely to attack in the next 30 years.

The slaughter of the oxen may ritually symbolize the deaths of the last generation of elders who have gone to join the ancestors, but who continue to guide and protect the tribe by warning, through the entrails of the oxen, where enemy invasions are likely to occur.

The Nitha, the tribal Rite of Passage, being complete, a new generation of Mursi are moved from boyhood to manhood. Those men who passed into manhood at the last Nitha, and who have enjoyed the status for 30 years, now range in age from 45 to 75. They are all automatically promoted to elderhood, and those who attained elderhood at the last Nitha are allowed to retire from public life.

While this system apparently works well for the Mursi, it unfortunately cannot be applied to the Pagan or Wiccan in contemporary society. Just as Coming of Age and Initiation must be two separate events for today's Pagans, even if they are celebrated at the same time, there are two different aspects to becoming an elder. One is to reach the age of retirement on the physical level, and the other is to achieve some goal worthy of elderhood, or complete some task within the Pagan community. Obviously, the first of these two aspects will necessarily occur in later years, while the second can occur at any time.

While the first aspect, attaining retirement age, is self-evident, the second, achieving a goal or completing a task, is usually agreed upon by members of the community, the immediate coven, all the daughter covens, or a larger segment of the community.

For solitary Pagans, this can become questionable. While on the one hand, as solitaries, we do not directly participate in Pagan activities within the community, so our position in the community is very irrelevant. On the other hand, even solitaries network with other Pagans, sometimes with vast numbers of them, and if such solitaries have made a major contribution to the Pagan community, they deserve to be recognized for it. Still others may know in their hearts what they have contributed or achieved, and need no more recognition for it but the love of the Gods.

In any case, elderhood means that we have attained our goal, completed our mission, and it is no longer required of us that we continue working for the Craft, though we are free to continue if we so desire.

In ancient times, one way to become an elder was to accomplish some heroic act or bring some new magick to the community. Legends and folktales are filled with stories of such heroes. "Dragon Slayer" is a typical tale. The story lines of these tales are very similar. The land was once terrorized by a horrible monster, often a dragon, which devastated crops, mutilated cattle and devoured citizens, until one day the wise ruler of the land arrived at an agreement with the dragon. The agreement was that periodically the king and country would offer up to the dragon a maiden chosen at random. Some tales seem to suggest that the maiden was more wife than dinner. The years passed and all was quiet and peaceful, except that the maidens of the kingdom lived in fear for their lives. And then, one day, it was the king's own daughter who was selected for sacrifice, but it also happened that there was traveling in the land a young prince, who accepted the king's challenge to slay the dragon and win the hand of the princess. This, of course, was accomplished, and the prince and the princess lived happily ever after.

It is interesting to note that in just about every tale of this type, the dragon dwells either in a cave underground, or in a well, or the sea. All of these are places which are traditional entrances to the shamanic underworld, or dwelling places of ancestral spirits, and it is only through this underworld that the upper worlds can be reached.

The fact that the ruler of this underworld is a dragon rather than a god of the dead, and that the dragon is slain rather than implored or outwitted, makes this type of tale different than the Goddesses' or Gods' descent into the underworld.

A similar tale is that of Jack, the Giant Killer, who slew no less than four giants. For slaying the first giant he received a magick sword which could cut through anything, and a belt with gold letters that stated,

> *This is the valiant Cornishman*
> *Who slew the giant Cormoran.*

For killing Blunderbore, the second giant, he received the keys to the giant's castle, which he gave to the three beautiful ladies he found tied by their hair in one of the chambers.

For slaying the third giant, the two-headed Tunderdale, he obtained a cloak of invisibility, a cap which answered all his questions, and shoes which were swifter than the wind.

When Jack entered the castle of the fourth giant, Galligantus, he discovered in the courtyard a beautiful, pure white deer tied to a hawthorn tree. When he slew the fourth giant, the spell was broken, and where the white deer had been there was a beautiful princess with a wreath of hawthorn blossoms in her hair.

The dragons or giants in such tales represent not evil, or death, but the naturally destructive forces of Nature, such as storms or earthquakes, which have a consciousness or spirit, but no real evil intent. Giants, in particular, are the sons of Mother Nature, and their function in the long term is to lay waste so that new life might arise, in much the same way that the Hawaiian Fire Goddess, Pele, causes destruction with volcanic eruptions, so that new land may be created upon which new life will flourish.

There are, however, times when such forces become too strong, upsetting the balance between the destructive and the creative functions of

Nature, and the magick or wit of such a hero as Jack is required to restore the balance. In the tale of the Giant Killer, Jack receives trophies from the giants he slays, and two of these are very interesting. One is a sword which can cut through anything. The sword is often associated with the element of fire, the element in which it was forged. Other trophies won were a cloak of invisibility, a cap (of wisdom) which could answer any question, and shoes that were "swift as the wind." All three of these magickal tools are very apparently associated with the element of air. The element of air is associated (in most traditions) with the direction of the East and with the Vernal Equinox, while the element of Fire represented by the sword is associated with the direction of South and Midsummer. Apparently, what Jack did was overcome the forces of death and destruction associated with winter, and prepare for the return of the Goddess in Spring; all the chores of a shaman or priest.

The Fool

In the tale of the Dragon Slayer, the dragon dwells in a cave, symbolizing the element of Earth and the direction of North; or in a well or the sea, representing the direction of West, the element of water and of death. The slaying of the dragon represents, once again, the balance restored so that life may continue, not, as so often told in later versions of the tales, the powers of goodness overcoming the powers of evil.

While Jack the Giant Killer was a rather bright fellow, his counterpart in another tale, "Jack and the Beanstalk," was a bit dull-witted, trading a cow for a handful of beans. Very often in such tales, the hero is a simpleton, which is a bardic formula for conveying the idea that the hero-to-be is innocent, pure of heart, and completely without guile. He is the Fool of the Tarot deck, just starting out on the path of life. After many adventures, through his own purity of heart, he overcomes all obstacles to be united, at the end of the legend of his life, with the Great Goddess, as portrayed on the final card of the Tarot, The World.

In the end, Jack, the Giant Killer, wed the beautiful princess, and to spare her from a life of worry and care, he gave up slaying giants, retired from public life, and, in short, joined the elders.

The theme of these tales, as opposed to those of the descent of the God or Goddess into the underworld, is the theme of the shaman who enters the world of Nature Spirits, often through the underworld, in order to obtain psychic gifts or overcome a troublesome spirit. Such is this tale of Odin, who is often referred to as a shamanic God.

In the myth in which Odin must obtain the Sacred Mead of Inspiration, which has fallen into the hands of the Etins (giants), it is Odin himself who takes the form of a serpent. In this form, he burrows into the base of the mountain, which is the abode of the Etin-wife who possesses the Mead. After sleeping with the Etin-wife for three nights, Odin is able to drink down the Mead from the three drinking horns in which it was stored. He then shape-shifts into an eagle and flies out through the top of the mountain to Valhalla, where he returns the Mead to the Gods, but on the way a few drops are spilled upon the earth where anyone might find them.

There is a difference between these two types of tales; those of the descent of the Goddess or God into the underworld in order to insure immortality for humankind, and those of the descent of the shaman into the underworld as an entry point to the higher realms of spirit, in order to obtain some secret (or treasure) for the betterment or well-being of the community. In the first type, the task needed only to be performed once by the Goddess or God. In the second, a similar task may be performed by anyone at any time. The successful completion of such a task would automatically promote the hero to a position of honor in the community. He would become one of the Elders.

In those long-lost days of humankind's youth, when giants and dragons could be seen for what they truly were, it was simpler to recognize the monster. And if one had the courage and the skill, the wit and the desire, one could ride out to slay the monster and return home a hero. Today the giants and the dragons wear the disguises of a technological society, and the citizens of the land, for the most part, neither know nor care about the old ways, so he or she who would be a hero has a difficult task.

There are yet dragons and giants, but to recognize them takes the eye of the shaman, and there is a community of Pagans in the land who care very much about the old ways and who are more than willing to honor those who conquer their enemies.

In many ancient religious cultures, one of the goals one expected to achieve was to make a certain pilgrimage. In these cultures it is the desire of each individual to visit a certain sacred site at least once in their lifetime. Among the followers of Islam, the sacred pilgrimage is to Mecca where a black meteorite is enshrined. For the natives of the Mongolian plains, it is to follow in the footsteps of Ghengis Kahn, which is the path delineated by the Great Wall of China. For the followers of the Hindu faith, the pilgrimage is to the sacred river, the Ganges, to bathe and be blessed in its healing waters, and to carry some home to share and possess its power. In Tibet there is a mountain known as the Snow Jewel, believed to be the dwelling place of the Gods. This pilgrimage around the sacred mountain is made to attain self-knowledge and spiritual perfection by both Hindus and Buddhists. The Bonn, an early shamanistic sect of Buddhists, make the pilgrimage by taking their measure every step of the way, that is, by lying full length on the

Snow Jewel Amulets.

ground and then, standing where their head had been, lying flat again. The pilgrimage made this way can take weeks. Protective amulets, which are stylized representations of the Snow Jewel, are placed above doors and windows of homes.

On the summit of Mt. Kinnabalu in Borneo is a lake which is believed to be the home of sacred dragons. Pilgrims to this site leave offerings, including coins. For a small tribe in Mexico, at least once in every lifetime it is desired to make a pilgrimage, led by the village shaman, to their ancestral hunting ground. Where their ancestors once hunted the sacred deer, they now ritually shoot arrows into deer tracks, and gather the peyote buttons for another year. The various tribes of North American Indians had sacred sites to which they made, and still make, pilgrimages periodically. Fahata Butte in Chaco Canyon must surely have been such a sacred place to the Anasazi. Today, many sacred places are being threatened by lumber companies and big businesses.

The early Pagan inhabitants of Europe had many sacred sites, some of which are still marked by stone circles and other megalithic monuments. According to some, these megalithic structures are aligned on straight paths or "ley lines." If this is so, then it might suggest that these structures were stopping points along a path of pilgrimage.

One of the best known of all pilgrimages undertaken by European Pagans is that which began in Athens and ended at the Temple of Demeter in Eleusis. The 14-mile walk is dotted with sacred caves and shrines, many of which have had churches of the new religion built upon their sacred foundations; but it is still easy enough to see through the thin veneer of Christianity and recognize the Pagan symbolism beneath. This pilgrimage was undertaken by those who would be initiated into the Eleusian Mysteries. They left Athens at dawn to follow the ancient path, stopping at shrines and grottos along the way, to arrive at the Temple of Demeter in Eleusis by dusk. Here, the mysteries, given by the Goddess Herself, would be revealed to them at their initiation. They were sworn to secrecy, these initiates of Eleusis, but they left Demeter's temple rejoicing in the certain knowledge that death is not an end. The fact that not a single initiate of Eleusis ever revealed the secret of the mysteries is testimony to the truth and power they contained. The fact that the Temple of Demeter now lies in ruins, destroyed as it was by Christian zealots, almost 2,000 years ago, also testifies to the truth and power it once contained.

For today's Pagans there are sites, both old and new, that are becoming once again the destination for a pilgrimage. Stonehenge is probably one of the most popular places for today's Pagans to visit at least once in the present lifetime. Glastonbury is another. Many Pagans who cannot, for one reason or another, travel to Europe, can visit such American sites as Circle Sanctuary or Salem, Massachusetts.

The ruins of the Temple at Eleusis.

Other places of pilgrimages were believed to be the birthplaces or dwelling places of particular divinities, or the sites important to their myth. To follow in the footsteps of the Gods is to tread the Magick Circle, to dance the round dance and to walk the wheel of the year. For those of us who wish to make a magickal pilgrimage but cannot, here is a rite that can be performed instead. Select a series of sites from the mythology of your tradition; six or eight would be ideal. Then within the area you have chosen for the ritual, symbolically recreate the sites. An outdoor space with lots of room would be ideal, but a nine-foot Circle or even smaller would do just as well. The preparations for this rite are as important as the rite itself. The idea is to recreate the sites in miniature. For example, if your tradition is based on the myth of Demeter, it begins with the abduction of her daughter, Persephone, by Hades, Lord of the Underworld. There is still in Greece a sacred site, a cave which is believed to be the entrance to the underworld, to which many come each year. To recreate this, gather a few stones and arrange them to resemble a cave entrance, at the Eastern point of the Circle or your starting point. The next part of the myth is that Demeter was so stricken with grief that she allowed Nature to die and the Earth to become barren. This could be represented by an earthenware bowl filled with sand. As she searched the Earth for her lost daughter, she stopped to rest at the well of Eleusis, where she was treated with kindness by the daughters of the king. This site could be represented by a cauldron of water, surrounded by blocks of stone in the Western part of the Circle, and so on through the myth.

This rite should take one night for each site recreated, so it would be a rather long ritual, but not nearly as long as some pilgrimages that are made by the faithful. In any case, if privacy is a problem, one site could be set each evening in the appropriate place, but if privacy is not a problem, then all of the sites might be recreated and the Circle left cast for the duration of the rite. When all has been prepared and the Circle has been cast, approach the first site, seat yourself before it and, by candlelight, meditate on that particular portion of the myth, then make an offering at the site. Remember, you are not recreating the myth or impersonating a deity; you are making a pilgrimage, and would therefore do what a pilgrim would do (short of having your picture taken at the site).

For many of us, it is not possible to visit the ancient sacred sites, to follow in the footsteps of the Gods as they lived out their mythologies; but, as Pagans, we know that all of Nature is a manifestation of the Gods, and therefore every site is a dwelling place of the Divine Spirit. While the shrine in the backyard might not be imbued with the power of an ancient site that has been venerated for thousands of years by untold numbers of devout pilgrims, it is still a dwelling place of the God or Goddess.

One of the most intriguing elements in the old literature on the Craft of the Wise is the traditional familiar. The term instantly brings to mind images of the lonely Crone in her enchanted woodland cottage, befriended only by a toad; or the bearded wizard in his tower, conversing with an owl or crow. What is not as well known is that the familiar, or familiar spirit, may occur in forms other than the traditional animal or pet, and it is in these other forms that we begin to recognize the familiar as a universal and important element.

One of these forms is that of the discarnate entity. That is, the spirit of one who has lived before on the material world, but who is currently free of the physical body. Such a discarnate might become attached to a living person, and be able to communicate with that person telepathically, or through other means. This type of discarnate familiar, such as the invisible character Louise in the hilarious film *Vibes,* is the invisible playmate of childhood, the Christian's "guardian angel," and the "spirit guide" of the spiritualist, the medium and the channeler. Their magickal work might include divination or prophecy, or acting as a go-between or an interpreter between the Witch and the spirit world.

A second type of familiar is the nonphysical entity, one that has never been incarnate, but one that can occupy, or be made to occupy, a nonphysical object such as a bottle, a mirror, a wine glass, or a Ouija board. In this group are the famous genie or djinn of Syria, Persia, and Baghdad, as well as the

Objects which traditionally might contain a "familiar."

talking mirrors, rings and basins of European folk and Faerie tales. These objects, believed to contain familiar spirits, are called by anthropologists "fetishes." Many an old "Grimoire" or Book of Shadows gives directions for attracting to, or trapping within, an object such as a mirror or a ring, a non-physical entity, for the purpose of predicting the future or communing with the spirit world.

But for the warmest companionship and purest love, the traditional Witches' familiar in the form of an animal or a pet is not to be surpassed. The two most typical pets today are the cat and the dog. Aside from their love, their loyalty, and their beauty, cats have always been valued for their psychic abilities. In the presence of a ghost, cats often respond with fear and the usual defensive posture, with back arched, teeth bared and claws extended. It is from their acute awareness of the spirit world that the traditional Halloween decorations of the "Scaredy Cat" or the "Scratchy Cat" were drawn. It was in Egypt that the cat was first domesticated, and so beloved were they that their bodies were mummified, just like humans, and buried in cat cemeteries. The Cat Goddess, Bast, is the Egyptian counterpart of the Greek Moon Goddess, Artemis, and the Roman Diana, who herself took the form of a cat in order to seduce her brother, Lucifer, the Light Bringer. Black cats have been associated with Witchcraft since ancient times, because they are the symbolic color of the Goddess in her Crone aspect, but other writers on the Craft tell us that probably the first cats to be the familiars of Witches had brindle markings, as the original wild cats must have had. Today there are pink-nosed white cats, green-eyed black ones, and blue-eyed beige and brown Siamese, but one of the types of cats that is still surrounded with myth and mystery is the old fashioned, nonpedigreed calico. Marked with patches of black and orangy-red on white, she carries the colors of the Goddess, red, white, and black, and to call a calico "she" seems quite appropriate, because legend tells us that all calico cats are female.

The bond between Witches and cats is so great that often, when people were convicted and executed for Witchcraft, their cats were tortured and executed along with them. Dogs are the other most popular pets, and anyone who has known the love of a dog knows why. To gaze into the dark eyes of a dog is to see unconditional love, which is probably why the Goddess Diana chose dogs for her symbol and companion, but to see a dog turn its eyes upward to return the gaze is to see the white crescent Moon of Diana herself.

As dogs are the companions of Diana the Huntress, when Herne, the Horned Hunter of Men, is seeking his prey, it is his hounds that are heard leading the hunt, and they have been companions to hunters throughout the world. Natives of Papua, New Guinea, when starting out on a hunting expedition, perform a ritual that includes chanting and breathing into the nostrils of their canine hunting guides in order to insure a successful hunt. But it is as

Several versions of the Halloween Scaredy-Cat.

a guide in the spirit realms, as well as on the Earth plane, that dogs are to be valued as well. There have been instances when a dog, in perfect health and in the prime of its life, has died suddenly, only to be followed in a few weeks or months by its lifelong human companion. It is believed that in such situations the dog simply went on ahead to act as a scout and guide for the spirit of its human companion. For this reason, in the Colima culture of South America, small clay figures of dogs were placed in tombs to act as guides for the spirits of the deceased.

Other traditional familiars are rabbits and hares. Rabbits are becoming very popular household pets, because they are intelligent, affectionate, and can be trained to use a litter box like a cat. The rabbit and the cat were at one time considered to be the same animal, and sacred to the Goddess in her aspect as Goddess of fertility. The slang or folk names for both, the cat, or "pussy," and the rabbit, or "cunny," still reflect this association with the Fertility Goddess; in fact Coney Island, New York, was so named for the huge population of wild rabbits that once lived there. Eventually the two animals were differentiated, and the cat, because of its nocturnal habits and acute psychic awareness, became associated with the Crone at Samhain and the rabbit, because of its obvious fertility and its wild mating behavior in spring, became associated with the Maiden at the time of the Vernal Equinox, Eostre's rabbit, or the Easter Bunny. For this reason, many women were accused of shape-shifting into the form of a rabbit.

While dogs, cats, and rabbits are the most popular pets, and therefore familiars today, in earlier times, and certainly during the persecution, less conspicuous animals were kept as pets and familiars. Among these, toads and spiders seem to be traditional. Toads are nocturnal creatures who hide from the heat of midday, but who, when darkness comes, are quite friendly and unafraid of humans. Dan and I have, as mentioned in a previous book, had one, or a series of incarnations of one, living in the stone wall behind the herb garden. It has come out at night to sit at our feet like a tiny dog, leaving only to catch a slug or an insect. If a toad is kept indoors, it might hide by day and keep the house free of insects by night, but whether kept indoors or out, a bowl of water must be provided for it, and it must be a bowl which it can easily get in and out of, or it might drown. A traditional familiar to Witches, the toad produces a poisonous substance from its skin which was known and used by Witches in ages past.

While the toad is keeping the floor of the house insect-free, a spider might be doing the same for the ceiling. Night after night these spinners of silk produce their cobwebs in order to trap their prey. Like the Triple Goddess, they spin a silken thread of unbelievable strength, weave it into intricate patterns of exquisite beauty, and, when an insect is ensnared, they cut the thread of life. But while the cobweb weavers produce the stuff with which horror films and "Great Expectations"are draped, it is the orb-weavers who recreate each night one of the most powerful symbols of the Old Religion. Like Ariadne, who produced the thread which enabled Theseus to penetrate the very center of the Labyrinth, slay the Minotaur, and then retrace his steps, the orb-weaver spins first a frame and then a few radial lines. She then produces a continuous thread, beginning at the center of the web and spiraling around and around until the web is complete. When daylight comes she retraces her steps, consuming the web she wove and recycling her silk.

As the spider is associated with Ariadne and her thread in the labyrinth, Ariadne, consort of Dionysus, is very likely another version of Arianrod, Goddess of the Spiral Castle, as well as Aradia, Goddess of Witchcraft.

Cobweb or Orb-Weaver, trap-door spider or tarantula, all spiders are members of the Class *Arachnidae,* which is named for the beautiful Arachne who dared to challenge the Goddess to a weaving competition. Arachne won, but Aphrodite turned her into a spider for her audacity.

People who live with and love their pets don't usually think in terms of "using" them, but that is the purpose of having a familiar. It is not "using" your pet to be aware of its behavior and to know that dogs and cats can see a world that is, for the most part, invisible to us. They often try to communi-

An Agripe Spider in her Web.

cate to us the presence of Faerie-folk or unfriendly spirits, and by attempting to understand their subtle body language and eye signals we can, through our beloved pets, begin to sense the invisible world of Nature Spirits that surrounds us.

There are a couple of insects that might be mentioned here because they have special significance, and because insects have been kept as pets and familiars. The first of these is the much loved "Lady Bug." Lady bugs feed on aphids, which live by sucking the vital juices from plants, so the lady bug has long been recognized as the gardener's friend, and especially the organic gardener's. It is widely believed that the lady bug was named for Mary, the mother of Jesus, who is often referred to as "Our Lady," but in all likelihood, this adorable little insect, like so many other plants and animals, was originally considered to be sacred to the Pagan Goddess, long before being reassigned by the new religion, and the obvious clue to this is that she still wears the colors of the Triple Goddess; red, white, and black. Knowing this, however, does little to shed light on the nursery rhyme that was to be chanted when a ladybug landed on you.

> *Ladybug, ladybug, fly away home,*
> *Your house is on fire, your children are gone.*

The ladybug is in the beetle family, along with the Scarab beetles which were sacred in ancient Egypt.

Keeping insects as pets was not confined to the Middle Ages or the Burning Times. My mother tells a story of being in a fine shoe store in Manhattan in the 1940s, when a very well-dressed woman walked in with a praying mantis on a leash! The mantis is another insect that is welcomed in any garden because, though not as selective in its diet as the ladybug, it has a huge appetite for insects. Its great size does little to reveal its location because of its leafy green coloration and its twig-mimicking appearance, but it is probably the mantis' strange, swaying walk that helped it earn its English name, "soothsayer." It is easy to imagine a mantis in the midst of cast runes, rocking back and forth, going from one rune to another, spelling out a prophecy.

In earlier times it was traditional to give an animal pet as a familiar when a person was initiated into the Craft. Today it is considered unwise, and rightfully so, to give anyone a pet without their complete approval first. It is recognized that elderly persons who have pets live longer than those who do not. Anyone who has and loves a pet can understand this, knowing that the love of a pet is worth living for, and the simple soothing act of petting a cat can lower blood pressure. So an ideal gift for an elder, provided of course that it is with their full consent, is the gift of a lovable pet. It is the gift of life given twice, once to the pet which may have been obtained from the animal pound, and once to the elder who will receive it.

Aside from the familiar, or pet, another traditional gift for the elder is the staff. This magickal tool can serve a dual purpose. On the mundane level this staff might aid the elderly in walking. In Egypt such a walking stick was found which was inscribed with the words, "O stick, support me in my old age." The symbolism of the staff, as a device used by the elderly for support in walking, is conferred when such a magickal tool is given to one who has attained Elderhood before reaching an advanced age. In such a situation, the staff suggests that the recipient has attained the wisdom or the experience usually associated with great old age.

On the magickal level, the staff is a large version of the magick wand, a tool whose function, as mentioned earlier, is to draw unto itself magickal power or energy, in the same way that a television antenna attracts a signal, and to send that energy where it is pointed, and directed, by the will of the magician.

Because the staff is intended to function on both the mundane and the magickal levels, there are certain woods which are more appropriate than others. A staff of oak or ash has both the strength required of a walking stick, and the magickal associations of a powerful wand. Birch and willow are powerfully magickal, but too flexible as a long staff to be of any support for anyone who needed it. Hazelwood is ideal; however, finding a long enough piece of this bushy shrub can be a problem. If it can be found, it will be worth it, as hazelwood was the wand of the Druids, and it is associated with the Crone aspect of the Goddess, the wisdom of great age, and the messengers of the Gods. Another wood that is surprisingly strong and magickal is the very old trunks of grape vine. Sacred to Dionysus, the grapevine often grows in a natural spiral. The smooth wood needs only to have the bark removed. The traditional Witching-stick of the Pennsylvania Germans is of course the staff around which a vine such as honeysuckle has grown, causing the wood to grow in a natural spiral. As mentioned in Chapter Five, this Witching-stick is usually of maple wood, but for the Elder with advanced magickal power, this staff should have five, rather than three turns to the spiral. Such a Witching-stick having a single twist might be given at a Coming of Age or Initiation rite, the staff of three twists at Midlife, and the staff of five turns when Elderhood is achieved. It may be supposed that each turn or twist of the Witching-stick represents 13 years of life, one twist being thirteen years of age or the Coming of Age, three twists equaling 39 years or Midlife, and five turns of 13 years each representing the 65 years to retirement or Elderhood. In other words, the Witching-sticks of one, three, and five turns represent the Maiden, Mother, and Crone aspects of human life.

Regardless of the kind of wood the staff is made of, it is the besom and the wand. It is the Tree of Life and the symbol of the shaman. As we become more advanced in age and in our magick, we may begin to shed the physical trappings we once found so necessary to the performance of our magick, in favor of simpler, more shamanic methods; and for this reason, many of the symbolic objects associated with the Elder, the Wizard and the "Master Magician" are quite the same as those associated with the shaman. The magickal staff then might be tipped with a crystal or capped with a headpiece. It might be carved with symbolic figures to enhance its natural shape, or inlaid with wire or precious metal. Or, the staff might be adorned with amulets and symbols of the elements; acorns and feathers, shells and crystals, bones and beads, and holey stones may dangle from it on multi-colored ribbons, yarns and twine, each adding its own unique magick to the power of the staff and the Elder that wields it.

Another article usually associated with the elder is a cloak or cape. This is the magician's mantle, the Crone's cape, and the ceremonial robe of the wizard and the alchemist. It is the prayer shawl of the Jewish faith and the surplice of the Catholic priest, and it has its roots in the traditional robe of the shaman in almost every part of the world.

The basic cloak of the Pagan or Wiccan Elder is a black one, expressing the association of the Crone aspect of the Goddess with this phase of life, but as every illustrator of Faerie tale books knows, the basic black cape may be adorned with Suns and Moons and stars, just as the robes of shamans were decorated with the symbols of the Sun, the Moon, and the planets. It may be adorned with the signs of the zodiac, as the alchemists robe was decorated with the alchemical symbols of metals. These designs may be painted on, stenciled, or embroidered. Like the staff, it might be adorned with feathers, expressing the association of the Elder with the messengers of the Gods, or it might be fringed with ribbons, which in shamanistic cultures represent snakes, and which express an association with the underworld and the ancestors.

The term spinster is one that is often applied to an elderly, unmarried woman, but *Webster's Dictionary* tells us that it also means an evil woman. This is a very interesting combination of ideas. It has been said that the first definition is derived from the fact that an elderly, unmarried woman, after her parents had passed on, would live with her various married sisters and brothers, and earn her keep by doing the spinning for the family, but the art of spinning is one that has long been associated with Witchcraft and the Triple Goddess of the Moon, who controlled the destinies of mortals and determined when their time would end.

The art of spinning is a sacred one, and as every spinner knows the act, whether performed on a drop spindle or a great wheel, generates magickal power, just as a steam-driven turbine generates electrical energy.

This was apparently true in other parts of the world as well as Europe, because in the sacred caves of Central America, those known to be used for ritual acts because of the nature of the paintings on their walls, little clay spindle whorls have been found in great numbers. In Japan the spinning of silk by aristocratic ladies was considered a very noble act.

To return to the mythology of Europe, it may have been the wishful thinking of the maiden, combined with her attempts to spin straw into gold, that conjured the dwarf Rumplestiltskin to come to her aid, and it was definitely a prick from a spindle that put Sleeping Beauty to sleep in her castle for a hundred years. It was also a thread, handspun, that Ariadne gave to Theseus when he entered the Labyrinth of the Minator. As Theseus trod the maze of the Labyrinth he unwound the thread, marking the path with it, just as Hansel marked his path into the forest with bread crumbs so that afterward he could find his way home by following his trail. Unfortunately for Hansel, birds had eaten his trail of bread crumbs, and we all know what happened then! What most people don't know, however, is that an older non-Christianized version of the tale has an entirely different ending. In this older version of the tale, the young hero is named Hop-O-My-Thumb. The story begins the same way as the all-too-familiar tale of Hansel and Gretel, but instead of being just a tale to frighten boys and girls into being obedient children and staying out of the forest where real magick still dwells, the story ends with Hop-O-My-Thumb coming to the castle, where he finds the magickal Seven League Boots. After some adventures he returns home the hero, with the boots and finds his evil stepmother dead and his father happy to see him.

A collection of pre-Columbian spindle whorls. The large one on the left is from Mexico, the group on the right is from a sacred cave in Quatamala.

Theseus, likewise, returns from the Labyrinth after defeating the Minatour, by following the magickal thread given him by Ariadne, consort of Dionysus, who himself defeated death in the underworld. There can be little doubt Ariadne is Arrianrhod, the ancient Celtic Goddess of Death, and also Aradia, the teacher of Magick. The wicked Witch of Hansel and Gretel, then, might be seen in a new light.

To retrace the thread of this tale then, the unmarried elder woman who spins for her sisters, and the evil woman of Webster's definition (evil simply being another term for magick used by those who don't know its secret) are both simply the elder male or female who knows the secret ways of the wise, who has felt and used the power of Magick, and who has experienced all three aspects of the Triple Goddess; youth, midlife, and old age.

And so, another appropriate gift for one upon whom the title of Elder is about to be bestowed is a spindle; not an ordinary spindle, but an enchanted one. To make an enchanted spindle, first purchase an ordinary drop spindle from a fiber craft supplier. Smudge it with the smoke of wormwood or wash it with a wormwood infusion to cleanse it, then tie to the base of its shaft a few feet of your own handspun yarn and begin spinning some fleece on it. If you are not a spinner, just tie a bit of thread to the top of the shaft and spin the spindle, always doesil, chanting words like:

> *Spin Spin*
> *Spindle spin*
> *Round round*
> *Magicks bound.*

While visualizing the spindle glowing with radiant magickal power, spin and chant, chant and spin, until you feel the spell has taken. Then bless the spindle with the four elements and in the sacred names.

One more traditional gift for the elder is the retirement gold watch. This symbol of the Sun and its movement through the 12 signs of the zodiac marks the minutes and the years of our lives. It was given to a boy when he became a man and held the promise of the years that lay ahead. Now it is a reminder of the time that has passed, and how little is left to us as we enter our golden years, but as Pagans we should remember that every ending is a new beginning. Time is a Circle and the spirit never dies.

When we have entered our "golden years," and the greater portion of our life lies in the past, we may begin preparing a place for ourselves in the next life, in the Spirit World.

This is a chore that may take some time, and it also takes an extremely clear idea of what it is that we truly want. To begin the process, choose a time and a place in your home where meditations can be performed on a regular basis, perhaps weekly. Set aside an hour, let's say each Friday evening at

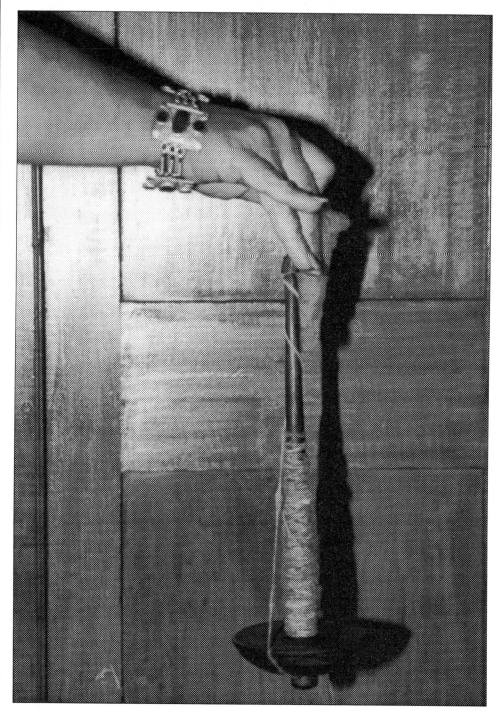

An Enchanted Drop Spindle.

dusk, to sit by the fire and prepare our future home. The traditional way for someone on a shamanic path to enter the world of spirits is through an actual opening on the material plane. This opening, a rabbit hole at the base of a tree, a cave entrance, or a hollow log, is the entrance to the underworld, the dwelling place of the ancestors, which leads to the spirit planes. This entrance place in the physical world is usually selected in advance, before the meditation is begun or the trance is induced. For those of us on a Wiccan path, a more traditional entrance point is a fireplace chimney. If you do not have a chimney, a window, door, or any entrance point you know of on the material plane can be selected. Prior to the appointed time for the meditation, study the place with your physical eyes. Become familiar with it so that you won't have to waste time recreating it during meditation, but do not open it or see what lies beyond. If you do have a fireplace chimney, gaze up it, if possible, while smoke is drifting up.

Now, when the chosen time has arrived, light a candle of violet or white, seat yourself comfortably in the chosen place, take hold of your besom and begin to breath rhythmically. (Some find a drumming tape helpful.) Visualize your chosen entrance point. When you clearly see the entrance before you go through it, you will find yourself in a long earthy tunnel, or chimney. At the far end is a light. Feel yourself drifting, like smoke or mist, toward the light, a light as brilliant as the Sun, but not blinding. There is no need to blink or squint, just go toward the light. Eventually you will find yourself on an open plane, a sunlit meadow of incredible beauty and radiance. Beyond this open meadow are gentle and beautiful hills.

Ask yourself now which way in this land of beauty is home. Go where you feel led until you come to the place that you will recognize. Gaze at it for a few moments. Soak in its feelings. Become familiar with it. In all likelihood, you have seen this place before, in a fleeting vision, or perhaps in a long forgotten dream.

This should be enough for the first visit. Retrace your steps back to the meadow and across it, back to the entrance point, back to your seat by the fire, the flickering candle and the broomstick by your side.

During the time between your regular visits to your home in the spirit world you will be able to plan each visit in advance. There will be much to think about. Is there a dwelling there? A dwelling is not really necessary, but if you feel you will want one, its design is entirely up to you. It might be a stone castle from the time of Arthur, a log cabin from a previous incarnation, a thatched roofed hut right out of a Faerie tale, or just an idealized version of the home you live in and love now. If a dwelling already existed, now is the time to begin cleaning, renovating, and remodeling.

How about the furnishings? Ultimately, your dwelling place in the land of Fee will be furnished with the astral bodies, or ghosts of furniture here on the material plane. You may fill your bookshelves with rare grimoires and herbals, and line your cabinets with jars of roots and barks and magickal herbs.

What were the surroundings like? Now is the time to plant the gardens, and there is nothing that won't grow well in Summerland. Seeds planted now will be the established herb garden, oak grove, or rain forest when you arrive. While the land beyond the veil is without limit or boundary, remember to use only what you really need. You might even draw the garden plans on paper until the gardens are firmly established on the spirit plane, and you can see them clearly and in minute detail on your weekly visits. Then, when the garden is well-grown and the furniture is all in place, burn the plans and charts to ashes so that they may be transformed.

Who else dwells nearby? We all have loved ones on the other side, and they must look forward to being reunited with us just as surely as we long to feel their presence once again. We may prepare a guest cottage for our parents or an extra room for a grandparent, and plenty of places by the hearth for all our dogs and cats.

Each weekly visit should, from this point on, consist of two parts; reexamining the work done on the previous visit so that the details will remain clear in the eye of the mind—study each new planting or furnishing; and second, do the work planned for the present visit—clean a room, stock a shelf, or plant a tree. On every visit be sure to notice any changes that have taken place, and attempt to understand their meaning.

When all the details have been completed and your dwelling place in the Spirit world is just as you want it, you may continue to visit it mentally until the day you finally take up residence there. Just as we plan our homes here in the material world, as places apart, where we wish to spend our lives, to grow old and die, so should we plan our homes in the spirit world, as the place where we will grow young, and eventually leave when we are born again.

As a very wise fortune cookie once said, "Old age does not a sage make, only an old man." Growing old alone does not guarantee wisdom. A life lived sheltered from the world will never give us the knowledge that we seek. Experience is a great teacher, but only if one is open to the wisdom to be gained through the experience. It is important for those of us on the Pagan Path to live our lives as a quest of wisdom, but it is equally as important to recognize wisdom when we find it.

Still, the years of a single lifetime, regardless of the number, or the way in which they were lived, are only truly significant as an extension of a series of lifetimes. For this reason, one very young in years lived in a present lifetime may seem to be what is usually called "wise beyond their years," while others of very advanced age seem to go through life acting in an immature, or even an infantile manner. This is not to say that those who seem to be more wise than others their age are "old souls," or that those whose behavior is less than mature are "new souls"; it is simply to point out that the number of years of a single lifetime, or for that matter a series of incarnations, is really irrelevant. Once again, it is how those years and those lives are lived that is important. One can probably gain great wisdom in a relatively few incarnations, just as one can probably fail to recognize wisdom even after relatively many lifetimes. It is probably just as true that we cannot judge another's "karmic lessons" or "karmic debt" by their behavior. Even those who have the ability to look into the past lives of others can only see the physical acts, they cannot know the deepest thoughts, feelings, and motivations of another. For these reasons we cannot judge others, not in terms of years of age or of lifetimes lived, not in terms of physical behavior or of acts committed, nor do we have the right to. In the end, we can only pass judgment on ourselves by looking deep within.

When we look back over a life lived magickally, whether it has been 60 or 80, or only 10 or 20 years, we can realize that we do control our destinies and that what we wish for is what we get. Unlike others who might have society, karma, or Satan to blame for their problems, those who live a truly magickal or charmed life accept the responsibility for their own lives, and in doing so gain control of their lives and themselves. When we see how we have controlled our past and created our present, we can begin to understand the incredible power we have to control our future in this life, the next, and the one after that.

As we prepare to enter the next world, and the incarnation which will follow that, we might consider the effects of karma. Karma is a Sanskrit word which is intricately entwined with the idea, or the belief in reincarnation, but it is a word, a term, and a concept which is often greatly misunderstood. To begin to truly understand karma, all that is necessary is to examine our own recent past, and how we got to where we are at the present moment. Consider all of those little things that go to make up our present condition. Isolate each one and retrace the steps of how it came to be. Each of those things— our home and personal surrounding, our marriage partner, our career and the degree of its success—probably all began as ideas, desires, wishes, or even fears.

As an example, several years before Dan and I found the old stone farmhouse that came to be Flying Witch Farm, we sat down and had a long discussion. We decided exactly what we wanted in a house. We even made a list of the features we wanted, the number of rooms, the amount of land, it had to be built in the 18th century, and there were some real specifics, like a south-facing slope where Dan could grow wine grapes. Among the features there were two we disagreed about. I wanted a studio/gallery separate from our home, Dan wanted it to be in our home, and I wanted a fireplace in our bedroom. Dan didn't, because he was certain we'd burn up in our bed. We were living in this old house for several years before we found the list of features again, and even a sketch Dan did. The house fits every feature we wanted, and when you're looking for an 18th-century house in our price range then you don't get to be too choosy! But most interestingly, the two features we could not agree on were settled for us over 200 years ago; our studio/gallery is the summer kitchen, a part of the house but with a separate entrance, and there is a fireplace in the bedroom, but it's sealed off!

In the East, the practitioners of Zen have a saying, "Desire generates karma." It is the purpose of this discipline to eliminate any kind of earthly or material desire in order to eliminate karmic debt and achieve Nirvana. Among Pagans and Witches it is exactly the same law, the law of karma, that we use when we practice magick. The more clearly, the more intensely, and the more repeatedly we express our desires magickally, the better magick works, and as we all know, magick always seems to happen naturally. It never (well almost never) occurs instantly, with a puff of pink smoke. Unfortunately it is this same law of karma that we are using, even when we are not working magick, and it is not unlike the law of threefold return.

How many of the situations in our lives presently are the result of wishes made casually, or fleeting thoughts repeated, when we thought the Gods weren't listening? Understanding this, then it is possible to see that the tragedies in our lives can be the result of lifetimes of negative thinking or careless wishing.

We cannot control others, we cannot control the world, but we can control ourselves, and we must begin with our thoughts. As we enter the final years of our life, prepare to pass into the next life and the incarnations that will follow, we can begin to eliminate karma that might accumulate, with a few simple rituals.

At regular intervals at about the same time, or as a part of daily meditation, you might want to do the following ritual. Light a white candle inscribed with the Rune ᛏ and burn a purifying incense and review the previous day or period. If you meditate evenings, review the day that is about to conclude. Each day is usually divided into a series of events. Review each event in terms of emotional reactions. Note the negative responses, feelings of anger, resentment, or fear. Now mentally recreate the event, replacing the negative feelings with positive, more logical ones. This does not mean that you should change your emotional responses to be the opposite of what they are; they just might be expressed in a more positive way. For example the thought, "I hate him!" might be replaced with "don't bother me," or "I probably deserve this" could be replaced with "it beats the alternatives." If you keep a daily diary or journal this is the perfect time to cancel out each negative thought or feeling with a positive one. It does not have to be put into writing, it is a simple mental exercise that can be done as you record the physical event. Finally, on white paper, in red ink, write the negative response in one word. Then in black ink write a positive word over it, and burn the paper in the candle's flame.

As we prepare to write the final chapters in the legend of our life, it is a time to reflect, to look back on a life lived magickally, and one lived in accordance with the law: "An it harm none, do what ye will!"

It is also a time to look forward, to all the rest of our life. Having retired from years of work, our children grown with children of their own, we may now devote ourselves more than ever to the ways of magick, the ways of the Wise. We may once again play, as we did when we were children, only this time the magick will be real.

And we must also look beyond the limit of our years, to the time when we will pass beyond the veil to enter Summerland. We must consider what will become of those physical objects and beings that we will be leaving behind. To begin with, we must make a will. This is a good idea at any age. For those of us who are fortunate to have a family that will continue the tradition of the Craft for us, there will be very little problem. For others there are several things to settle.

First, there are our magickal tools of which to dispose. As Elders, we have already shed many of the trappings that we considered necessary and the tools we now possess are minimal. We may choose to leave our tools to our heirs within the Craft, whether they are our descendants or simply kindred spirits, or we may choose to have certain tools interred with us to confound some future generation of archaeologists. Or, we may simply choose to deconsecrate them, and allow them to retire as we have done, to rejoin the mundane world. Certainly, any object containing a familiar spirit should be destroyed to liberate the entity within. Traditionally, a Witch's Book of Shadows is destroyed upon her death, but it might also remain in the Witch's family. In either case there might be others on the Path with whom certain parts, or the entire book might be shared, and if so then others might be invited to copy these passages before the book is gone.

There is an old rede which states that no Witch can die until she has passed on her knowledge, and considering some of the ways there are to die, its best to heed this warning, I suppose, rather than lingering on the threshold. Of course, for any Witch who has worked with a coven, instructing newcomers to the Old Ways, this task has already been completed: for others who have committed their knowledge to paper in the form of a book, published or not, this also has been accomplished, but for those who have practiced, in solitary, secrets that have been handed down, there is still time to find someone worthy of receiving the knowledge.

Finally, of all things to be considered as we prepare to leave this life and go on to the next, it is those animals that have shared our life and our love, but whom the Gods have decided will outlive us, that most need to be provided for. One way to insure this is to specify in a will as generous an amount of money as possible to provide for the animal for the rest of its natural life-span, the amount to be paid only if these conditions are met.

Regardless of the precautions we take in our lifetime to see to it that our intentions concerning our magickal tools and our beloved pets are carried out, our best insurance is to appoint as executor of our estate, one who is sympathetic to our beliefs and the Old Religion. Having dealt with these considerations, and being assured that our intentions will be carried out should we unexpectedly find ourselves in Summerland, we are free now to celebrate our Elderhood, and live happily ever after.

To celebrate the elderhood of a member of the immediate community or coven, one who, through service to the community or the Old Gods, has earned the title of Elder, regardless of age, the following rite might be used. To prepare for the rite, inscribe or delineate as large a circle as possible. The altar placed in the north will be arranged simply with a cup of wine, a loaf of bread, and the basic elements of the tradition. There should also be the cloak and the staff which will be presented to the Elder.

Before the circle has been consecrated on the night of the Full Moon, a spiral of as many turns as possible (at least three, but as many as nine) shall be arranged with red yarn on the floor or ground within the Circle. Beginning in the east the yarn will spiral to the north, then west, and so on, widdershins around and inward to the center of the Circle where a seat of honor will be placed.

When the rite is about to begin, priest and priestess take their places at the altar within the circle, but not within the spiral. When the circle has been cast in the ways of the coven and the coveners have entered and taken their places about the circle, the priest or priestess, whichever is the opposite sex of the elder, will escort the elder into the Circle, treading the spiral of yarn widdershins (either the pathway between the rows of yarn or with footsteps on either side of the yarn, but not on it) to the center of the Circle where the elder will be seated. If the elder is a woman the priest will then return doesil to the altar and announce something like:

> *Before our high Gods,*
> *Within this Circle*
> *Protected by the Guardian Spirits*
> *Of the four directions,*
> *Do we gather on this night*
> *To honor one among us*
> *Who is worthy of this rite.*

The priestess then replies:

> *Lord and Lady*
> *We have gathered here this night*
> *To honor the one who has been known to us as*
> (Craft name).
> *From this night forward,*
> *In recognition of her service*
> *Unto you, O Mighty Ones,*
> *And to us your children,*
> *Shall she be known as* (new Craft name)

Now the blessing of the loaf and the wine will be performed and priest and priestess will share it with the Elder before passing it to the rest of the coven. When the loaf and the wine have been shared, the priest will take up the cloak, saying something like:

> *Here do I hold the Cloak of Darkness,*
> *With the protection of its Magick*
> *May* (new Craft name)
> *Pass among the Shades and Shadows of the night,*
> *Unharmed by malignant powers,*
> *And move unseen among her enemies by day.*
> *And may its color, black as ebony,*
> *Remind us all that she is now sister to the Crone.*
> (he is now brother, if the Elder is a man,
> of the Holly King, etc.)

Now the priest places the black cloak of the Crone about the shoulders of the Elder. He stands by her side while the priestess takes up the staff, saying words like:

> *Here do I hold the Tree of Life*
> *Whose trunk connects the Three Worlds,*
> *Of Above, Below, and Middle.*
> *As* (Elder's new name) *came to these ways*
> *Like the youthful Fool, bearing the burdens*
> *Of the mundane world, now is she relieved*
> *Of her burdens. Having followed the ways of the Wise.*
> *Now does she wield the Staff of Wisdom.*
> *Let it symbolize to us that she is free*
> *To go her way and merry part,*
> *Or like the Hermit on the hill,*
> *Remain a beacon in the night.*

The priestess then presents the Staff to the Elder. The priest then takes up the end of the yarn nearest the center of the Circle and, handing it to the Elder, says something like:

> *You who have sat at the center of the Circle,*
> *Long may the thread of your life be.*
> *Take and wind it as you will,*
> *And live happily ever after.*

Then priest and priestess slowly escort the Elder doesil, around and around the spiral as the Elder winds the yarn as a spinster would, (the priestess will have to hold her staff as the winding will take two hands). When the spiral is complete the three return to the altar and the elder places the cord on the altar, takes up the bowl of salted water and blesses the priest and priestess, making the sign of the Sun wheel on their foreheads with her forefinger, and then blesses the rest of the coven likewise and they present her with gifts or tokens of respect.

The following rite has been designed to celebrate the passage into Elderhood by virtue of age, of any member of the Pagan community, regardless of any goals that might have been achieved.

Sixty-five is generally accepted as retirement age, and as the age that one passes from midlife into elderhood. This is entirely compatible with magickal thinking, because, as we came of age at about 13 years, or one times 13 years of age, we entered Midlife at about 39, or three times 13 years of age, and now we enter elderhood at 65 or five times 13 years of age. To celebrate this passage into what some call our "golden years," everything about the rite should be of black and silver and gold. The black is to remind us of the Crone aspect of the Goddess with which the celebrant is about to be identified, and of the spirit world nearby; the silver reminds us of the Triple Goddess of the Moon, who is the measurer of time on a monthly basis; and the gold is a reminder of the Sun which measures time on a yearly and on a daily basis.

On a night of the Full Moon nearest the celebrant's 65th birthday, in the center of the Circle, a long table will have been arranged, long enough for all of those gathered to be comfortably seated. This table may be covered with a cloth of black and adorned with gold candlesticks, black candles, and silver cups.

At one end of the table a seat of honor has been placed. At the other end a small altar has been set up with the tools and symbols of the tradition. The priest or priestess, whoever is the opposite sex of the one being honored, will be seated at this end. If the one about to become an Elder is a man, then the priestess will preside, her priest sitting next to her on the right.

When the Circle has been cast and the coveners have entered the Circle according to the ways of the tradition, the celebrant is escorted to the seat of honor as the priestess, standing, announces something like:

> We have gathered this night
> Within this Circle
> To honor one who is about to pass
> From Midlife into Elderhood.

Priestess and priest then bless the cakes and wine according to their tradition, and after the libations each covener receives some of the wine in her or his cup, and the celebrant receives a large portion. Then the priestess drinks to the honor of the Gods and the Elder, toasting him with words like:

> To the glory of the Old Gods
> And to the honor of one
> Who has served them long and well
> Do I drink this blessed wine.

And after taking a sip she continues :

> To mark this passage,
> Shall the one who has been known to us,
> As (old Craft name), from this night on
> Be known as (new name) to us,
> And to the mighty Gods!
> Hail (new name)!

And the coveners repeat the salute. Then the priestess continues

> As this wine has become fine with age
> So has our brother (new name)
> Refined and attuned himself
> With each turning of the Sun Wheel.
> And it is this which we celebrate this night.

To this, the priestess might add some comments about her personal experiences with the Elder. Then the covener to her left will toast the Elder by his new name, sipping some of the blessed wine, a gesture returned by the Elder; and the covener will recall his or her experiences with the Elder, presenting him with some symbolic token of the event. This will continue doesil around the table until the Circle is complete and the final toast is left to the priest, who will also present the Elder with a token amulet, such as a gold watch, that will mark the occasion for all time.

The priest might conclude his remarks with words like:

As our brother (name), *on this night*
Enters the realm of the Crone,
Let us all remember that our lives
Are measured by the turning
Of the Golden Wheel
And the spinning of
The Silver Cord.
Elder (name) *we wish you long life*
And happily ever after!

And the coven replies;

So Mote it be!

And now, having received a new name to mark the passage, and an amulet of Elderhood, the newly made Elder might thank the coveners for the honors they have bestowed upon him, and the Gods for the years of life that have been given, and for those that are yet to come.

The autumn days grow shorter, and there is a strange, familiar chill in the air. Lengthening shadows slowly creep across the landscape of our lives as we hurry to gather the last fruits, the final harvest, before grim cold winter freezes hard the earth. The golden years and sunny days of our lives fly away like dry leaves in the autumn breezes.

Chapter Eight

The Final Passage

The Final Passage

The Sun of late October sinks in the Western sky. As purple shadows lengthen into night and Jack-O-Lanterns smile their smile of candle-light to welcome wandering spirits, little children with painted faces and colorful costumes shuffle through fallen leaves to beg "trick or treat" from door to door. In earlier times these children might have been begging "a soul cake, a soul cake," a Christian echo of a far more ancient practice, on this the most sacred night of the Pagan year.

When the Jack-O-lantern's candle has burned down, when the pale Moon has risen high in the midnight sky, and the wind sighs down the chimney in the wake of the Crone, in the homes of the followers of the Old Faith, little offerings have been lovingly left for the spirits of recently deceased loved ones. By hearth-sides or lounge chairs, at dinner tables, or on TV trays are offerings of a favorite food and drink; a slice of crusty bread and a glass of red wine for a father, a square of carrot cake and a cup of tea for a grand-mother, all are lovingly placed by a favorite seat, because on this night of nights the veil between the worlds is very thin and the spirits of loved ones on the other side can easily pass through.

It is this same veil that every child of the Gods, each one of us, must part and pass through at the end of every lifetime. And it is this final passage that is celebrated in almost every culture as a Feast-of-the-Dead.

In Egypt candles are lit to guide the spirits of the deceased back from the City of Osiris. In Japan, candlelit paper lanterns are hung on garden gates to welcome the spirits of the ancestors. Families pack picnics and take them to cemeteries, where a pleasant day is spent picnicking and cleaning graves. When the day is done, a fond farewell is bid the spirits, and they are sent off with paper lanterns lit to guide them, set adrift on rivers and streams and ocean waves. In Tahiti, on the feast-of-the-dead, graves are covered with fresh white sand.

Bidding the Final Farewell.

When the Spanish arrived in Mexico, conquering and converting the native population, and enforcing the celebration of Christian holidays, the date of November 2nd was given as All Souls Day. This date, which was adapted by the church from Pagan Celts in the first place, was perfectly acceptable to the Mexican natives, because it coincided exactly with their Day-of-the-Dead, *El Dia de los Muertos.*

The Mexican celebration actually begins on October 31st, when women spend the day preparing special foods and treats, while men prepare small altars of clay upon which the food and toys are placed. At midnight ,it is believed, the Angelitos, spirits of children that have died, come and take the essence of the offerings.

Meanwhile women are busy preparing a greater feast for the spirits of deceased adults who arrive by the following dawn. For this celebration, altars are more elaborate, and are decorated with marigolds and with skulls made of bread or marzipan; they were once decorated with the actual skulls of ancestors. And everywhere are the *Calaveras,* mementos of death. Neighbors and relatives visit one another to speak lovingly of the deceased, who are by now close about. As the day draws to a close, meals are eaten and the candles are extinguished. November 2nd, The Day-of-the-Dead, is spent quietly until evening, when every member of the community gathers food, tequila, and candles for a candlelight procession to the village cemetery, accompanied by musicians. Here, after a mass is said by the village priest, the villagers gather by their family graves to rest and share food with their departed loved ones, celebrating together until midnight.

Our own American Feast of the Dead, Halloween, has its roots in the Celtic festival of Samhain, and our many traditions have their ancient origins, some obvious and some quite obscure. The tradition of Trick or Treat, with its costuming and masking, probably was at one time the begging for Soul Cakes, an English Christian tradition, which almost certainly originated in earlier Pagan times as wassailing, or the begging from door to door practiced at Yule, in which children acted as proxies for the spirits of the deceased to whom offerings could be made. This Samhain tradition, moved to the Winter Solstice, has its counterpart in the Beltane, or May Day processions of Europe in which children also beg treats from door to door in exchange for fertility. The costuming and masking come down to us from the shamanistic practice of wearing and dancing about in the skins and horns of animals slain for food which needed to be appeased, a practice vehemently opposed by the early church.

The Jack-O-Lantern, the fat, orange pumpkin with flaming eyes and jagged teeth is, of course, the American version of the candle lit as a beacon for the wandering spirits who are trying to find their way home. In Egypt, Mexico, and Ireland, candles are used. In Japan paper lanterns, and in western Europe, it is said, turnips were carved and used as lanterns on All Hallows Eve. There are many old German Halloween decorations that depict a man made of vegetables, with a deep red turnip for a head. Turnips, along with other root crops such as carrots and potatoes, and the vegetables in the Cole family; cabbages, cauliflower, Brussel sprouts, etc. are all seasonal vegetables which were grown for winter storage and as a vital food supply. In Europe figures of "vegetable men" were made as Halloween ornaments and represent the Foliate God fully ripened. He is a close relative to the sacrificed God of the Grain, and his American counterpart, the adorable scarecrow, stuffed with straw and smiling the benevolent smile of Ray Bolger who protected Dorothy from the Wicked Witch of the West in the Land of Oz, is none other than The Wicker Man. He may be disguised as Guy Fawkes, who, in 1605, attempted to blow up The House of Lords, and who has been-burned in effigy on November 5th ever since, replacing the spiritual Samhain fires of the Celts with the political bonfires of Britain, but he is still the sacrificed Son of the Great Mother, the Vegetation God who, though cut down at the harvest will rise up again in the spring fresh and new and green, so that the cycle may be repeated. He is the Lord of Death and Resurrection.

In an attempt to convert our Pagan ancestors to the new religion by giving Christian names to our Pagan sabbats, Samhain, the Celtic Feast-of-the-Dead became All Souls Day, a day on which the souls of all the martyred

"Calaveras" used in the Mexican celebration of the Feast of the Dead.

Christians were honored and remembered. By some strange coincidence, today, as more and more of us are finding our way back to the Old Religion, and reclaiming the old traditions, Halloween seems to be the time when we not only celebrate the Feast-of the-Dead in honor of our recently deceased ancestors, but of our spiritual ancestors as well who were martyred, tortured and murdered for their faith, the Old Religion.

One of the fundamental beliefs of the Old Religion is the eternal cycle of birth, death, and rebirth. The spirit never dies, but when physical death occurs the spirit is reborn into another world where it continues to exist, a world much like this one, until it is reborn again into physical life.

To the followers of ancient ways this world of spirit has many names. To Norse Pagans it is known as Hel, the underworld, or Valhalla, the hall of the Valiant who died heroically in battle. To English Pagans it is Annwyn, or Avalon, the Isle of Apples, where it is always summer and where one's youth is restored. To others it is Caer Arrianrod, the Castle of the Silver Wheel, presided over by Arrianrod, Goddess of Death, who is probably the same Goddess as Ariadne, wife of Dionysus, Greek God of Resurrection, and who was abandoned by him on the Isle of Naxos, which might be the Isle of Nixos, Night or Darkness. To the Greeks the after-world was known as Hades, presided over by Hades, or his Roman counterpart Pluto, where Dionysus defied death and won resurrection for all mankind. Later Greeks divided the world of the after-life into several areas, the most wonderful of which is the Elyssian Fields, a place where the deceased found true bliss. The Irish deity Manannan, usually thought of as a sea God, presides over his land "beyond the sea." While the Isle of Mann was named for him, his land is probably the Irish counterpart of Avalon.

Manannan feeds the Gods in his land beyond the sea, the flesh of pigs which renew themselves as soon as they are eaten. This sounds remarkably like the feasting which takes place in Valhalla nightly, on the flesh of a pig which each morning is reborn.

All of these places, almost without exception, are located across a river, or across the sea. The Norse Hel is approached by Bifrost, the rainbow bridge; while Avalon, Manannan's land beyond the sea, and even Ariadne's Isle of Naxos, are clearly islands. Hades' or Pluto's underworld is approached through a cave, but is still surrounded by the River Styx. The Egyptian Necropolis, or City of the Dead, is across the Nile River to the West, and to Eastern Europeans, the land of spirits lies across a vast ocean that all the rivers of the world flow into.

What is it like, this land beyond the sea, this Isle of Avalon, or Summerland? According to mythology, it can vary from a dark place of silence and of shadows, to a beautiful landscape of bright sunshine, sparkling water, green grass and flowers, trees and hills of unspeakable beauty, filled with exquisite music and peopled by radiant beings. It is a place where it is always warm, and there is always plenty to eat, where heroes can fight their battles again and again, and the hunter and the hunted can dwell together in harmony and bliss.

This description seems to be supported by those who have clinically died, gone to another plane of existence, and then were revived and lived to tell of their experiences. What is most remarkable about these accounts is the amazing similarity between them. With almost no exception, these people have found themselves first free of their body, and then suddenly being propelled through a dark tunnel toward a bright light at its end. The majority then describe a radiant landscape of exquisite beauty, filled with the fragrance of flowers, and the music of the universe; a place where they wish to go and never return, where all pain is gone, and all wisdom is given. Most who are given the privilege of a preview of Summerland are greeted by loved ones who have gone on before, and, most convincingly, a number have encountered those who had died, but whose deaths could not possibly have been known, unless they met in spirit. These loved ones usually appear radiant, and in the prime of their lives, healthy and youthful, even though they may have died of a wasting illness or advanced old age. Ultimately, the spirit traveler is convinced by their deceased loved ones, or thoughts of loved ones left behind, to return to their physical body and the world of mundane reality. The majority of those who have had this experience, however, are changed for life. They no longer fear death, and are able to live a life free of fear.

The image of the light at the end of the tunnel seems to be a consistent one, and sounds very much like a description of birth; of being propelled from the warm, safe darkness of the womb through the birth canal into the cold, bright light of a physical, independent existence. It is usually with reluctance that we are born into this life, and we enter it crying and screaming; but for those who have gone through the tunnel, to be born into the world of spirit which we call death, it is with peace and with willingness.

Perhaps those shadowy areas in the underworld are for those who have tried to turn back to the world of physical reality.

Perhaps these are the spirits that haunt, but for those who enter the world of spirit, every ending is a new beginning.

An abiding belief in an afterlife has caused Pagan people all over the world to bury with their loved ones all that they will need in the life that follows death. The earliest known burials were done by the Neanderthals, 40,000–70,000 years ago. They buried their dead, and presumably loved ones, on their sides in the fetal position, which strongly suggests a belief in rebirth. These burials also include tools and joints of meat, and in one famous Neanderthal burial site in a cave in Iraq, the corpse was apparently strewn with eight different species of flowers, including wild relatives of the bachelor's button and hollyhock. All eight species of flowers are still used in that part of the world today for their medicinal properties. The tradition of funeral flowers is an ancient one, indeed.

"Give my spirit beer and onions," states an ancient Egyptian prayer. Food was probably the most common grave offering ever made, since the first Neanderthal lovingly placed a joint of meat beside a corpse. While the food itself has not survived, the containers in which it was buried appear in a great many grave sites. The ancient Egyptians placed baskets of food in the tombs of their dead, and also built funerary temples adjacent to some tombs, where offerings could continue to be made. In prehistoric burial mounds of North America, bones of deer, elk, squirrel, wild turkey, geese, swans, ducks, and many species of fish are found. The food offered varied from culture to culture, but it was probably the staple food of the living that was placed in the graves for the dead as well.

Even when food was placed in a grave, the tools necessary to hunt, gather, and prepare food were often included as well. The ancient people who have been named the Maritime Archaic, and who fished and hunted marine mammals in the icy waters of the Atlantic from Maine to the Arctic Circle, have left a wealth of grave goods to testify to this. In one site known as the Nevin Site, in Maine, the harpoons and bone dagger found, all decorated with geometric designs of aligned drill holes connected by incised lines, may have been more ceremonial than practical. In other sites in Maine, delicately decorated plummets, or net sinkers, and polished slate gouges used for boat-making, were discovered ceremonially arranged. Other sites contain lance points and barbed harpoons as well as highly stylized stone effigies of killer whales. What is interesting about these stone carvings is that the dorsal fin of the orca is so exaggerated as to be the same size as the front end and back end of the whale. If it were not for the delicate facial features on these carvings they would give the appearance of a three-pointed star. None of these sites, however, contained skeletal remains, due to the acidity of the New England soil, and so it was not known if these sites were actually burials until the discovery in 1968 of another similar site in Port-au-Choix, Labrador, which did contain skeletons, proving that these were grave sites. What it was that all of these sites had in common was that they all contained similar artifacts related to deep sea fishing and marine mammal hunting, and they all contained large amounts of red ochre, about which more will be said shortly. These sites have been radio-carbon dated to 7,000 to 7,500 years old. This culture has been compared to simular cultures along the coasts of Norway and Denmark, but they are probably not related. They were apparently a people with a shamanistic belief system and were megalith builders.

In the courtyard of an ancient temple at Cuello in Belize, in Central America, archaeologists have made some interesting discoveries. It was the

Pre-Columbian grave goods. The smaller two vessels contained offerings of copal.

Mayan practice to rebuild their temples periodically, each new temple being built around the previous one, so that at the core of every temple is its earliest section. As the archaeologists dug into the graves in the courtyard at Cuello, they found some of the graves containing collections of pottery bowls; and the food containers also contained some remnants of the corn that was the basic food of the Mayan people. As they dug down through layer upon layer of grave sites, the earliest, of course, being the deepest, they realized that they were digging down through the history of corn itself. The corn in each successive level of graves was an earlier variety, dating back over 4,000 years.

Just outside the stone chamber of a Sumerian tomb in Ur were found the bones of animals which had been left as offerings. At a Celtic cemetery unearthed at Hallstatt in Germany, and dating to the Iron Age (ca. 700 B.C.E.), almost a thousand graves were excavated. The majority of them contained vessels or bowls that may have contained food, as well as animal bones, suggesting that meat was placed in the graves. There were also tools and weapons of both bronze and iron.

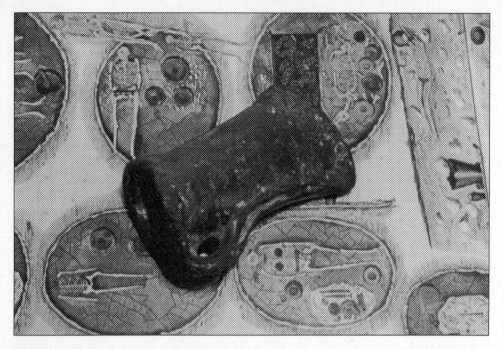

A miniature bronze ax head from a Celtic burial near London. In the background is a 19th-century drawing of the Celtic burials at Hallstatt, Germany.

While many of the weapons and hunting tools found in graves are of stone or flint, iron, or bronze, and may be the actual weapons or tools used by the individual in life, some seem to be more ceremonial than practical. For example, miniature hollow bronze axe-heads have been found in graves in Britain. From a La Téne (Celtic 5th century B.C.E.) burial there is a shield of thin, beaten bronze, inlaid with red glass. There is also the gold dagger with its richly ornamented hilt and sheath found in the tomb of Tutankhamen, and there is the gold dagger with a solid lapis lazuli hilt adorned with gold studs and protected by a sheath of gold openwork found in a shaft grave in Ur, in Sumeria. It is possible that the highly decorated bone harpoons and daggers found in the Maritime archaic mound burials of New England and Labrador were more ceremonial than practical. All of these objects seem to bring to mind the athames of today's Wiccans, which are never to cut anything but air.

Along with weapons, jewelry is among the most universal of grave offerings. This instantly brings to mind, once again, the 1350 B.C.E. tomb of Tutankhamen and the fabulous jewelry found within it; the gold collar in the form of the vulture Goddess Nekhbet, inlaid with colored glass, the solid gold vulture necklace filled with tiny pieces of red and blue glass, the gold pectoral with a winged scarab, its green chalcedony body and inlaid wings supporting a solar boat of gold and lapis, and golden falcon inlaid with red and blue glass and holding the symbols for life and infinity in its talons. There are also the headdress of Queen Shub-ad, whose tomb of 3000 B.C.E. was in Ur. These consist of beech leaves of beaten gold, suspended from strands of lapis and carnelian beads, clusters of three gold willow leaves suspend from a four strand band of lapis beads, gold discs with lapis centers on strands of lapis beads and tiny gold rings hung from a triple strand of red carnelian and lapis beads. A crown of gold laurel leaves adorned the head of a warrior's wife in a Thracian tomb of 4000 B.C.E. A few thousand years later, in the same part of southeastern Europe, King Philip of Macedonia, father of Alexander the Great, was buried and with him his crown of pure gold oak leaves and acorns, symbols of the Oak God. Beside him was his wife and her crown of exquisitely delicate gold myrtle blossoms, sacred to the Goddess of Love and Beauty.

In the rich singular burials in the round barrows that are contemporary with Stonehenge, individuals of apparently high rank were buried with much finery, including beaten gold breast plates and belt buckles. In the La Téne culture first discovered in Switzerland, torques of gold and silver were found only in the graves of women, suggesting that men passed theirs on to

Burial beads from three ancient cultures: (left to right) pre-Columbian, Egyptian, and Sumerian.

their sons. In the oak coffin burials of Bronze Age Denmark have been found wonderful examples of bronze ornaments, including many pins which work like modern safety pins, and other articles of jewelry adorned with spirals. The earliest examples of gold treasure ever discovered buried in a grave were found in a large cemetery not far from Varna, in what is today Bulgaria. The find is about 6,000 years old. The ornaments include rings and beads, some highly stylized horned animals that are perforated, probably in order to be attached to clothing, and a large number of ornaments that seem to resemble pairs of goats' horns.

So far, we seem to have been discussing the burial jewelry of the rulers and nobility, but in most cultures even the poorest commoner would have some ornaments or jewelry buried with them.

For the ancient Sumerians there were clay burial beads of black, white, and grey. For the ancient Egyptians there were beads of faience in shades of white, tan, and turquoise. Some say the sand of Egypt is filled with it. Among the pre-Columbian people of Central and South America, there were burial beads of terracotta in shades of pink, tan, red and brown, and there were large beads of jadeite and quartz, carnelian, and shell. The Mound Builders of North America buried with their dead thousands of shell beads, ornaments of mica, fresh-water pearls, and wooden ornaments covered with copper foil. For many of the early people of Europe there were beads of amber and necklaces of wolves teeth and seashells.

An Egyptian frog lamp, and a funerary cone
inscribed with prayers for the deceased.

Colima Dogs

Aside from jewelry and weapons, food and storage vessels, other practical items were included among grave offerings. Greek and Roman makers of clay oil lamps made special miniature lamps to be buried with the deceased, to light their way to the next world. Many of the Roman period lamps found in Egyptian tombs are decorated with the images of frogs. In the Colima culture of South America, small figures of dogs were buried with the dead to act as their guides from this world to the next.

In addition to lamps and dogs to light or guide the way into the next world, the deceased was often provided with a vehicle with which to make the journey. For the majority of Pagan cultures, the afterworld was believed to be located beyond a large body of water, and so, for the most practical of purposes a boat was often provided for the journey of the deceased. Possibly the oldest examples of these are to be found in Northwest Thailand. Here, far from any physical body of water, high up a hillside in a dense tropical jungle is a place that is called Spirit Cave. Deep in a recess of Spirit Cave, where now only bats dwell, are to be found a number of wooden boats. Each of these boats has been hewn from a single tree and measure 14 feet long by 2 feet wide. Each has been intentionally placed in an east-west position. These boats were used as coffins and the earliest of them date to 12,000 years old. There seems to be evidence that Spirit Cave was used as a burial site for 10,000 years.

According to an ancient Norse myth, one day in the far-distant past a small boat containing an infant lying on a bed of corn drifted ashore. He was named Scyld Scefing by the country folk who found him, and he grew up to be king. When he died he was given a Viking's funeral. As he came into this world, so he left it, set adrift in a boat, his body surrounded with weapons and with treasure. Viking funerals are legendary. Heroes' bodies were arranged in ships surrounded with all their worldly possessions, weapons, and all the foods of a feast, and the ship was put to sea, often first being set ablaze. Not all such ship funerals were set adrift. In 1880, a small Viking ship was discovered buried in Vestfed, Sweden. It is believed to be the tomb of King Olaf Geirsta-da-Alf, and is one of a number of ship burials in northern Europe. There have also been found in cemeteries graves that are shaped like boats.

In ancient Egypt "Spirit Boats" were placed in tombs. These boats were believed to rise in spirit, carrying the Ka, or spirit, of the deceased, along with the immortals to accompany the Sun God, Ra, on his journey into the underworld each night. Also called the solar ships of night, these "spirit boats" were usually small models made of wood and clay, but in 1854, in a secret chamber at the base of the Great Pyramid, 100 feet below ground level, a full-sized Egyptian ship was discovered. It is almost certain that the boat was built by Cheops or Kufu, the fourth dynasty king whose reign was about 2,800 B.C.E.

In other cultures, however, other vehicles besides boats were provided. Celtic tombs, for example, sometimes contain chariots ornamented with gold.

Death masks are an almost universal grave offering, and may have served to magickally preserve the facial features of the deceased in the next world. We are all familiar with the spectacular mask of deep blue glass and beaten gold that covered the face of the boy king, Tutankhamen. Lesser known Egyptians had death masks of "cartonage," or painted plaster, usually a portrait of them done in life. The nobility of South America had death masks covered with bits of jade, while some natives of North America had death masks of stone or wood. When Heinrich Schleimann discovered, in his digs in Mycenae, the beaten gold death masks of ancient Greek nobility, he wrote, "I have gazed upon the face of Agamemnon" (which he hadn't, because the grave site turned out to be far to early). In many of the 6,000-year-old tombs in Bulgaria there have been found clay masks with gold features and ornaments, which may be likenesses of the deceased or images of the Mother Goddess, buried to insure rebirth.

Of all of the objects found buried in ancient tombs, surely the most fascinating to us are those with a purely magickal intent.

The Woodland Indians of the central basin of the United States built grand burial and ceremonial mounds. In some of these mysterious amulets called bird stones and boat stones have been found, and there are fetishes which represent the four directions; the mountain lion–North, the white wolf–East, the badger–South, and the black bear–West.

In a Bronze Age mound burial north of Copenhagen, Denmark was discovered the traces of the body of a man with his sword placed across his chest. He had worn a twisted gold band on his left wrist, and pinned to his garment, over his heart, was the remains of a leather pouch and its contents. Among these were a bronze knife with a crooked blade, a flint blade stitched up in leather so that it could not be used for cutting, and a stick of wood, wound around with strips of skin. While these objects may not be of great importance to archaeologists, to the Wiccan or Pagan reader of the description of such a find, it is quite clear that these are ritual objects similar to our own athames and wands. In another Bronze Age burial mound, along with the burned remains of a man, was found a leather bag, remarkable in itself because it was closed with what might be the world's first zipper. This bag contained such items as an amber bead, a conch shell, a flint flake, a falcon's claw, a cube of wood, and an assortment of roots and bark, as well as many other items, including another flint knife stitched into a length of intestine. Bags with similar contents have been found in about 30 Bronze Age graves throughout Denmark. Some of the items in this bag come very close to sounding as if they might represent the four elements; the cube of wood, the falcon's claw, the flint, and the conch shell might represent respectively, Earth, Air, Fire, and Water.

In other mound burials have been found miniature bronze figures of a horse drawing a wagon, and upon the wagon is a bronze solar disc. Both the horse and the wagon have wheels which are Sun wheels, a rim with four spokes which join in the center at a round hole. The only surviving solar disc is covered on one side only with beaten gold, and on the dark bronze side is a spiral design. This would suggest that the solar disc, depending upon which side is shown, represented the waning or the waxing Sun, or death and rebirth. Paintings in other tombs suggest that annual rites held at Midsummer and midwinter involved actual horses drawing a wagon bearing a solar disc of some kind. Furthermore, these rites may have taken place on the flattened tops of some of the burial mounds themselves. In still another of these tombs a bronze drum has been discovered, its head ornamented with concentric rings, between which are straight lines forming sharp angles, suggesting the radiant power of the Sun. The drum is supported by ten Sun wheels around its base. This drum and other pieces like it originated in southeastern Europe. Its symbolism found its way to the Danube delta and into Denmark, both named for the Goddess Dan, or Danu. Here women of the Mound builders wore the bronze Sun wheel as a dress pin and introduced its design into central Europe. Here, too, people buried their dead in hollow oak log coffins, within sacred ceremonial mounds. Perhaps this symbolized, as it does elsewhere, the active male principle of the Oak and Sun

God planted in the earth mound womb of the Mother Goddess, and the union of the two assuring the rebirth of the deceased.

No other culture has more magick surrounding death and the afterlife then the Egyptian. Even the pre-dynastic Neolithic Egyptians made amulets of shist, some in animal form, and laid them on the breast of the deceased. A book could be written on the subject of Egyptian burial rites, and in fact, it has. It is the Egyptian Book of the Dead, and it contains prayers and charms for every step of the ritual that the deceased must perform as he passes from this life to the next. A similar book is the Tibetan book of the Dead.

While the Egyptian rituals surrounding the preparation of the body and tomb can fill volumes, I shall mention only a few. First, vital organs were removed from the body cavity, and four of these were placed in containers called canopic jars. The lids of these jars are carved to represent animal heads; and the jar containing the stomach had the head of a jackal, the jar containing the lungs had the head of a baboon, the one containing the intestines had the head of a falcon, and the one containing the liver had a human head on its lid. These four heads and prayers inscribed on the jars invoked the protective powers of the four sons of Ra, the Sun God, and small amulets of these four heads on the figures of mummies were also stitched into the wrappings of the mummy for added power.

The heart was removed from the body, and in its place a large scarab inscribed with prayers was placed within the wrappings. The heart was sought by Annubis, the Priest God of the Dead, and taken to be weighed against the Goddess Maat's Feather of Truth, before the deceased was allowed entrance into the afterlife.

The symbol of the scarab is an interesting one. The insect rolls a ball of elephant dung with its hind legs into a hole it has previously dug. Within the hole, underground, the female deposits her eggs on the ball of dung, which the larvae feed upon after hatching. Twenty-nine days later new scarabs emerge from the underworld, no doubt symbolizing to the ancient Egyptians, as it would to us, the miracle of resurrection.

It was believed by these ancient people that life in the afterworld was much like it is in this one; that grain had to be planted, irrigated, and harvested. In order to avoid the toil and labor of agriculture in the afterlife, Egyptians had buried with them, small mummiform figures called *Ushabti*. In the tombs of the nobility small boxes containing 365 Ushabti might be buried, one for each day of the year, but in the tombs of the less fortunate, fewer were placed. It was expected that these Ushabti, when properly enchanted or inscribed, would take the place of the deceased if he or she were called upon to toil in the fields of the afterlife.

There are three other amulets which were of great importance in Egyptian tombs; the Ankh, the Djed tower (see artist's rendition on page 217), and

Amulets of the four sons of Ra, made to be stitched into mummy wrappings.

Ushabti

the amulet of Anubis. The ankh is the Amulet of Life, and every Egyptian god seems to carry it. The Djed tower has been interpreted as representing the backbone and ribs of the God Osiris, but an earlier interpretation is that it represents the hollowed tree trunk in which Isis hid the slain body of Osiris to protect it for all eternity, and the four bars at the top represent the four directions to which she traveled in search of his severed parts after Set had scattered them.

This interpretation brings to mind the legend of the spell cast over the wizard Merlin by the enchantress Morgana, who then hid him in the trunk of a hollow oak tree. This Arthurian legend suggests that the Queen of the Faeries did not kill the wizard, but enchanted him, and one day the hollow oak will open and the wizard will return from the Land of Faerie. This story calls to mind the oak coffin burials of Denmark and Northern Europe.

But to return to the amulet of the Djed Tower; the amulet had to be dipped in water in which certain flowers had been steeped, and then placed on the throat of the mummy so that the deceased would become a perfect spirit in the afterworld. One ancient papyrus shows an ankh rising up from a Djed tower, with the disc of the Sun above it, seeming to symbolize life rising anew from the Djed.

And finally, the amulet of Anubis is not, as one might expect, a representation of a jackel, but of the inflated skin of an animal hung from a post which terminates in a lotus bud. This enigmatic symbolism might refer to an ancient ritual which was performed annually in Egypt to unite the Pharaoh with the God Osiris, in order to renew his vitality, and in so doing insure the fertility of the land. In this ritual the pharaoh symbolically died, was laid out and mourned, and then was ritually reborn by being wrapped in the skin of a cow symbolizing the Goddess Nut, "The Cow of the Heavens," who is also painted on the ceilings of some Egyptian tombs.

Could there possibly be any connection between this ritual rebirth known as the Egyptian Mysteries, and the fact that the majority of bodies buried in oak log coffins in the mounds of Northern Europe are wrapped in cow or ox hides? If so, then the cow hide almost certainly was placed in these graves to insure rebirth, or reincarnation.

On the other side of the world, among the Mayans, a similar grave offering was made, and its intent was clearly to insure rebirth. These people are known for their incredible and intricate weavings filled with symbolic figures, and among these is a fragment of a burial shroud which shows a human figure within the womb of a much larger figure. Later, the descendants of the Maya, who have continued the ancient crafts of spinning and weaving, have produced figures known as grave dolls. Dressed in the ancient textiles and adorned with parrot feathers, these figures are of a mother with a child on her back, and one in her arms or belly.

Fragment of a Mayan burial shroud, showing rebirth symbolism.

These grave dolls seem to suggest a strong belief in rebirth and some sort of magickal ritual to insure it. They also seem to echo the Cycladic figures found in graves in the Greek Islands of the Cyclades. These highly stylized figures, eagerly sought by collectors of antiquities, are usually discovered in pairs in the graves where they are found, and one of the pair is usually larger than the other. This has caused some archaeologists to call them Mother and Daughter figures. They were probably intended to represent Demeter and Persephone, "The Two who are One," and no doubt were buried with the deceased to insure their return from the underworld, just as Persephone returns to Demeter every Spring.

In the Maritime Archaic mound burials of New England and Labrador, mentioned earlier in this chapter, there is another grave offering that must surely have been placed in those graves to insure that life would return to the deceased. That is the mineral pigment red ochre. This pigment was sprinkled so liberally in the ancient graves that 7,000 years later, after a heavy rain, red ochre was still bubbling to the surface, forming pools that looked as "though filled with blood." In fact, it was these "pools of blood" that led to the discovery of the burials in the first place. This is not the only culture to use red ochre ritually in a burial. Later, in historic times, the Delaware Indians who in prehistoric times had wrapped the bodies of their dead in sheets of bark, buried their dead in log coffins in which a notch was cut near the head. This notch was filled with red ochre. In Lebanon, the dismembered bones of deer were discovered arranged on a bed of stones, and covered with the powdered red pigment. There can be little doubt that this ritual grave was intended as a shamanistic rite to insure the re-birth of the deer.

Red ochre is a powdered or pulverized ore of iron, usually Hematite, which was discovered thousands of years later to yield the metal, but which was used in the meantime for its magickal properties. Red ochre not only looks like blood, it *is* the red pigment in blood, and it is the pigment that was sometimes used to magickally give life to Runes. Chemically, red ochre is iron-oxide, and it is this same pigment that is used today to make the artist's color "Indian Red," whether it is oil paint, acrylic, casien, or water color. The easiest way to obtain the pigment today for magickal purposes is to purchase a tube of Indian Red watercolor. It can be made into a liquid by putting a dab in a container, adding water, and stirring until the desired consistency and amount is obtained, or it can be made into a powder by emptying an amount onto a nonporous surface and allowing it to dry thoroughly, then crushing it with a mortar and pestle. This then can be used to give life to magick spells, or it can be sprinkled or scattered on or in graves, as it was in ancient times to insure rebirth.

While all of these grave offerings were made in order to provide the loved one with all that would be needed in the next life, as well as insuring that the deceased would eventually be reborn into the tribe from which he or she had departed, probably the most important offering of all was the grave itself.

While it is difficult to know exactly what a Neanderthal tomb looked like when it was finished, the majority of stone age tombs were probably simple earthen mounds. The symbolism of burying a body in the earth, from which all life comes, combined with a belief in rebirth or reincarnation, expressed itself in many ways.

In ancient Sumeria where Ishtar was Goddess, and where she descended into the underworld and returned, the royal burials at Ur were in shaft tombs. Here a great square pit was dug with an earthen ramp to reach the bottom level, where a domed tomb or miniature house was built to receive the body of the deceased, along with grave offerings and human attendants. Of the 1,000 graves discovered at the cemetery of Ur, about 16 were royal tombs, the rest surrounding them were the tombs of commoners.

In ancient Greece there were built tombs called "beehives," of corbelled stones placed layer upon layer in ever-decreasing circles—so that the tombs

A Mayan "grave doll" and spindles full of colored thread, from a Mayan burial.

rose gradually into great vaulted domes. In Eastern Europe, the grave of 1000 B.C.E. is a simple mound. In one cemetery of 150 graves, in Bulgaria, nearly 50 of the graves seem to be symbolic burials. They contain grave offerings of metal, and pottery arranged as if around a body, but the corpse itself is absent. In Northern Europe in the Bronze Age, tombs were also mounds. Within these mounds of earth were sometimes a single grave and sometimes a small grouping. The great majority of these graves consist of an oak log coffin placed on a bed of stones, and within the hollowed trunk of oak the body of the deceased lay wrapped in the hide of a cow or an ox, and surrounded with its finest possessions.

In the British Isles, the mound burial took many forms. Among the earlier forms is the long barrow, or ditch and barrow—a long barrow with a ditch on either side, such as one in West Kennet. Within the long barrow is a chamber tomb, constructed usually of upright stone slabs covered with a roof of stone slabs. These stone cairns are all that remain of the barrow when the earthen mound erodes away, and within these cairns were buried the remains of a number of individuals. The earliest of the mound burials, however, are to be found in County Meath in Ireland. Here in the Valley of the River Boyne lies a cemetery of enormous proportions, known as Brough na Boinne. It includes three legendary Neolithic tombs; Knowth, Dowth, and New Grange. The Knowth tomb and its surrounding satellite tombs were only discovered in the 1960s, while the other tombs have been known for hundreds of years. All three are what are known as passage tombs and have a similar construction. The base of the burial mound is delineated with a ring of huge, roughly rectangular curb stones, with an opening at the entrance to the tomb. The purpose of the curb stones is to stabilize the mound. At the entrance of the tomb begins a passageway into the core of the tomb itself. This passageway is composed of parallel rows of upright stones, roofed with stone lintels, and it is many yards long. The passage ends in the central burial chamber, which is constructed in much the same manner as the Greek "beehive" burial chambers described earlier. These central burial chambers are of two types. The first is the simple, undifferentiated chamber and the second is a chamber having three small niches off the central area, giving the tomb a cruciform floor plan. Ancient rites must have been performed in these niches, since some of them still contain ornamented stone basins. The passage and the central chamber are covered over with alternate layers of stones and earth and sod. The curbstones at Knowth are highly ornamented, as are some of the uprights at the tomb's entrance, with deeply "pocked" designs of spirals, concentric circles, lozenges, triangles, and zig-zags. Of all the megalithic tombs of Neolithic Ireland, certainly the most significant is the New Grange passage tomb. During its restoration, above the huge upright stones ornamented with spirals and circles, and the lintel stone that capped them, was discovered a horizontal slit. Here, on the Winter Solstice, following the darkest night of the year, the rays of the rising sun filter through this slit in the stones, and for a few brief moments flood the burial chamber with sunlight as it has for 5,000 years.

Following the period of the construction, in the British Isles, of the passage tombs and long barrows, a new form of burial was begun. This was the causewayed enclosure, of which there are a number of examples in Wessex. These consisted of a ditch and a bank or barrow forming a ring, with causeways across the ring to form from one to four entrances to the inner circle. In some cases the ditch was inside the ring, in other cases it was outside. In either case, funerary rites must have taken place within these rings, because the soil within the ditches is filled with human bones and grave offerings, and in some cases human skulls have been found ritually arranged about the circle, in the ditch. About 2700 B.C.E., contemporary with Stonehenge, the round barrow burial came back into use, but instead of chambered cairns these smaller barrows contained single graves. Among the grave offerings found in one of these mounds were flint arrowheads, gold earrings, a copper dagger, and decorated pottery vessels called "beakers," for which the people who made them were named.

While the ancient megalithic tombs of western Europe, great earthen mounds surrounded by rings of curbstones, with bases that cover more than an acre, are awe-inspiring and impressive, certainly the ultimate burial mounds are the pyramids of Egypt.

Regardless of the structure of the tomb or the materials of which it was built, for our Pagan ancestors the methods for disposing of the body were many, and the ways came and went as cultures changed and grew.

The earliest-known human burial occurred among the Neanderthal ca. 40,000 B.C.E. In this first known grave the body was arranged lying on its side in the fetal position, suggesting a belief in rebirth.

In India, cremation was, and still is, the preferred method of disposing of a body, and there is a sound spiritual reason for this. The spirit is the integrating force which binds our body. Once the spirit begins to leave, the body begins to disintegrate, but the spirit is never completely free of the body until the body is entirely disintegrated. And so, in India, that most spiritual land, the body is cremated so that the spirit is liberated.

There are, however, two major traditions in which just the opposite approach has been taken in dealing with the body of the deceased. These are the ancient Egyptian and the Roman Catholic. Among the Egyptians, the physical body, through the process of mummification, was preserved for all time, and every step of the process was accompanied by religious ritual. First, the organs were removed and preserved separately in canopic jars, and the body cavity was filled with preserving chemicals. For the pharaoh and members of the aristocracy, the process took weeks, but for the less fortunate there were simpler processes. When this was done the body was wrapped with linen into which charms and amulets and magickal spells were stitched. Then a mask painted with the likeness of the deceased was placed over the face of the mummy case, which also bore the likeness of the departed. Finally, this coffin was placed in a stone sarcophagus within a chamber, the walls of which were painted with scenes of the daily life of the individual, prayers for his journey into the next world, and even some scenes suggesting resurrection or rebirth. This chamber was then filled with provisions and personal possessions, all that one would need in the next life, and sealed for all eternity.

The reason for all these elaborate preparations and preservation was to give the Ka, or astral double of the deceased, a recognizable body to return to. As long as the body was preserved, the spirit would never be free.

It is very likely that the ancient Egyptians believed in reincarnation just as much as the majority of Pagans do today. However, Egyptians might have seen in their greatest monument, the Great Pyramid, a reflection of their social structure; at the apex is a single capstone representing the pharaoh. The further down the pyramid, the more stones there are, until the very lowest tier, the 13-acre base, which bears the burden of all the rest. Since the lower classes, like the lower stones of the pyramid, were in the vast majority, and since it was they who bore the burden of toil, tilling fields, carrying water, and cutting stone, an individual's chances of reincarnating further up were pretty slim. If one had to choose between remaining on the astral planes or returning to the mundane world, the choice was pretty simple, especially for those further up the social pyramid. And so the body was preserved, and daily life was recreated on the walls of the tomb, so that the ka could remain in the afterlife for all eternity and not reincarnate.

As 3,000 years of Egyptian civilization were drawing to a close, another power was beginning to organize itself in Rome. In another 300 years it became the Roman Catholic Church. It is a fundamental belief of the Catholic Church that eventually, there will be a judgment day, at which time all those living will be assumed bodily into heaven to be judged and all of those who have gone on before will rise bodily from the grave to be called to judgment. While this conjures visions of the now-classic film *Night of the Living Dead*, it is probably the reason that the Catholic Church (until Vatican II) forbade cremation. The basic teaching of the church is that those who are obedient and good will go to heaven and those who sin will go to hell, to be tortured for all eternity. There is no second chance, no next incarnation, perhaps in more just circumstances, in which to try again, having learned from one's own mistakes. There is only one life to live—and it will be judged.

While the ancient Egyptians and the Catholics had their reasons for preserving the bodies of their dead, for the vast majority of Pagans the object has always been to return the body to the elements as quickly and as easily as possible.

In the ancient British Isles bodies were left exposed to the elements, and to predators and scavengers, in a process known as excarnation, and when the bones were cleaned they were gathered up and placed in such communal tombs as the long barrows and the ditches of the causewayed enclosures. This method of returning the body to the elements of nature causes the bones of different individuals to be mixed together, but the skulls, probably because they were believed to be the seat of the human spirit, were often arranged separately in a special chamber of the tomb. A similar method of excarnation is used in areas like Tibet where below freezing temperatures prevent burial and a lack of fuel prevents cremation. Some of the natives of North America also used excarnation, placing the bodies of their deceased loved ones on platforms of poles and hides, surrounded by their possessions. The bones that remained after birds and wild animals devoured the flesh may have later been gathered and buried in communal graves.

The Vikings disposed of the bodies of their heroes by sending them off in treasure-laden ships. But water was not always the only element involved. Fire is the element that transforms. Sometimes the ship was set ablaze before it was set adrift, and sometimes the deceased was cremated and the remains put into a container before being placed aboard the ship.

Probably the most traditional element for receiving the body of the deceased is the element of Earth, the womb of the Earth Mother. From that most ancient Neanderthal burial with the corpse lying in the fetal position, our ancient ancestors have left monuments that seem to echo down the years to us an unshakable belief in the eternal cycle of birth, death, and rebirth.

At the great Irish Passage tomb of New Grange on the morning of the Winter Solstice, in secret and in silence for 5,000 years, the rays of the rising Sun have flooded the burial chamber with warmth and light. On this day that marks the birth of the Divine Child, the New Solar Year, the Sky Father has entered the womb of the Earth Mother so that life can be renewed.

On a Danish farm, a mound of earth rises like the belly of the Earth Mother, and within her womb an oak log coffin, symbol of the Father God contains a corpse. The burial was no doubt intended as a magickal rite to cause the deceased to be born again.

On the other side of the world ancient Indians of the central plains and the New England coast alike buried their dead in great mounds of the Earth Mother, while their descendants, the Delaware, laid their dead to rest in shallow graves, in the fetal position, ready to be reborn.

Anyone who has ever known the love of a pet knows that an animal has a spirit, just as any human does. Certain followers of the new religion, in what can only be called religious arrogance, believe that what sets us apart from other species is that we have a soul (a soul being something like spirit, but somehow intricately associated with sin and guilt). In the early years of this century a zealous follower of the new religion set out to prove, scientifically, that animals do not possess souls, or spirits. All he managed to prove is that at the moment of death a dog loses a fraction of an ounce of weight. One wonders, with a shudder, what experiments this zealot performed to prove his thesis.

One of the fundamental beliefs of Paganism is that all of Nature is a manifestation of the Gods, and therefore everything in Nature has a spirit—especially our beloved pets. So loved were cats in ancient Egypt that when a family cat died its people shaved their eyebrows as a sign that they were in mourning. These Egyptians mummified their pet cats and buried them in large cat cemeteries under the protection of the Goddess Bast, who was identified by the Greeks with the Goddess Artemis, and who was called by them, The Mother of All Cats.

For anyone who has lost a pet, the rites given at the end of this chapter to mark the final passage of a loved one can be performed for an animal as well with very little alteration.

It is with great delight that skeptics often use the apparent contradiction between the belief in the reality of ghosts and apparitions, and that of reincarnation, as evidence that those who believe in such things are too ignorant to understand that the one might cancel out the possibility of the other. But in fact, there is no contradiction at all. Here the law of "as above, so below," or the longer version, "that which is above is like that which is below, and that which is below is like that which is above," seems to apply. In the East, where a belief in reincarnation is taken for granted, it is also accepted that since on average a person needs to sleep about eight hours each day, or one-third of every day, and therefore one-third of every lifetime, then on a more cosmic scale an individual must spend a period of about one-third the length of their lifetime between their most recent incarnation and the next. According to this belief then, those who die in early childhood are able to reincarnate quite quickly.

Regardless of rules about the length of time between incarnations, it is during the period between lifetimes, obviously, that certain individuals are able to make their presence known to those still in the physical realm.

As Pagans and Wiccans we all seek, from time to time, to contact the world of spirit in one way or another, and encouragement to do so is part of our training, but we also live in a physical world of high technology that denies such things, and considers them ignorant superstition or the aberrations of an unbalanced mind. One of the greatest challenges to today's Pagans is to be able to feel comfortable in both worlds, and to always keep the doorway between the worlds open.

This doorway between the worlds is often the Magick Circle. It is within the Magick Circle that most of us are able to enter that state of mind which allows us to accept the reality of the Spirit World. The Magick Circle is a meeting place between the worlds, but there are also others. For those on a more purely shamanic path there is a personal entry point which actually exists on the physical plane, but which one enters only in spirit, and there are entry points into this world that are known and used only by those in Spirit.

It is through these entrance points that we are most likely to enter the world of nature spirits, totem animals, Faeries, the spirits of trees and rivers, the heroes of folk-tales and legends, and the makers of myth. It is here that some of our most magickal experiences occur, but the memories of them do not always return with us. Vague fragments only remain in our minds, and when we attempt to visualize them we often fail. For me, the closest description is that images of beings in that world seem to be composed of luminous living vapor, in constantly changing rainbow colors and shifting shape, as if each atom of vapor is a pinpoint of light, and somehow the mechanism of my mind is able to recognize this living nebula of pure being as an oak tree (or whatever). And even this description falls far short of the actual experience. However, personal messages received while on this plane are often recalled quite clearly, even if they are not understood for years to come.

Still, there are other ways, too, to experience the world of spirit. One of these is to visit a place that is believed to be haunted, (unless you happen to live in such a place, as we do). To experience the presence of a ghost is one of the most convincing proofs that the spirit of the individual does survive the death of the physical body. I will use our own ghost, Mrs. Hunt, as a perfect example of many of the arguments for survival.

Dan and I became aware of Mrs. Hunt in 1977, a year after we had moved into the old stone farmhouse, which at that time was on the verge of ruin due to years of neglect and abandonment. After a year of hard work I noticed a familiar figure walk past the kitchen window. I had seen this figure dozens of times in the past year, but shrugged it off as a shadow or a bird when no one knocked at the door. The moment I was consciously aware that I had seen a ghost, I called Dan into the kitchen and told him what was going on. He agreed that he too had seen her many times but also shrugged it off and forgot about it. Dan and I promised one another then and there that we would never tell anyone about our ghost. We were new in this very rural community and already considered strange for being artists, and so it was for another year or so, until one day we hired a young man to do some yard work for us—in plain view of our kitchen window. In a short while he came into the house and told us that all the while he was working outside, he kept seeing a woman, whose description matched ours exactly, come around the corner of the house, pass the kitchen window, and vanish at the back door. Dan and I had sworn an oath never to tell any of our neighbors about our ghost, and we never did. Here was absolute proof that Mrs. Hunt was not the product of a hallucination caused by suggestion.

For this reason, we made it a point never to tell first-time visitors about our ghost, yet month after month, year after year, visitors have given us descriptions, verbal and written, that match our observations of Mrs. Hunt in startling detail.

And month after month, year after year, Mrs. Hunt continued her haunting. It was always the same. She could be glimpsed coming around the corner of the house, walking past the kitchen window, and vanishing at the back door. This is what parapsychologists have called a "classic haunting." In such cases the ghost, which always repeats the same activity, without any deviation, is completely unaware of those living people who are present.

The haunting has been explained by many as an "imprint" made upon the "atmosphere" of a place where a violent or traumatic act has occurred. But there are no less than three problems with this explanation.

For one thing, if this materialist explanation were true, then places like historic battlefields would have tourists seeing ghostly reenactments of the battle far more frequently, and predictably, than is actually the case.

Another reason that this explanation doesn't work, is that the majority of hauntings seen are of ghosts repeating such mundane acts as sweeping the floor. Hardly an act violent or traumatic enough to "leave an imprint."

And finally, ghosts are far more frequently seen in the homes and other places they lived in life, rather than where they died, regardless of how violent or traumatic their death might have been.

This brings me back to our own ghost, Mrs. Hunt, who came to our house, in life, as a bride in 1825 and lived here all the years of her long life, until, in her 89th year, she went to visit her son in a nearby town for a vacation. On her return trip she was crossing the bridge half a mile from home when she collapsed. She was taken to her daughter's home on the other side of the bridge where, after a few days of illness, she died.

How can there be any doubt that as Mrs. Hunt lay dying, her one wish was to return home? A wish that was only granted when death released her spirit. Why does she still haunt the house? It was the home she loved, the one her husband built for her, and the greatest joy she could imagine was to return here and stay. (I can understand this. I love this house myself, and when my body dies, I might just stay on too.)

If the comparison between sleep and death is an accurate one, and we believe it is, then hauntings are probably to be compared to a restless sleep,

Mrs. Hunt comes around the corner of the large section of the house, and disappears at the back door.

such as we have all experienced, especially when the thought of something that must be done keeps us tossing and turning. But when the dreamer is rewarded with the completion of the task in the dream, what joy then, what peaceful sleep. Until the dream begins again. This is the feeling one gets from Mrs. Hunt, not the sense of desperation, but of peaceful relief, each time she arrives at her own kitchen door. If returning home was her fondest wish, than surely having it granted again and again must be her greatest joy.

While there are many who believe that ghosts who haunt are trapped between the worlds, unaware that they are dead, and that it is the duty of the living to send them on their way, this may not necessarily be so. If a ghost seems to be reenacting some horrible moment, suffering some awful pain again and again, then certainly the only kind thing to do is to attempt to contact them and explain, telepathically, that they need not continue suffering. However, if a ghost seems to be cheerily going about their own business, blissfully unaware that others now reside where they once lived, then who are we to banish them from the heaven they have chosen?

This haunting may prolong the period of death that is traditionally one third of a lifetime, between lifetimes, but since the spirit is eternal, that doesn't really matter.

So far, we have been discussing haunting ghosts, those that repeat the same activity again and again, seemingly oblivious to those observing them, or to physical obstacles placed in their way, but there is another type of ghost as well, one who actively participates in the affairs of the living. These are the ghosts of our deceased loved ones who may appear to us after their passage, to reassure us of their well-being, and their continued existence. They include the mothers and fathers, grandparents, sisters, brothers, and others, who appear to us at unexpected times, to warn us of impending danger, or to deliver some specific message. For many, they appear in dreams to give their messages, but most often they appear visibly, often in bright daylight. These are apparitions.

One very strange, but not uncommon, phenomenon, is the ghostly phone call. In these instances, a living person receives a phone call from the spirit of one on the other side. Usually, the voice is easily identifiable and familiar expressions or special names are used. Often the one receiving the call interrogates the one on the other side, without ever disproving the identity of the caller. Such a phone call, within our own family, lasted almost twenty minutes.

The basic difference between a haunting and an apparition is that a haunting ghost is one who usually repeats the same action again and again, completely unaware of changes in their surroundings, or of the living who are their witnesses, while an apparition is one who interacts with the living, often giving warnings or information that the living could not receive through ordinary means. While some may continue to dismiss the former with such explanations as "imprints on the atmosphere," it is the latter, the apparition, that is sometimes considered evidence of survival.

Interestingly, our ghost, Mrs. Hunt, crossed the border one night, from the haunting variety of ghost to one who interacted with us in a very startling way. After seeing Mrs. Hunt walk past our kitchen window for more than fifteen years, Dan and I were sitting on our back porch one summer evening. We were examining a collection of vintage clothing that had just been given to us by a neighbor, because some of it had originally come from our house. The air was hot and still, not a leaf was moving, when I picked up a beautiful brown satin blouse. Realizing that the style of it dated to the later years of Mrs. Hunt's life, I said to Dan, "I wonder if any of this clothing belonged to Mrs. Hunt, and if so, will she be more active because its here." In the next instant we both heard something take hold of the thumb latch on our back screen door, and, without opening it, bang it as hard as possible at least five times.

As I said, the air was still that night, there wasn't a breeze, and our screen door has never done that in all the years we've lived here. We had no choice but to consider this a ghostly answer from Mrs. Hunt. It was also the only time she ever seemed to be aware of our presence, or interacted with us in any way.

Aside from hauntings and apparitions, there are those who call themselves mediums or channelers, who are sometimes able to give stunning evidence of the continued existence of the spirits of the deceased. The medium may be one who, in a state of trance, receives telepathic messages from the spirit world and may also be able to see and describe the spirits with whom she is communicating. Or, she may be one who allows the spirits to use her physical body, to speak with her lips and vocal apparatus. Such mediums may seem to speak with the accent, expressions, and even the voice of the deceased. There were also, in the past, mediums who produced what was called ectoplasm, which seemed to be some sort of solidification of the medium's own aura, and which seemed to emanate from the medium's mouth or finger tips. To my knowledge, any ectoplasm that was ever taken for the purpose of scientific study evaporated in a few days, but ectoplasm doesn't prove survival of the human spirit and ectoplasm now seems to be a relic of the Victorian seance room.

One of the most studied and gifted of mediums in recent times was Eileen J. Garrett, who passed beyond the veil herself in 1970. Reading her work today, in the light of ancient wisdom, her visions, especially those of her earlier years, are clearly the visions of a shaman. She had dedicated her life to the scientific study of her mediumship, but in the end, despite the incredible accuracy of her messages from the spirit world, she went to her grave uncertain of what it was that she received.

It will never be in the science laboratory that the existence of the human spirit will be proven to exist or not exist, but on that deepest level of human consciousness which is the spirit world.

We need not, however, rely on mediums to give us messages from our discarnate loved ones. There are a variety of tools at our disposal with which we might receive messages, if we ourselves have not developed the skills of mediumship. I have discussed all of these methods at length in previous books, but at the risk of repeating myself, I feel they must be mentioned here again.

Probably the first device that comes to mind is the Ouija Board, which has an undeserved sinister reputation. For anyone who is not familiar with the Ouija Board, it is simply a board upon which the alphabet, numbers from one to ten, and the words yes, no, and goodbye have been printed. A plastic pointer, called a planchette, is placed upon the board, and all present rest their fingertips, lightly, upon the planchette, which will begin to move of it own accord from letter to letter, spelling words and forming messages.

Ouija Boards now come in a round as well as a rectangular format, but there are several homemade devices that work as well, if not better for the effort. One of these is the Wine Glass, which is just that, an ordinary wine glass inverted on a smooth surface, surrounded by letters of the alphabet. These letters might be jotted in marker pen on torn bits of paper, cut from a magazine, or carefully hand-lettered. The wine glass is worked in the same way as the Ouija Board, by each participant placing their fingertips upon the upturned base of the glass, which will begin to move, touching letters and spelling words.

A more solitary version of this is to lay out letters in a semi-circle rather than a complete circle, and holding a pendulum just over the center of the semi-circle, allow it to swing from one letter to another. With any of these methods, the message must be recorded one letter at a time, because they often go in unexpected directions and are sometimes remarkably long. For anyone who is trying to recall the message without loosing the psychic connection, this can be quite difficult, so a tape recorder is advisable.

One more traditional method of spirit contact is table rapping. In this method participants touch hands on a table top and enter a trance state, while spirits converse by knocking on the table to spell messages; one knock for A, two for B, and so on. The problem with this method is that while the spirits may have an eternity to deliver a message in, we usually don't have that much time to receive it. However, there might be other manifestations as well. One evening, while Dan and I were experimenting with table rapping with a friend in her haunted Victorian mansion, the center of the cardboard top of the old card table began to breathe. The table then lifted up off three of its legs, and began to turn, almost pushing our friend off her chair. To break the spell, we let go of one another's hands, and slowly the table settled back down to the floor.

One problem with all of these devices is that there is no way of knowing who, or what for that matter, is coming through. There are a whole host of discarnates on the other side waiting for an opportunity to express themselves, and they are not necessarily our deceased loved ones. While discarnate entities are not especially dangerous in themselves, they can exert powerful psychic influence if allowed to. While these devices are not dangerous, they are not parlor games and should not be experimented with by those who are afraid, depressed, or unstable in any way. Also, even those on the other side are not all-knowing just because they have passed over. If recently deceased Uncle Artie was a financial failure in life, chances are he still is, so the world of discarnates is not to be allowed to make our life's decisions for us. That is what we are here to do for ourselves.

Finally, using any of these methods takes practice. In the beginning messages may just be a series of letters that spell only an occasional word, but eventually the spelling will improve, as will grammar and content. The problem will still remain of contacting the spirits of the deceased loved ones that you wish to contact. The following method may be useful.

Cast a Circle according to your ways, at a time "Between," such as the stroke of Midnight, or the Full or New Moon or Samhaintide. If this can be done in a place the spirit knew in life, all the better. Have upon the altar an image of the person if possible, and hold a token, an object that they once possessed. Burn candles of indigo.

After gazing at the image on the altar for awhile, close your eyes and visualize them. See their face, at first as it was in the photo, then animated, as in life. See them smile, hear them speak, feel their touch. Softly call their name.

With eyes still closed, place your fingertips upon the planchette or wine glass. See their hands join yours. Now ask, not the traditional, "Is anyone here?" but "(the person's name) are you here?" Repeat the question, but keep your eyes closed until the planchette begins to move. If there is no response, don't persist. Let the spirits rest.

When the spirits of the deceased in Summerland have rested, when they have finished dreaming their dreams of life in the mundane world, and haunt the living no longer, it must be then that they awaken, at the dawn of their spiritual existence, to a world in which they grow, not older, but younger, until it is time again to be reborn.

In cultures in which the belief in reincarnation is of great importance, there are also many explanations of how it works. While the belief in reincarnation is one of the basic beliefs of Wicca, as expressed in the old rede, "Every ending is a new beginning," the explanation of how it operates seems to have been lost along the way, and so we must look to the ancient wisdom of the East for answers to certain questions.

One of these questions concerns how the spirit reenters a new body. The theosophists tell us, sensibly, that as a spirit prepares to return to the material world, it will naturally be attracted to the physical body that will best enable it to pursue its life's work. For some this might mean a body with certain physical characteristics, or parents in a certain income bracket. It might also mean being born with a specific astrological natal chart. It may also mean, especially to Wiccans, being born in the same place and at the same time as others we have known and loved before, so that we may meet, and remember, and love again. When the body has begun to form, when the egg has been fertilized and the cells of the embryo begin to multiply in the womb of the mother, the spirit will be attracted to it from time to time, to begin to get a feel for its future environment. Later, as the fetus develops, the spirit of the one about to be born will enter its new body occasionally and with more frequency as time goes on. When the spirit is not in the fetus, it might hover about its mother and might telepathically communicate to her its ideas and plans for its own future. At some point, some believe early in the third trimester, the spirit becomes more or less permanently attached to the physical body that soon will be born, leaving it only occasionally, as we leave our bodies when we astrally project.

It is an ancient belief that those in the spirit know the future, and so, should anything happen to terminate a pregnancy during the final months, then in all likelihood the spirit had already left it, or never entered it in the first place.

For those of us who can recall our previous lifetimes, it is easy enough to believe in the continuity of the human spirit. While there are those who have framed their religious beliefs around the idea that reincarnation is an evolutionary process, and that each new lifetime brings us closer to perfection and to Godhood, for the majority of Pagans it is sufficient to believe, simply, that we reincarnate. Still, there are some who require proof (and these are often the same people who cannot accept proof when they are shown it).

For all of us who recall scenes from our previous lives, it is advisable to research details given in the visual recall. These sometimes prove to be not only historically accurate, they may also give added information about the lifetime. Often when one has been given a glimpse of a previous lifetime, confirmation of historically significant details come from startlingly unexpected directions. For example, a lifelong friend and I seem to share a memory of living and working in a large stone room, with several fireplaces along one end. We discussed this once or twice between ourselves but never with anyone else. Then one day, another friend (who had never met the first friend) returned from a trip to England with a large stack of photos. "Here," she said, "I took this one for you. I don't know why, but when I walked into this room I thought of you, so I took this picture." There was our great stone room, with a row of fireplaces.

The architectural details, colors of clothing, species of plants or animals, all might give added information about time and place, and support the authenticity of a past life recollection.

Not surprisingly, the one event the great majority of people seem to recall from a previous life is the moment of death. It is also true that the majority of people who claim to recall a previous life, do *not* believe that they were anyone famous; a king, a pharaoh, or a high priest. Most seem to recall the simple life of one whose name would never have been recorded in a history book. Occasionally, though, a past life recall seems to explain the origin of a talent, skill, fear, or habit that affects the life of the individual in their present incarnation.

While some people seem to come into their present lifetime with memories of a previous life, and others have the details of a former lifetime revealed to them in a flash through meditation or some other means, there may still be many who believe in reincarnation, but simply cannot remember. For such people there are alternatives. There is past life regression through hypnosis, and there are psychics who seem to have the ability to see events in the previous lives of their subjects.

Hypnotic regression into previous lives seems to have been discovered by various hypnotists while regressing their subjects back to early childhood. While many in the scientific community deny the validity of past life regression, it is still being done to explore and correct harmful habits or fears, and there are hypnotists who are willing to help individuals explore their previous lives for their own sake.

Psychics who give past life readings are dealing in an area that is extremely difficult to substantiate, and so information gained in this way should be applied with discretion. However, if such a psychic gives information that strikes a chord or confirms information given by another psychic, it could be considered evidential. Ideally, information given by a psychic reader of past lives can be used to confirm your own memories of your previous lifetimes.

In the end, there is nothing so convincing as our own memories of a past life, and the certain knowledge that they are just as much a natural part of us as our memories of our first puppy or our high school prom.

Just as some of us are able to see into the distant past, many of us receive warnings or omens when someone we know or love is about to die, or when a family member who lives at a great distance passes beyond the veil. One of the most common of these messages is a loud knock at the door. If the door is answered, no one is there, but when the door is closed there may be another knocking, louder than the one before. If a person receives such a warning of death, often that person will continue to receive such warnings throughout their life.

Possibly a related phenomenon to the knock at the door is the loud bang that sometimes accompanies the moment of a person's final passage. This "bang," which sounds like a sonic boom, is not only heard in the vicinity where the passage occurs, but may be heard simultaneously many miles away by a relative or loved one of the deceased. It may occur at the moment of passage, or it may precede it by a few minutes to several hours. Many years ago, when Dan and I were first married, and were sharing a house with several elderly people, one stormy night we heard the death bangs. Three of them that were so loud and frightening we thought someone was trying to batter down the doors. Our elderly landlady, who had been very ill at the time, was completely recovered by the next morning. We have reason to believe that the loud bangs we heard were her husband, who had died twenty years earlier, and who had returned to take her back with him. She never heard the sounds but something, possibly our presence, or her unwillingness to die, stopped him and sent him back. Five years later when we no longer lived there, on the same date, she made the final passage.

These "sonic booms" have been interpreted by some as being caused by the spirit departing, and by others as being caused by the spirits coming to guide them to the other side.

Such death omens seem to be given to certain people and to certain families, and they seem to be consistent, occurring in the same way, and remaining with the same family for generations.

Another consistent death omen is the clock which stops at the exact moment of the death of a family member, regardless of how far away the person was at the time of their passing. Dan was once commissioned to do a painting of a group of family heirlooms that included a clock which had been in one family for several generations, and which had stopped a number of times at the moment of a family member's death.

Another fairly common death omen is a ball of light which will appear in a closed room, and dance and bob about as if trying to attract attention, before fading away. Known in parts of the South as fetch lights, their name suggests that these lights are coming to take the spirit of the dead, they are not the spirits themselves.

The sudden howling of a dog may be taken as a sign that the dog's master, or a close family member, is about to die. Presumably, this does not apply to dogs that howl rather than bark, but only to dogs that bark normally.

Possibly one of the most commonly accepted death omens is a bird, but there are many variations on this theme. I've had several experiences with this omen, and with people who believe in it, and those who do not. My first experience was in art school in the 1960s. "Someone in that house is going to die," said a classmate of mine with absolute certainty, and she pointed out the pure white pigeon sitting among the gray ones on the roof of the house next door to the studio. That was on a rainy Friday afternoon. When we returned to the studio the following Monday morning the house next door was being emptied of its contents. The elderly doctor who had lived there alone had passed on over the weekend.

Sometime after that I was visiting a friend one evening and he decided to light a fire in the fireplace. Unfortunately, he forgot to open the damper. As the room filled with smoke he reached up the chimney, feeling for the lever, and pulled it. There was a lot of squawking and flapping, and when the smoke cleared there was a starling, singed and bewildered, in the middle of the floor. My friend captured the bird and coated it with aloe, fed it, and cared for it. Three days later we were attending my friend's father's funeral, although none of us made the connection at that time. (Months later the starling's feathers had grown back, and its blackened bill and feet were once again yellow, and my friend released it.)

The years passed and Dan and I were married, and we inherited a white pet dove. He lived with us for many months with no problems. Then one day

Dan and I decided to take him to visit my mother-in-law. She had a guest at the time, an older woman, who became hysterical when we brought the bird into the house. She began screaming that it was a death bird. She died in three days.

Dan and I had the dove for several more years before finally releasing it at an aviary where it could be with other doves of its kind, but none of our family members died.

There are apparently several different beliefs concerning birds as death omens:

* If a pure white bird roosts on a house, someone living in that house will die.
* If a wild bird of any color enters a house some member of the family will die.
* If a white bird enters a house, someone in the house will die.

The belief in birds as death omens is an ancient one, and has its roots, no doubt, in the ancient belief that birds are messengers of the Gods. Many an ancient alphabet originated as a means of receiving messages from the spirits, or the Gods themselves, and the shapes of the letters were inspired by the flight patterns of birds, or their footprints on the earth. Hermes, the messenger of the Gods, was inspired to create the alphabet by watching the flight of cranes. Birds such as cranes and herons were believed by ancient Europeans to take the fertility and life of Nature away with them when they flew south on their fall migrations, and to bring with them the resurrection of Nature when they returned in the spring. Among the Germanic people, the spirits of those slain in battle were carried to Valhalla on the backs of swans, and in Russia the spirits of those who died valiantly were transformed into cranes. At the other end of this cycle, of course, is the folk tale that newborn babies are brought by the stork. The stork is a bird related to herons and cranes, and has the peculiar habit of nesting on chimney tops. The chimney, of course, is the place where a Witch was believed to leave her house on her broomstick to attend the sabbat meetings, just as the smokehole of the shaman's yurt or igloo is sometimes the entry point into the spirit world. And so, the belief in birds as death omens, which has its roots in ancient traditions, is firmly held by many today, and with good reason.

While Pagans of an Anglo-Saxon or Mediterranean background might have birds as death omens, Celtic Pagans have a whole assortment of death omens uniquely Celtic. Among these are the Banshees and Pookas.

The Banshee is a type of spirit, the suffix "shee" meaning faerie, that usually attaches itself to a particular family, sometimes continuing this attachment for many generations. Traditionally, whenever a member of the family is about to die, the banshee wails, a terrible mournful wail, announcing that death is imminent.

There are also Pookas, sometimes dark shadows, whose appearance announces that a death is about to occur. Like the Banshee, the Pooka is of the Faerie folk and is related to, or the same as Puck, a nature spirit who is the Celtic counterpart of the Roman Faunus and Greek Pan. Puck's symbol, the black goat which was ritually honored, its horns and hooves gilded and its neck adorned with flowers, clearly tells us that this was once the Lord of the Dead, the Horned God who presides over the spirits of the departed, the most ancient of all Gods.

Pookas also appear sometimes as large black dogs. These dogs may follow or stalk the one who is about to die, or simply be there, watching. The dog as a death omen has a double meaning. For one thing, the dog may act as guide to the spirit world, for another, the black dog is one of Herne the Hunter's hounds, and Herne is, of course Cernunnos, the Horned One. (Herne and Cerne may have originally been one name.) Cernunnos, the Horned God of the Hunted, who wears the circle of the Goddess on his horns or about his neck, became Herne, the Horned Hunter of men whose hounds may still be heard in Windsor Forest. His hounds, the hounds of Annwyn, also bear a stunning resemblance to Anubis, the Egyptian God of the dead who is symbolized by a black dog or jackel, and depicted with the head of a dog. The Greek counterpart of Anubis is Hermes. It is Hermes who guides the spirits of the dead to the underworld.

For anyone who has lost a loved one, it is clear that no amount of flowers, no number of sympathy cards, or mourners at a wake can help to reduce the pain of loss or the hopelessness of grief. But Pagans know, too, that every ending is a new beginning. As we are born to die, so do we die that we may be born again, and so, for any of us who may unfortunately have to endure a "mainstream" traditional funeral for one who shared our love but not our ancient faith, it might be helpful to focus on the traditions with which we will be surrounded, traditions which may have Pagan origins, and which most definitely have Pagan significance.

The first and most obvious of these is flowers. No funeral is complete without them. So great is the association between flowers and funerals that some people claim they dislike the smell of flowers because it reminds them of funerals. This is unfortunate because flowers at a funeral no doubt serve the same symbolic purpose as they do at weddings. Human fertility and the blossoming of vegetation have always been closely connected magickally. Flowers at a wedding insure fertility so that the couple may have many children, and flowers at a funeral may also insure fertility within the clan of the mourners gathered, so that in due time the spirit of the departed one will

WHEELS OF LIFE

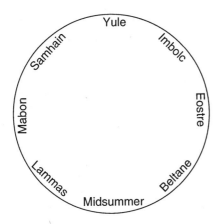

The Wheel of the Year

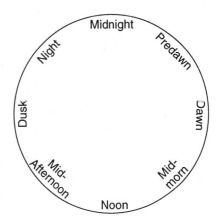

Times of Day

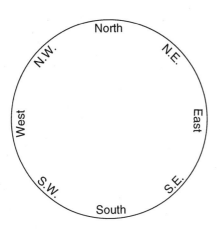

The Magick Circle

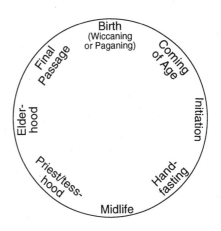

Rites of Passage

eventually be born again among those whom they have loved, that they may again know, and remember, and love again. We may never know what was in the minds of that gathering of Neanderthals who lovingly placed flowers about the corpse of one of their own members, but we can know what was in their hearts: that they and their loved one would one day be reunited.

Among the horseshoes and the baskets of flowers, the spikes of gladiolas and spicy-scented carnations, there are candles. Their bright dancing flames in the dim stillness of a funeral home are like the bright shining ones of the spirit realms, and they serve to guide the spirit of the deceased to the next world; a world of spirits and radiant beings where all pain is gone, and where, eventually, youth will be restored. The bright flame of a candle, like the light of a Jack-O-Lantern, is a symbol of the spirit, and as it will serve magickally as a guide for the spirit to return when again the veil between the worlds is thinnest, so does it guide the spirit now as it hovers close about the mourners yearning to console us.

Finally, as we look about the room, filled with swollen eyes and tear-streaked faces, we are aware that the majority of us are wearing black. To others in the room black is the color of negativity, of sadness and grief, of death and evil. For those whose faith causes them to fear death, this is understandable, but to those of us who love a kinder God, and who know that death is not an end, the color black is not negative in any evil sense, it is the color of Spirit, and we wear it with honor and respect for the deceased, as we wear it with pride most of the time.

In fact, as we look about the room, with the exception of a symbol of the new religion here or there, we seem to be surrounded by far more Pagan symbolism, and while this cannot remove the pain of our loss, it can give us some comfort.

Even the cemetery, with its headstones in neat rows, seems to recall the cairns and menhirs of our ancient Pagan past. One of the traditions which has sometimes drawn much ridicule from those less spiritual or understanding is the so called "Irish wake." It has been a tradition among Catholic people (not necessarily Irish), until recently, to bury the body of a loved one on the third day after death. At a time when there were no funeral homes and when the bodies of our deceased ancestors were laid out in the houses in which they lived, it was the custom for the family to keep a vigil with the corpse, sitting up, all night, for the entire three-day period. A custom, incidentally, which is reflected in some of the Halloween traditions which last three days. It was also customary among the Eskimo people that for three days following the death of a family member no sharp tools or weapons were used, and no loud noises made, for fear of harming the spirit of the deceased.

The word wake is an archaic term which means at once; a vigil kept with a corpse, a feast, and a ritual; but whether or not the word actually comes from the fact that the object was to stay awake is not clear. What is clear is that the term is an old one. The "Irish Wake," however, puts an emphasis, not so much on the vigil with the corpse as with a feast (including drinking and generally rowdy behavior). It is just possible that the so-called "Irish Wake" has its roots in Celtic Paganism, the number three, as the number of days of the wake being sacred to the Celts, and possibly it was believed that it took three days for the spirit of the deceased to withdraw from the body. Furthermore, for any Pagan people who believe in the continued life of the spirit in a world free of pain and suffering, reunited with those loved ones that have passed on, and also in the cycle of birth, death, and rebirth that guarantees that we will be together again, the passing of a loved one can be a cause for celebration.

A feast of a simpler sort is a part of traditional Greek funerals. When the coffin has been lowered into the ground and some Earth has been thrown into the grave, the mourners gather to share a simple meal prepared of whole grain, wheat, nuts, and the ruby red seeds of the pomegranate. It was the seeds of the pomegranate that Hades gave to Persephone to eat, insuring that she would return to him in the underworld. And it is these same grains that were soaked and sprouted in dishes called "the Gardens of Adonis," by the women of the area, at the time of the Vernal Equinox, to insure the renewal of life.

The whole grain wheat, of course, is sacred to Demeter, the mother of Persephone, the raisins are grapes, sacred to Dionysus, and the almonds are sacred to Attis, Phrygian God of resurrection. While modern Orthodox Greeks have a Christian myth to explain the tradition of the eating of Kolyva, it is clearly a Pagan rite performed to bring about the return from death of the deceased. Furthermore, while Kolyva is sometimes eaten at the funeral, it is also traditionally eaten 40 days after the death, one year, and again three years after (or in some areas five and ten years after the death), and it is also eaten by families of the deceased on the Greek All Souls Day, which is the first Saturday of Lent. Lent, among Christians, begins 40 days before Easter, and since the date of Easter is based on Eostre, the Vernal Equinox, then this places the Greek All Souls Day at about mid-February, or Lupercalia, an ancient Pagan fertility festival at which time the Luperci, or priests of Dionysus, performed rites to insure fertility, especially for women who were barren. This clearly suggests that the eating of Kolyva, made of so many ingredients sacred to Pagans, and traditionally decorated with a solar cross, is, as it has always been, a Pagan rite of rebirth.

The recipe beginning on the following page is one of many variations of Kolyva.

Kolyva

2 pounds of whole wheat (kernels)
1 teaspoon of salt
½ pound of sesame seeds (toasted in a moderate oven)
2 cups of white raisins
3 or 4 cups of walnuts (finely chopped)
3 cups of confectioners sugar (1½ pounds)
2 teaspoons of dried parsley (flakes)
2 teaspoons of dried Basil leaves (crumbled)
1 tablespoon of ground cinnamon
¼ cup of fresh pomegranate seeds
½ pound of white Jordan almonds

Place wheat kernels in a saucepan with one teaspoon of salt. Cover this with a generous amount of water and simmer for about 2 hours, stirring frequently to prevent burning or sticking, until wheat is soft. Drain wheat, and towel dry any excess moisture.

In a large mixing bowl, combine the wheat with the sesame seeds, white raisins, walnuts, parsley, basil leaves, cinnamon and pomegranate seeds along with 1½ cups of the confectioners sugar. (If needed, add a little more confectioners sugar until the mixture has a slightly sweet taste.)

Place this mixture on a large tray about 12" x 16", and sift the remaining confectioners sugar evenly over the top of the Kolyva. Carefully press the sugar down firmly with wax paper or a spatula.

Now, using the Jordan almonds (and possibly raisins), decorate the top of the Kolyva, making a large solar cross (even-armed) within a circle, and possibly add the initials or name of the deceased. Extra designs might be added as borders or corners with the remaining almonds/raisins. After the Kolyva is prepared it may be stored in the refrigerator. It can be served in cups to the mourners, and is traditionally eaten with spoons.

When this graveside meal is completed and the coffin has been covered with a mound of freshly turned Earth, there is one last offering to make. There on the cold damp earth a fresh white egg is placed. There can be little doubt about the Pagan origins, meanings, and intent of these simple Greek burial rites.

There are other, older customs too, that are only now beginning to fade away. Our own house and many others like it here in the Delaware Valley have a peculiar architectural feature, two front doors. The basic floor plan is simple. On the ground floor are two large rooms. One is the kitchen, or keeping room, with its huge "walk-in" fireplace, where all the family activities

Kolyva

took place, and the other is the parlor which was kept sealed off from the dust and soot of everyday life. The parlor, with its small formal fireplace, was only used for special occasions; holidays, weddings, and it was here that the dead were laid out and wakes were held. One front door leads into the kitchen and was used every day. The other door leads from the parlor and was never used except on certain occasions. It is called the "coffin door."

For Pagans who have lost loved ones not of the Old Faith, and who have endured the sermons of ministers at the grave site of someone he or she has never met, it can be very helpful, and healing, to perform a memorial rite of their own, a Pagan rite, soon after the "mainstream" funeral.

The purpose of the following rite is threefold; first to call upon the deceased in order to complete any unfinished business in the material world, second to dispose of the remains in a traditional manner, and third, to bid a final farewell before sending the spirit of the departed one off to Summerland. The rite would best be performed outdoors, ideally in a Pagan cemetery where such traditional methods as an open funeral pyre or mound burial would be permitted. Since this idea probably will not manifest until sometime in the distant future (although, people are working on it), there are other methods that might be substituted. Probably the majority of Pagans would prefer to be cremated. The ashes then might be scattered (which is illegal in many places, but done nonetheless), or they might be interred along with traditional grave offerings. If the loved one is not a Pagan, the body will have been disposed of according to other traditions. In this case a substitute grave might be made to receive offerings, or a cairn might be built by each of the mourners contributing a stone, or a menhir might be erected. If the rite must be performed indoors, then a coffin-like box might be used to receive the offerings, to be kept as a reliquary or buried at a later date. The rite may be performed by as few as a solitary individual or by as many as would wish to participate, and it may be performed to bid farewell to a Pagan, a non-Pagan or beloved pet.

Finally, there are no secret words, no magick wand that can take away the grief and pain of the loss of a loved one. No matter how deeply we believe in the continuity of spiritual life, no matter if we ourselves have experienced death and fear it not, there is no pain as great as the loss of a loved one, and the emptiness of knowing that we will never again see them in this lifetime. Perhaps this is more true for Pagans than for anyone else, for we have made a practice of knowing our own true feelings, more than most. This is not a time to be strong and brave and to hide our grief, it is a time to mourn and weep and be totally self-indulgent, and then to be done with it so that our loved one can move on.

This rite should ideally be performed as soon after the third day after the death as possible. A Waning Moon would be preferable, but not necessary.

The Circle is cast in the usual manner and on the altar is a photograph or image of the deceased if possible. If he or she was of the Craft, then their Craft tools should be on the altar. A device such as an Ouija Board, wine glass, or pendulum might be present, if desired, and there should be candles and holders enough for everyone present. The priest or priestess conducting the rite might be the person who was the closest to the one being mourned. The altar and the Circle might be adorned with oak and holly, willow and birch, or whatever trees and flowers symbolize death and rebirth in the tradition of the loved one or the coven.

When the Circle has been cast and everyone has assembled within, the priest/ess might begin the rite with words like:

> *Lord and Lady, Father and Mother of All life,*
> *We have cast this Circle at this darkest hour*
> *To bid farewell to one of your children*
> *Who stands now at the threshold.*

> *Grant now God* (name) *and Goddess* (name)
> *That your child* (Craft name)
> *Be permitted to enter this place between the worlds*
> *That we may bid our final farewells.*

The priest/ess then goes to the Western Gate and cuts a doorway, saying something like:

I open now the gateway
Through which we all will pass one day.
(Craft name) *we invite you to join us,*
With the blessings of our divine Mother and Father.
Retrace your steps through the Western Gate
To be among us once again.
Accompany me now to the center of the Circle.

Then, as the priest/ess spirals slowly, widdershins from the Western Gate to the center of the Circle, the group might light their candles, forming a ring of light, and visualize the presence of the departed one entering the Circle.

When the priest/ess has reached the center of the Circle, the group gathered might begin something of a chant, beginning with the person closest to the Eastern Gate and going around the Circle sunwise, each person intoning something like:

Welcome (Craft name)

or

Come to us (Craft name)

until the presence of the departed one is felt and acknowledged, or until a sign is given that the spirit is present. The priest/ess might then state something like:

(Craft name) *we have called you up*
To bid you fond farewell.
We have gathered here in this sacred place
To commune with you once more.
Before you return to that place
Where we may not yet follow,
Hear beloved (brother)
The words we have in our hearts.

Then, beginning again with the person nearest the Eastern Gate, each member of the group might give their final message. Such messages as:

I'll always love you
I'll miss you
I'll never forget you
I forgive you
We will be together again.

The priest/ess will be the last person to speak, and when the messages have all been given, it will be time for the spirit of the deceased to communicate. The priest/ess might say something like:

We have spoken to you (brother),
Now shall we listen.
Speak to us (Craft name) *and*
Make known to us your final message.

These final messages may be received with the use of one of the devices, such as the Ouija Board previously brought into the Circle, or there may be a period of meditation during which each member of the group might receive a personal message telepathically.

When this part of the rite has ended the priest/ess will state that this is so by saying something like:

(Craft name) *our time together*
Has drawn to a close.
No longer can you remain
Among us, for you have been
Called away.

Let us now prepare the tomb
For your earthly remains.

The priest/ess shall stand, holding either the cremated remains of the deceased, an offering at an actual grave, or at a reliquary which will symbolize for the rite an actual burial place. The priest/ess might begin this portion of the rite with words like:

Here are the mortal remains of our beloved brother (Craft name)
But as followers of the Old Faith we know
That the spirit never dies but is eternal.
Even now the spirit of (Craft name) *is here*
Within this Circle, moving among us.

Witness these rites we hold
In honor of your final passage.
Your body shall return to the Elements
So that your spirit shall be set free.

(At this point, if there are cremated ashes to be scattered it shall be done), The priest/ess going to the East might say:

Guardians of the East whose element is Air
Accept the remains of our brother (Craft name).
So that when the time has come for him to be
Reborn, you will give him the breath of life.

Going to the South:

> *Guardians of the South whose element is Fire*
> *Accept the remains of our brother* (Craft name)
> *So that when the time has come for him to be reborn*
> *You will give him the fire of life.*

And so on around the Circle, and then when the elements have been addressed, the priest/ess again faces into the Circle saying something like:

> *O ancient Goddess*
> *One of your children has returned to you.*
> *Accept his mortal remains*
> *And enfold him within your womb*
> *Which is the Cauldron of Rebirth.*

> *O Great Mother,*
> *Who brought forth our brother* (Craft name)
> *At the beginning of his many lives*
> *Accept his body now,*
> *That through the magick of your Mysteries*
> *He may be born anew.*

And now, that our brother may be provided for in his journey through the underworld, let us present our gifts.

Now, beginning in the East as before, each mourner might present an offering to be placed in the grave, beneath the cairn, or in the reliquary. Some examples might be:

> *I give this candle* (Craft name) *to light your way*
> *Through the darkness to the pure light of the Spirit World.*

or

> *I offer this food to nourish your spirit*
> *So that you may be renewed and refreshed.*

or

> *I place this egg, symbol of rebirth, upon your grave*
> *So that in some future time you will return.*

or

> *I place these flowers among your worldly possessions*
> *So that like all of Nature in Spring, you will be born again.*

When all of the mourners have placed their offerings upon the grave or in the reliquary, the priest/ess who was the closest one to the departed shall make the final offering, and if the loved one was a member of the Craft, their Craft tools might be a part of this offering. When this is done, the priest/ess might conclude this portion of the rite with words like:

Now (Craft name) has your body become one
With the four Elements,
And your flesh become one
With the Great Goddess
Hail, Farewell, and Blessed Be!

This might be followed by a symbolic act such as throwing earth into the grave, placing stones upon the cairn, or closing the urn or reliquary. The priest/ess might then begin the final portion of the rite with words like:

The body of our brother
Has been returned to the Earth
But yet his spirit lingers.

(Craft name) hear me now.
Your spirit has been called
To the realm of our Horned Father,
He who has removed your pain
And put an end to your suffering.

Now must we sever the bonds of our love
And free you from all earthly matters.
Let our love not hold you here,
But send you on your way.

While we who must remain behind
Shall miss you, so do we know
That ere the sun shall rise tomorrow
You will be in Summerland.

And as you shall grieve to leave us behind,
So shall you rejoice, to be reunited
With those who have gone on before.

O, ancient Father, Lord of Death
And of the realms beyond,
Welcome our brother (Craft name).
Bid him enter your land of spirit,
That he may feast in your great hall
Among the Shining Ones.

May he wander in your lovely land
Of sunlit meadows and fruitful orchards,
Beyond the rivers and the seas.

And when his time has come again,
When his wounds have healed

And his youth has been regained,
Through your magick, Spirit Father
And the mysteries of our ancient Mother
Shall he be reborn
That we may Merry Meet
Merry Part, and Merry Meet Again!

Now shall each mourner, beginning in the East, repeat "Merry meet, merry part, and merry meet again," and then extinguish their candle, as the priest/ess slowly walks, spiraling sunwise to the Western Gate, salutes the spirit, and then returns to the altar where a special ceremony of cakes and wine might take place. The cakes at this rite might be the Kolyva mentioned earlier, or a bread made of sprouted grains, symbolizing rebirth. When the cakes and wine have been blessed according to tradition, and distributed among the mourners, a simple toast might be proposed, something like:

On this night do we drink this wine
From the holy grail of immortality
And eat this meal (of Kolyva)
From the Cauldron of Rebirth.
For on this night the veil between the worlds
Has been rent, to allow one of our own
To pass through.

(Name) *now feasts, among the Mighty Gods*
And we, on our side of the veil,
Join him in that feast.
And let us remember
That when the year Wheel has turned,
And the veil again is thin at Samhaintide,
(Name) *will be free again to be among us,*
And we will be prepared to welcome him.

Conclusion

J ust as surely as the Sun will rise a bit earlier on Yule, bringing with it joy in the morning, so will we be born again. We will Come of Age just as Nature stirs again in the silent earth of Imbolc, and should we again find the hidden path of the Old Ways we will be spiritually reborn as the Sun rises at Eostre. We may meet and remember and love again, and be bound to our own true love in Handfasting, just as the Lord and Lady are joined in the Sacred Marriage at Beltane. We may achieve fortune and glory and reach our peak as the summer Sun at Solstice, and we shall reap the harvest of our lives as the Lammas loaf is blessed. Unless we are cut down sooner, we shall wither with age as the golden leaves of autumn before passing once again beyond the veil of Samhain, that we may Merry Meet, Merry Part, and Merry Meet Again.

STAY IN TOUCH

On the following pages you will find some of the books now available on related subjects. Your book dealer stocks most of these and will stock new titles in the Llewellyn series as they become available. We urge your patronage.

To obtain our full catalog, to keep informed about new titles as they are released, and to benefit from informative articles and helpful news, you are invited to write for our bimonthly news magazine/catalog, *Llewellyn's New Worlds of Mind and Spirit.* A sample copy is free, and it will continue coming to you at no cost as long as you are an active mail customer. Or you may subscribe for just $10.00 in the U.S.A. and Canada ($20.00 overseas, first class mail). Many bookstores also have *New Worlds* available to their customers. Ask for it.

Llewellyn's New Worlds of Mind and Spirit
P.O. Box 64383-119, St. Paul, MN 55164-0383, U.S.A.

* * *

TO ORDER BOOKS AND TAPES

If your book dealer does not have the books described, you may order them directly from the publisher by sending the full price in U.S. funds, plus $3.00 for postage and handling for orders *under* $10.00; $4.00 for orders *over* $10.00. There are no postage and handling charges for orders over $50.00. Postage and handling rates are subject to change. We ship UPS whenever possible. Delivery guaranteed. Provide your street address as UPS does not deliver to P.O. boxes. Allow 4-6 weeks for delivery. UPS to Canada requires a $50.00 minimum order. Orders outside the U.S.A. and Canada: Airmail—add retail price of book; add $5.00 for each non-book item (tapes, etc.); add $1.00 per item for surface mail.

FOR GROUP STUDY AND PURCHASE

Because there is a great deal of interest in group discussion and study of the subject matter of this book, we offer a special quantity price to group leaders or agents. Our special quantity price for a minimum order of five copies of *Rites of Passage* is $38.85 cash-with-order. This price includes postage and handling within the United States. Minnesota residents must add 6.5% sales tax. For additional quantities, please order in multiples of five. For Canadian and foreign orders, add postage and handling charges as above. Credit card (VISA, MasterCard, American Express) orders are accepted. Charge card orders only ($15.00 minimum order) may be phoned in free within the U.S.A. or Canada by dialing 1-800-THE-MOON. For customer service, call 1-612-291-1970. Mail orders to:

LLEWELLYN PUBLICATIONS
P.O. Box 64383-119, St. Paul, MN 55164-0383, U.S.A.

Prices subject to change without notice.

ANCIENT WAYS
Reclaiming the Pagan Tradition
by Pauline Campanelli, illus. by Dan Campanelli

Ancient Ways is filled with magick and ritual that you can perform every day to capture the spirit of the seasons. It focuses on the celebration of the Sabbats of the Old Religion by giving you practical things to do while anticipating the sabbat rites, and helping you harness the magical energy for weeks afterward. The wealth of seasonal rituals and charms are drawn from ancient sources but are easily performed with materials readily available.

Learn how to look into your previous lives at Yule . . . at Beltane, discover the places where you are most likely to see faeries . . . make special jewelry to wear for your Lammas Celebrations . . . for the special animals in your life, paint a charm of protection at Midsummer.

Most Pagans and Wiccans feel that the Sabbat rituals are all too brief and wish for the magick to linger on. *Ancient Ways* can help you reclaim your own traditions and heighten the feeling of magick.
0-87542-090-7, 256 pgs., 7 x 10, illus., softcover   **$12.95**

CIRCLES, GROVES & SANCTUARIES
Sacred Spaces of Today's Pagans
Compiled by Dan & Pauline Campanelli

Pagans and Wiccans have always been secretive people. Even many within the Craft have not been allowed to enter the sacred space of others. But within the pages of *Circles, Groves & Sanctuaries*, you are given the unique opportunity to examine, in intimate detail, the magical places created by Pagans and Witches across the country, around the world and from a wide variety of traditions.

Take guided tours of sacred spaces by the people who created them, and listen as they tell of the secret meanings and magical symbolism of the sometimes strange and always wonderful objects that adorn these places. Learn of their rituals that can be adapted by the most seasoned practitioner or the newest seeker on the hidden path. Become inspired to create your own magical space—indoors or out, large or small.

Accompany an Irish Count on a vision quest that led to the creation of a shrine to Poseidon. Read of the Celtic-speaking Fairies who dwell and practice their arts in Florida, and learn of the logistics of building a wood-henge in suburban New Jersey and a stone circle in the heart of the Bible Belt.
0-87542-108-3, 288 pgs., 7 x 10, 120 photos, softcover   **$12.95**

Prices subject to change without notice.

WHEEL OF THE YEAR
Living the Magical Life
by Pauline Campanelli, illus. by Dan Campanelli

If you feel elated by the celebrations of the Sabbats and hunger for that feeling during the long weeks between Sabbats, *Wheel of the Year* can help you put the joy and fulfillment of magic into your everyday life. This book shows you how to celebrate the lesser changes in Nature. The wealth of seasonal rituals and charms are all easily performed with materials readily available and are simple and concise enough that the practitioner can easily adapt them to work within the framework of his or her own Pagan tradition.

Learn to perform fire magic in November, the secret Pagan symbolism of Christmas tree ornaments, the best time to visit a fairy forest or sacred spring and what to do when you get there. Learn the charms and rituals and the making of magical tools that coincide with the nesting season of migratory birds. Whether you are a newcomer to the Craft or have found your way back many years ago, *Wheel of the Year* will be an invaluable reference book in your practical magic library. It is filled with magic and ritual for everyday life and will enhance any system of Pagan Ritual.

0-87542-091-5, 176 pgs., 7 x 10, illus., softcover $9.95

WITCHCRAFT TODAY, BOOK ONE
The Modern Craft Movement
edited by Chas S. Clifton

For those already in the Craft, and for those who stand outside the ritual circle wondering if it is the place for them, *Witchcraft Today 1* brings together the writings of nine well-known Neopagans who give a cross-section of the beliefs and practices of this diverse and fascinating religion.

- "A Quick History of Witchcraft's Revival" by Chas S. Clifton
- "An Insider's Look at Pagan Festivals" by Oz
- "Seasonal Rites and Magical Rites" by Pauline Campanelli
- "Witchcraft and Healing" by Morwyn
- "Sex Magic" by Valerie Voigt
- "Men and Women in Witchcraft" by Janet and Stewart Farrar
- "Witches and the Earth" by Chas S. Clifton
- "The Solo Witch" by Heather O'Dell
- "Witchcraft and the Law" by Pete Pathfinder Davis
- "Witchcraft and Shamanism" by Grey Cat
- "Being a Pagan in a 9-to-5 World" by Valerie Voigt

Also included are additional resources for Wiccans including publications, mail order suppliers, pagan organizations, computer bulletin boards and special-interest resources. The Principles of Wiccan Belief are also restated here.

0-87542-377-9, 208 pgs., 5 1/4 x 8, softcover $9.95

Prices subject to change without notice.

THE URBAN PAGAN
Magical Living in a 9-to-5 World
by Patricia Telesco

Finally, a book that takes into account the problems of city-dwelling magicians! When preparing to do ritual, today's magician is often faced with busy city streets and a vast shortage of private natural space in which to worship. Technology surrounds, and fear and misunderstanding still exist about "magic" and "witchcraft." This leaves even experienced spiritual seekers trying desperately to carry a positive magical lifestyle into the 21st century. With the help of *The Urban Pagan*, we all can learn to incorporate earth-aware philosophies of days gone by with modern realities.

The Urban Pagan is a transformational book of spells, rituals, herbals, invocations and meditations that will help the reader to build inner confidence, create a magical living environment, and form an urban wheel of the year. It updates interpretations of symbolism for use in sympathetic magic and visualization, shows how to make magical tools inexpensively, provides daily magical exercises that can aid in seasonal observances, shows practical ways to help heal the earth, and explains the art of cultivating and using herbs, plus much, much more.

0-87542-785-5, 336 pgs., 6 x 9, illus., softcover   **$13.00**

LIVING WICCA
A Further Guide for the Solitary Practitioner
Scott Cunningham

Living Wicca is the long-awaited sequel to Scott Cunningham's wildly successful *Wicca: a Guide for the Solitary Practitioner*. This new book is for those who have made the conscious decision to bring their Wiccan spirituality into their everyday lives. It provides solitary practitioners with the tools and added insights that will enable them to blaze their own spiritual paths—to become their own high priests and priestesses.

Living Wicca takes a philosophical look at the questions, practices, and differences within Witchcraft. It covers the various tools of learning available to the practitioner, the importance of secrecy in one's practice, guidelines to performing ritual when ill, magical names, initiation, and the Mysteries. It discusses the benefits of daily prayer and meditation, making offerings to the gods, how to develop a prayerful attitude, and how to perform Wiccan rites when away from home or in emergency situations.

Unlike any other book on the subject, *Living Wicca* is a step-by-step guide to creating your own Wiccan tradition and personal vision of the gods, designing your personal ritual and symbols, developing your own book of shadows, and truly living your Craft.

0-87542-184-9, 208 pgs., 6 x 9, illus., softcover   **$10.00**

Prices subject to change without notice.